D1732823

Contemporary India and South Africa

Legacies, Identities, Dilemmas

Editors

Sujata Patel
Tina Uys

Routledge
Taylor & Francis Group
LONDON NEW YORK NEW DELHI

First published 2012 in India
by Routledge
912 Tolstoy House, 15–17 Tolstoy Marg, Connaught Place, New Delhi 110 001

Simultaneously published in the UK
by Routledge
2 Park Square, Milton Park, Abingdon, OX14 4RN

Routledge is an imprint of the Taylor & Francis Group, an informa business

Typeset by
Star Compugraphics Private Limited
5, CSC, Near City Apartments
Vasundhara Enclave
Delhi 110 096

Printed and bound in India by
Sanat Printers, Kundli.

British Library Cataloguing-in-Publication Data
A catalogue record of this book is available from the British Library

ISBN: 978-0-415-52299-1

This book is printed on ECF environment-friendly paper manufactured from unconventional and other raw materials sourced from sustainable and identified sources.

Contents

PART II. The Contemporary Contradiction of Nation-States: Democracy, Education and Environment

PART III. Relating to Each Other as Regional Nation-States

Preface and Acknowledgements

November 2010 marked the 150-year commemoration of the arrival of the first group of Indian indentured labourers in KwaZulu-Natal, South Africa. The arrival of Indians in South Africa 150 years ago provided the impetus for the Centre for Sociological Research (University of Johannesburg) and the Centre for Indian Studies in Africa (University of Witwatersrand) to host an international conference in October 2010. The conference sought to reflect on South African and Indian dialogues on social justice and contested transitions. It was conceived out of a broader theme than the mere commemoration of 150 years of Indians in South Africa with the theme 'South Africa and India: Dialogues on Social Justice and Contested Transitions'. Over a period of two and a half days renowned scholars from both India and South Africa participated in pertinent and critical debates that bear historical relevance to both countries. The consensus that developed was that discussions such as the ones explored and analysed at the conference should be made available to a broader audience in the form of a published volume.

The idea of organising such a conference came from the Consulate General of India in Johannesburg. We would like to thank our fellow members of the organising committee of the conference namely Mr Vikram Doraiswami (then Consul-General of India in Johannesburg), Professor Adam Habib (Deputy Vice-Chancellor Research and Innovation, UJ), Professor Dilip Menon (Centre for Indian Studies, University of the Witwatersrand), Professor Shireen Motala (UJ) and Dr Mariam Seedat Khan (Department of Sociology, UJ) for their involvement as members of the Programme Committee in the coordination and preparation of the conference. Ms Annelize Naidoo (UJ), Projects Officer of the CSR and her team of students ensured that the logistics of the conference ran smoothly. We would also like to extend a special thanks to all who presented papers and chaired the sessions at the conference.

An event of this nature can only come to fruition if substantial financial support is provided and efforts and commitments given by individuals and institutions. We would like to acknowledge with gratitude the financial support given by the Public Diplomacy Division, Ministry of External Affairs, Government of India through the Consulate-General of India in Johannesburg. In particular we would like to thank Mr Vikram Doraiswami, who went the extra mile in providing financial and logistic support for the conference and the publication of the papers. Additionally, we would like to recognise the financial support given by the Centre for Sociological Research and the Faculty of Humanities at the University of Johannesburg, and the Centre for Indian Studies in Africa at the University of the Witwatersrand. We would also like to thank Prava Rai for helping with the copy-editing of the final manuscript.

We attach the following disclaimer from Mr Vikram Doraiswami:

As is often the case with independent intellectual discourse and in keeping with the highest traditions of free speech, a good many things are said and discussed in a conference such as this that fall well beyond the positions and perspectives of any Government. Naturally, it should be understood that the mere fact of there being support of institutions of the Government of India for the event does not mean that the Government of India, or its constituent institutions either subscribes to or endorses the views in this book in any manner or form, either partially or wholly.

1

Legacies and New Identities: Contemporary India and South Africa Compared

Sujata Patel and Tina Uys

In 1860 the first Indian indentured labourers arrived in South Africa; 2010 marked the 150 years, a year chosen to commemorate this historic event. Set against this background, the book is an outcome of a group of Indian and South African scholars who set out to explore contemporary challenges in both countries through the prism of history. The collection of articles in this book are diverse and intriguing in their individual capacities. When taken together, however, they take on even greater significance. The first section deals with legacies and relates to the Indian experience in South Africa at the micro level. Contemporary studies in sociology of migration have tried to capture the complexities of these legacies of 19th-century out-migration from India to South Africa, Fiji, Surinam and other regions. This literature has emphasised the negative fallout of indenture and located it within the colonial structures of labour use (Northrup 1995). Alternatively recent studies in diaspora (Brah 1996) have highlighted the social imaginaries of these migrants and now citizens as they negotiate between a reconstructed notion of 'India' and their real present and future in the country of citizenship. Articles in the first section integrate these two perspectives that of migration and of diaspora when they explore South African-Indian 'lived experiences' through an examination of their history and subjectivities as class, caste and gender. Simultaneously and for the first time, we introduce the reader to the imaginary of indenture in the field of out-migration. This represents a research orientation that needs to be further advanced.

However, legacies and identities need not be examined only in terms of out-migration of Indians to South Africa and other regions of the world within the colonial auspices. The question of identity is much larger and concerns itself with exploitation and oppression of many groups, not only Indian-South Africans. Both South Africa and India have had a long history of group-based identity movements being organised against colonial and post-colonial states. While the Indian nation-state divides people of India into religious communities, caste and tribal identities, it is clear that these intersect with class, gender, language and regional identities. On the other hand, South Africa divides its population in terms of race (Black African, coloureds, whites and Indians). Race, of course, also intersects with class, gender, religion and region. Thus, any comparison regarding identities will have to locate how the two nation-states have structured identity formation in these two territories (Uys and Patel 2011b). The second section considers the national, or meso-level, context in which not only South African Indians with an indentured legacy but also those living in India were and are expected to operate as South African and Indian citizens. This citizenship has to do with democracy and the varied ways in which it has been institutionalised after 1947 in India and after the end of Apartheid in South Africa. The focus of the second section is on democracy and the difficulties of transition. Both states have tried to introduce democracy in tandem with the capitalist economic structures and elite-driven political projects. Both have placed value on education as a means of mobility. Capitalist economic structures have created further exclusions which exacerbated earlier exclusions. Now these have also led to environmental degradation. The second section explores the contradictory institutionalisation of democracy and its projects regarding education and its inclusive repercussions. It also highlights the environmental question that organises the capitalist processes.

In the final section, a macro, or cross-national analysis is undertaken from both Indian and South African points of reference. The key imperative here was to problematise the role of the two states — South Africa and India in the global South (IBSA) and in the global arena as regional powers (BRICS). From this, it is evident that this text begins to tackle critical questions at all levels of societal analysis, and does so with a great sensitivity to matters temporal, theoretical and methodological.

Migration, Indenture and Identities: Being Indian in South Africa

2010 provided an occasion for reflection on the experience of forced and voluntary movement of Indian labour in an era of colonial 'unfreedom'. This history of Indians in South Africa addresses questions of exploitation and dispossession as well as Indian participation in the struggles against inequality and exclusion. It is an attempt to capture the details and texture of the lives individuals and communities made for themselves under adverse conditions (Desai and Vahed 2010).

British colonial regimes' exploitative labour practices in both South Africa and India created a linkage and bond between the two countries that could never be broken. Some of the contemporary perspectives on the history and sociology of indenture is caught in ideological and political language. Since the late 20th century these perspectives have increasingly been used by political commentators and historians as well as other social scientists who, for example, argue that indenture is slavery (North-Coombes 1984). The new field of diaspora studies have tended to stereotype the cultural traits of the migrant, suggesting that all migrants share a similar culture and that they can be perceived as being part of one larger community of Indians.

The articles in this section debunk many of these positions by reformulating the questions regarding migration. The contributors open up their specific questions to the existing discussions and thus contribute substantially the study of the history of Indian migration in the 19th century, and the nature of the contemporary Indian diaspora. The articles portray the many tensions that inform the fragmented and collective identities of Indian migrants, who as contemporary South African citizens must explore and understand their new identities whilst steeped in historical memories. Therefore, the first set of articles in this section begins by introducing the present tensions that structure the identity of Indians in South Africa, as they negotiate being South Africans and Indians simultaneously.

Ashwin Desai and Goolam Vahed's article relies upon a combination of methods. On the one hand they excavate official archives and court papers, whilst on the other visual records (such as photographs to capture the 'life and times' of the indentured) are not ignored. The stories that they record suggest that the indentured were not simply victims of the 'system'.To survive and even challenge the strictures of indenture they employed ingenious ways. Desai and Vahed argue that the many stories of pain and abuse, the horrible living conditions, rampant disease, and suffering of the indentured must be contrasted with those who successfully made new lives in Natal. The stories that emerge should also raise serious doubts about continuing to see indenture as a new system of slavery.

Mariam Seedat-Khan provides a sociological story of indentured women's experiences. This article is based on rereading secondary literature in conjunction with 20 qualitative interviews conducted with Indian women in South Africa. It records how, on 4 October 1860, men, women and children boarded the *Belvedere* in Calcutta and set sail for the shores of Natal. Eight days later the *Truro* left Madras and both ships arrived at the port of Natal in November 1860. Soon more arrived in search of a better life: they were going to work under what they thought would be ideal conditions. The dream was shortlived. The pre-embarkation barracks were far from adequate. The conditions on the *Belvedere, Truro* and other ships were inhuman. Death and disease saw families lose loved ones. Women were raped and subject to hard labour. Conflict ensued and violence was commonplace on the ships. The article records harsh experiences endured and outlines how this experience contributed to the development and building of strong ties among the women and their families. Women were instrumental in maintaining and promoting a familial environment. These experiences strengthened their role in South Africa and within the Indian community. Women in particular were determined to maintain a sense of family, community, religion and identity.

V. Geetha's article discusses the various ways indenture was represented by different interlocutors and commentators in the late 19th century and early 20th century in Tamil literature and among nationalist and Dalit politicians. Her article starts with the narration of a dream of a lonely old woman in Madras, Subbulakshmi, before her death in the 1980s. In her dream, she hears a Tamil indentured woman labourer in South Africa beseeching her for help. This dream helps Geetha open up a new window to understand the desire and the helplessness of being in indentured labour, a desire to free oneself from caste and gender strictures and to search for freedom in a new land where nevertheless everything was uncertain.

Geetha's article attempts to track the figure of the woman as indentured labourer in South Africa (and elsewhere) as she appears and retreats in Tamil popular imagination during the early 20th century. It does this through a critical consideration of a mélange of texts and their contexts, of production and reception: Mahatma Gandhi's writings on the plight of indentured labour, Dalit responses to the indentured labour question, tales that circulated in the popular sphere, were the stuff of family and common memory, poetry and song that dwelt on life across the vast seas.

The next three articles highlight how the commemoration of 150 years of an Indian presence in South Africa has allowed the Indian community in South Africa to reframe their politics, and to interrogate the memories of their histories as migrants. This event has also facilitated greater understanding of their present and their future as South African-Indians and as global citizens. The articles discuss the two kinds of actors that have organised this event at the South African end. For the South African state, there was hope that the celebrations would help to consolidate links with India as well as strengthen its position within the South-South alliance. This event also allowed the Indian community an opportunity to be recognised as an integral part of South Africa's citizenry.

For some ordinary South Africans of Indian origin, 150 years of living in South Africa represented a milestone. This is the first time that they could celebrate their presence in South Africa as full citizens during a national event, fully acknowledged by the South African state (Thurman 2010). Yet, this moment also created ruptures and failed to generate a consensus among South Africans of Indian origin about themselves and their future. Rehana Vally attended the celebrations of the 150 years of Indian presence in Laudium, the erstwhile Indian township of Pretoria, and uses this as a backdrop to discuss and reflect on the reasons that led the residents to organise this event. Through intensive interviews with three generations of women, she discusses how the event has led many to the reopening of old debates on the forms, processes and opportunities/disadvantages of being migrants, of living as an excluded group in South Africa, of building solidarity with each other and the religious and/or generational divisions among them today.

For the former white rulers, the South African Indians were a homogeneous community, and because they presented a united front in opposing apartheid, the rest of the population also viewed them similarly. The post-apartheid democratic era is characterised by a resurgence of ethnic and sub-ethnic identities and in some cases a reinvention of the divisions of the 1860s. Brij Maharaj's article underscores the various divisions and tensions related to class, religion, language, geographic origins and associated changes that have structured the Indian community in South Africa. This division, he argues, has intervened in forestalling the creation of solidarities among Indians and has also affected the organisation in Durban which wanted to celebrate the 150-year events. Maharaj's article discusses how the divisions influenced the discussions regarding the purpose of celebration, who organised these events, and the roles the South African and Indian governments played. Finally, he asks if unity is possible and whether it should be strived for. Is it possible to build a democratic, progressive platform from the grassroots that could articulate the problems and challenges facing the community, without harking back to the ethnic politics and feuding of the past or becoming the surrogate of any political party?

What kinds of solidarities do the Indian community need to build? This question is answered by Lubna Nadvi through a discussion of the movement organised by informal traders (mainly but not exclusively from the Indian community) working at the Early Morning Market (EMM), a 100-year-old fresh produce market in the city of Durban (also known as eThekwini). The traders were informed by the city authorities that the market was going to be demolished in order to build a mall and that they would be relocated almost immediately. A vigorous civic campaign ensued with the EMM Traders Association combining forces with broader civil society locally, nationally and internationally and opposed the City of Durban. The author argues that this contemporary struggle is significant as it takes place 150 years after the first indentured Indians arrived in South Africa, many of whom had been involved in setting up and trading at the EMM once their period of indenture had ended. The indentured workers' early struggles bore fruit as they passed on the ownership of their fresh produce businesses to their subsequent generations, who prospered despite remaining amongst the working class. It is this current generation that once again has to revisit the struggles of their forefathers and mothers, and face the brutality of a neoliberal, still imperialist, corporate state agenda. The article attempts to document the journey that the campaign to 'save the market' has taken since the beginning of 2009 and suggests that the Indian community needs to rediscover its histories to fight contemporary battles.

The final article in this section by Ravindra Jain provides an anthropological critique of Indian diasporic integration in South Africa by considering historical processes and the limits of social justice. His narrative is steered by methodological considerations. First, two major modes of historical discourse are employed. The so-called 'presentist' history works its way backwards from the contemporary formation of the democratic Republic of South Africa in 1994 up to sustained political moves for dismantling the apartheid regime that was introduced in 1948. The other stream of historical narrative — broadly chronological (conventional history) — is built on the conceptualisation of (a) the formation of the South African 'nation' under the special historical conjuncture of three 'city states' of Johannesburg, Durban and Cape Town as the nuclei for a largely agricultural-extractive (big and small farms and mining) hinterland rather than a network of urban-industrial complexes as in much of European and North American historical development; and (b) the history of political conflict and cultural-linguistic accommodation and rivalry between the British and Dutch colonial powers. This is the backdrop ('historical anthropology' of the title) of the growth of a multi-racial, multicultural society in South Africa with particular reference to its Indian component. The latter narrative is marked by indentured immigration followed by interstitial mobility of Indian South Africans and traversed by the troubled history of international support (political alliance between the Indian National Congress and the African National Congress) as well as the cleavage (variations in the Indian boycott of the apartheid regime in South Africa) as the salient political dimension of the India–South Africa interface.

Methodologically, his analysis proceeds along a three-pronged path: (a) delineation of socio-cultural and politico-economic processes in diaspora rather than reliance on procrustean typologies as historical or cultural products; (b) commensurately, the interpretation of the India– South Africa interface diachronically and synchronically with a view of comparison in the social sciences as cultural translation; and (c) reading this interface by calibrating epistemology and ontology of this particular discourse on the same page. In other words, the method of historiography followed moves away from simply 'abstracting' generalities from 'raw data' (as in many positivist sciences) to sketching family resemblances among and between the phenomena (ontology) and analytical concepts (epistemology).

The Contemporary Contradictions in Nation-state: Democracy, Education and Environment

This section explores the challenges that are being faced by both countries today and provides evidence for shared experiences of contested transition as well as a compromised social justice. As scholars and citizens, we need to acknowledge that the two countries share similar attributes. First, both countries are poor with high levels of inequality. They share a colonial history, where resources were extracted for the benefit of the metropole. Additionally, they also share a commitment to install democracy in tandem with capitalist economic structures. And last, both countries are organising the economy and the polity through elite-driven political project(s). These processes have yielded contradictory trends in the two countries particularly with regard to the role of the state which has created and encouraged political divides and maintained inequalities.

In spite of these similarities, South Africa and India are generally considered very different societies. The most obvious differences relate to population and geographical size. They also experienced different forms of colonialism. While South Africa was characterised by settler colonialism combined with an influx of migrant labour from different parts of the world (including India), in India the British created an elite group to rule for them and India has been and still is a major exporter of labour. South Africa's economy advanced quite quickly during the first half of the 20th century, mainly on the basis of extensive mineral resources. A huge black working class developed and the economy quickly progressed to large-scale industrial production. However, the apartheid policies put in place formally by its nationalist government from 1948 when it came into power hindered the establishment of democracy in South Africa. Around the same time India became a democratic state and initiated a policy and programme of development to wipe out its inequalities, which its political elite argued came from colonialism. The Indian economy was mainly based on agriculture at this stage, with very little industrialisation. This was the first stage of transition for India and entailed transition from the colonial system to a democratic social order.

Transition also entails two further dimensions, the second being primarily economic and involving the worldwide expansion of capitalism as a result of the growing integration of national economies into a global market and a predominance of economic liberalisation. There is also a third dimension related to the transformation of unequal social relations, inherited from pre-colonial and colonial pasts. While these three transitions are happening simultaneously in South Africa (the so-called triple transition) in India they are several decades apart, the political having occurred in the late 1940s and the economic (in this sense) since the 1980s, with the social overlapping both transitions in different ways (Uys and Patel 2011a).

We consider three themes in the political dimension of the triple transition — all three related to the state: democracy (with associated concerns relating to citizenship), education and environment. We include articles that discuss how these divides can be understood in the context of the common history of injustice and exploitation that both nations were subject to. Critical issues of transition at economic, social and political levels are addressed. Issues such as exploitation, class and socioeconomic conditions are critical for both South Africa and India and there are important lessons that these articles articulate.

The first article by Janis Grobbelaar discusses how South Africans are currently — once more — anguished about their future; that the South African journey that set out from the 1994 momentous small miracle has begun to seriously beg the question of — where to. Underpinning the article is the ultimate question as to whether or not the post-1994 state is able to build a just, fully participatory, economically equitable and secure South Africa for its entire people in the light of the enormous disparities of wealth and life chances that have typified society since its inception. The article suggests that what South Africa has experienced since 1994 is a successful formal societal transition rather than a winning socio-political transformation. Five key elements of the negotiated revolution are explored in regard to the former: the political deadlock of the 1980s; leadership; existing institutional strengths that facilitated transitional triumph; the role of social dynamics, social capital and cohesion between people of the same place; as well as instruments devised for social transformation, amongst which truth commissioning was envisioned as being necessary. Contrary to expectations — and in the light of the process of a successfully negotiated official transition notwithstanding — South Africa's 300-year struggle for freedom from racial ordering, economic exploitation, political oppression and discrimination — the ongoing attempts to build a transformed polity — are facing key challenges. Four essential contestations in this regard are considered: the economy, crime, the persistence of race and the question of the undermining of core constitutional principles. The country's socio-political fabric is breaking down and it will continue to face enormous challenges. Whether South Africa will succeed in its quest for transformation is therefore uncertain.

Adam Habib picks up the same issue but in a new way. He explores the nature of the decade-long democratic experiment in South Africa which unfolds in the context of the confrontation between Thabo Mbeki (known for his pro neoliberal approach) and Jacob Zuma (populist leader supported by the left and ANC working class) over the leadership of the African National Congress. The South African struggle, he argues, was to create a human-oriented development and he investigates the broader structural political condition and especially the configuration of power that has organised its ideology and practices. His conclusion is that not only is human-oriented development a product of a political process, but it also requires an intricate mix of representative and participatory democratic elements. This mix is meant to create a substantive uncertainty, which is the political foundation that generates accountability between elites and their citizens, so necessary for realising a human-oriented development agenda.

Juxtaposing these arguments is an article from India on its democratic experiment by Ujjwal Singh. Singh argues that the historically specific form of the modern state in India has unfolded along processes which exhibit an expanding register of democracy both in the narrow sense of electoral democracy and the more substantive logic of redistribution and entrenchment of consti-tutionalism. At the same time, however, the registers of governance unfold in a way which is skewed towards the consolidation of the power of the state, and modes of legitimation which make for a 'silent erosion' of constitutionalism and the rule of law, and a weak democratic state. This article explores the ambivalences of the 'democratic state' in India, by examining in particular its legal-institutional and political responses to nationality struggles, and struggles by peasants and *adivasis*. The state in India uses repressive laws for creating democratic rule. For example, on the one hand electoral democracy is seen as a surrogate for the political resolution of the challenges in Kashmir but the use of extraordinary laws like the Armed Forces Special Powers Act and various Preventive Detention laws are in force simultaneously. The same is true in the case of the struggles by the *adivasis*, and in particular the armed struggles in states with large *adivasi* populations.

If democracy and inclusive citizenship are key themes for understanding transition, so is education, which is the theme of the next set of articles. Education has been used as a tool to reshape perceptions of unequal societies. Education in both India and South Africa has held equal importance for citizens. In both nation-states it has always been a means of accessing freedom from oppression and injustice. The role of education needs to be carefully explored as a mobilisation or advancement tool for citizens from both countries that have made their mark all over the world.

The discussion on education starts with an article by Padma Velaskar on India. She argues that though education was given a key role for reorganising the injustice of the past and present society, the Indian state's strategy of passive revolution and the pervasive influence exerted on the education system by the forces of domination and discrimination, even the minimalist state agenda of equal opportunity and affirmative action in education stands unfulfilled today. Thus patterns of educational distribution and attainment reflecting structural — gender, caste, class, tribe — and other ethnic inequalities make it amply apparent and well established that education plays a predominantly socially repro-ductive and culturally hegemonic role. But we must also state that subordinated groups of Indian society having suffered the indignities of state neglect and social oppression have turned education into a site of resistance and contestation in the context of their political struggles for emancipation. For them education commands powerful substantive and counter symbolic value, and has helped wrest social freedom and political advantage and construct alternate discourses of modernity. What has unfolded over the years is a complex social history of educational expansion and an equally complex social impact marked by reproduction, change, conflict and contradiction. This article aims at capturing and analysing key aspects of the changing situation which are especially significant to emancipatory agendas of the socially subordinated.

Anita Rampal discusses the way in which education has been used as a tool to reshape perceptions and understandings of unequal societies. Education in both India and South Africa has equal importance for citizens. It has always been a means of accessing freedom from oppression and injustice for both nations. The role of education needs to be carefully understood as a mobilisation or advancement tool for citizens from both countries. This begins to impact on broader issues of emigration, advancement and identity. In particular it is important to consider how the modernisation–indigenisation dilemma for education continues to reconfigure now in several countries, around differently nuanced curricular dimensions, ranging from the 'developmental–ecological' crisis, 'rational–moral' values, 'academic–everyday' knowledge, 'intellectual–manual' work, English or mother tongue as the medium, to the material–cultural politics of identity.

Derek van der Merwe discusses the role higher education is expected to play in strengthening South Africa's evolving democracy by providing skilled human capital. He suggests that this role is severely constrained by the challenges experienced by higher education institutions as well as the students enrolled for such studies. These include limited access to post-school educational opportunities, glaring disparities between universities in virtually every institutional activity, partly as a result of severe long-term under-funding of the higher education sector, high dropout rates and deeply-rooted governance problems facing the sector. It examines these problems within the context of developments in education in general, and higher education in particular, in South Africa. It analyses structural complexities within the higher education sector and resource constraints that inhibit pursuit of the developmental agenda, and suggests some approaches that could be considered to alleviate the problems. In particular, modern societies in a developmental state need to confront the essential paradox in education that sustained wealth creation is deeply dependent on a workforce that is skilled, knowledgeable and innovative; but that the wealth (resource abundance) required educating and training such a workforce is largely absent.

Last, how do scholars address the issue of modernity and development and what have been the consequences for the environment? Issues relating to water resources, conservation and environmental degradation following the emphasis on industrial growth in a developing economy have lead authors to question the models of development in the post-colonial world.

Kalpana Sharma discusses the environmental questions in urban India. India is urbanising at a rapid pace. By 2050, half of India's population will be living in urban centres. It is already evident that the growth rate of the smaller and medium-sized towns is outpacing that of the larger metropolitan cities. While the latter attract the attention of policy makers and the media, the former are growing in an unplanned manner. As a result, even those towns and cities that were once sustainable are now showing all the symptoms of unplanned urban chaos. They are following a pattern of development that has already been proved to be environmentally unsustainable in bigger cities in India and in many other parts of the world. Where does concern for environment fit into this chaos? Is it even possible, with the inevitability of global warming, for environmental factors to be integrated into future urban planning? What examples can India look to for such a pattern of development given its urban growth concerns are markedly different from the advanced industrialised countries, due to the size of the population and the extent of urban poverty?

These questions relate to an understanding of nature and environment. As a result, in the next article, Mahesh Rangarajan debates the problem of conservation in India. Part of the controversy arises from the very attempt to make spaces for nature in a country of over a billion people that also has the second fastest growth rate among the world's major economies. But much of it is rooted in a complex and multi-layered history. The vast expanse of state forests was a major legacy of British imperial rule as were the hunting grounds of princely rulers. Republican India, in balancing growth with conservancy, often relies on instruments of power rooted in the past. The last two decades have, however, seen an efflorescence of alternative approaches at different levels in society and in contrasting regions and diverse ecological settings. Will a rights-based approach or middle-of-the-road attempts combine transparency with a role for government? How far can science be given a critical role in a system driven by the forest and civilian bureaucracy? Most crucial is the question of how far devolution of forest rights can act as a check on commercial, especially industrial pressures. Reconciling ecological values with social justice makes for a rocky road. But it lies at the very heart of the challenge of remaking a vibrant democracy into the seed bed of a more just social order.

Globalisation and Regionalism: Relating to Each Other as Regional Nation States

In this last section the articles discuss bilateral relationships between India and South Africa and the challenges faced by these countries.

Rajen Harshe explores the different dimensions of Indo-South African ties and demonstrates likely possibilities of Indo-South African cooperation in the context of contemporary globalisation. The article discusses the possibilities that can help structure a firmer relationship between the two countries in the present context of globalisation given that it has today placed the two countries in the same situation — of being regional powers. While undoubtedly there are deep connections because of history — the migration of Indian indentured labourers, the role played by Mahatma Gandhi in the incipient struggle against colonialism and the subsequent support given by the Indian government for the anti-apartheid movement — it is the present connections that formed as a result of the global dynamics that is nourishing the relationship. The article traces the different theories of globalisation, the formation of regional blocs and highlights in this context the many convergences and divergences between the two countries. It concludes with an assessment where economic, political, intellectual and cultural contacts can be developed in the context of globalisation.

Priya Chacko discusses how India still persists in prioritising Southern multilateralism despite new partnerships with the North. This article examines India's attachment to Southern multilateralism by examining its membership in the IBSA (India, Brazil, South Africa) coalition. She argues that explanations which focus solely on economic self-interest or a desire to consolidate regional leadership are incomplete. Instead, she suggests that understanding India's enthusiasm for the IBSA must take into account the issue of identity. Drawing on insights from critical constructivist international relations theory which posits that foreign policy discourse enacts a state's identity and that identity forms the basis of a state's interests, she assesses the role that Southern multilateralism has played in the construction of India's postcolonial identity in the past and the present. The article suggests that both in the past and in the present Africa and South Africa in particular have played key roles in India's self-fashioning as a state pursuing an alternative modernity based on avoiding unequal relationships and pursuing less exploitative and aggressive relationships with others. At the same time, the selective, rather than universal, Southern multilateralism of the IBSA suggests an important shift in the ethico-political basis of India's foreign policy.

Finally, David Fig again looks at the IBSA from trilateral perspectives. He considers whether the IBSA Dialogue Forum served the peoples of its constituent countries by improving the position of the global South within multilateral fora. The article examines the purpose, workings and stated aspirations of the IBSA and discusses some of the challenges in forming a trilateral partnership embracing key countries in three regions of the world. In particular, it scrutinises the workings of the IBSA in relation to some of the controversial technologies that impact on the environment, such as agrofuels, GMOs (transgenic seed and crops), and more broadly, the field of science and technology. Finally, concerns about development, especially as expressed by formations of civil society in the three countries as they relate to the IBSA, are considered.

The article concludes that the IBSA Dialogue Forum is likely to remain in essence a consultative body, which, so as to extend its coherence, has established some collaborative programmes. It does not really play a role as spokesperson for the global South, nor is it essentially involved in producing a coherent South position on key global issues such as UN reform, the fulfilment of the Millennium Development Goals or the combating of global poverty, inequality and injustice. While it is not in a position to put forward a new global vision for sustainability and planetary justice, its summits and ministerial consultations may provide a focal point for civil society from the three nations to put forward their shared alternative vision through coordinated actions and interventions. It remains to be seen what impact South Africa's recent acceptance into BRICS will have on the continuation of the IBSA programmes.

Conclusion

South Africa and India are both major stakeholders in their regions today and have the potential to become serious players on the global stage. With increasing importance given to political processes, both bilateral and multilateral (such as the IBSA — India, Brazil, South Africa partnerships — as well as South Africa's recent inclusion in the BRICS countries) at the political levels there is a growing interest in comparative research between India and South Africa from both countries which has spearheaded various kinds of intellectual and educational collaborations.

First, there are a growing number of special editions of journals attempting to make social science scholarship accessible to audiences in both countries or to provide comparisons. From the Indian side there is a long tradition of studying Africa and South Africa from the perspective of area studies, while more recent initiatives have been undertaken by South African scholars to study India. Full-scale volumes and monographs devoted to this issue have been published (eg. Williams 2008). A special edition of the *South African Review of Sociology* (40 [1]) devoted to sociological scholarship in India, and a special edition of *Journal of Asian and African Studies* (44 [1]) containing essays by South African scholars comparing South Africa and India, appeared in 2009. Second, research centres and institutes such as the Centre for Indian Studies in Africa at the University of the Witwatersrand have been established. Collaborative teaching programmes such as the one on globalisation at the University of KwaZulu-Natal and the Global Labour University based at the University of the Witwatersrand in South Africa and the Tata Institute of Social Sciences in India have been introduced. Last, cultural and educational exchange programmes together with attendance at conferences, visits by scholars and institutionalised links such as 'Memoranda of Understanding' between the Indian Sociological Society and the South African Sociological Association, and between universities are more recent developments.

This volume emerged from similar exchanges that inaugurated a dialogue of comparing the transitions in India and South Africa.

In particular, the commemoration of 150 years since the first indentured labourers from India arrived in South Africa provided the spark for an India–South Africa conference held at the Soweto campus of the University of Johannesburg where scholars from India and South Africa debated ways to relate to each other. Given the context, there was a spate of papers on South African Indians and their search for a new South African identity, whilst simultaneously not relinquishing their links to India. On the other hand, the conference also included contributions from both Indian and South African scholars about contemporary challenges of nation-state dynamics in the context of global changes.

Apart from analysing the connected histories of India and South Africa, this volume also considers dilemmas that the two societies have in common, in particular those related to the state, namely democracy and citizenship, the environment and education. This comparative analysis of contemporary India and South Africa demonstrates how the dilemmas faced by each country are constituted by processes which are similar in certain respects. This provides the beginnings of an understanding on how to move forward in dealing with individual and collective challenges. The spirit of the 2010 celebrations has been captured in these pages, as has a promise of the potential of a more substantive Southern dialogue still to come.

References

Alexander, Peter and Sujata Patel (eds). 2009. Special edition on Indian scholarship, *South African Review of Sociology*, 40 (1).

Brah, A. 1996. *Cartographies of Diaspora: Contesting Identities*. London: Routledge.

Desai, A. and G. Vahed. 2010. *Inside Indian Indenture: A South African Story, 1860–1914*. Cape Town: HSRC Press.

Hofmeyer, I. and M. Williams. 2009. 'South Africa–India: Connections and Comparisons', *Journal of Asian and African Studies*, 44 (1).

North-Coombes, M. D. 1984. 'From slavery to indenture: Forced Labour in the Political Economy of Mauritius', Kay Saunders (ed.), *Indentured Labour in the British Empire, 1834–1920*. London: Croom-Helm.

Northrup, D. 1995. *Indentured Labor in the Age of Imperialism, 1834–1922*. Cambridge: Cambridge University Press.

Thurman, C. 2010. 'India and South Africa: 150 Years of History'. http://www.mediaclubsouthafrica.com/index.php?option=com_content&view=article&id=1977:india-011010&catid=43:culturenews&Itemid=112C. Accessed 17 May 2011.

Uys, Tina and Sujata Patel. 2011a. 'On Comparing the Contested Transitions of South Africa and India', idem (eds), *Exclusion, Social Capital and Citizenship: Contested Transitions in South Africa and India*. Delhi: Orient Blackswan.

———(eds). 2011b. *Exclusion, Social Capital and Citizenship: Contested Transitions in South Africa and India*. Delhi: Orient Blackswan.

Von Holdt, K. and E. Webster. 2005. 'Work Re-structuring and the Crisis of Social Reproduction: A Southern Perspective' in idem (eds), *Beyond the Apartheid Workplace — Studies in Transition*. Scottsville: University of KwaZulu-Natal Press.

Williams, M. 2008. *The Roots of Participatory Democracy: Democratic Communists in South Africa and Kerala, India*. New York: Palgrave Macmillan.

Part I

Migration, Indenture and Identities:
Being Indian in South Africa

Part I

Migration, Indenture and Identities: Being Indian in South Africa

2

Indenture and Indianness in South Africa, 1860–1913

Ashwin Desai and Goolam Vahed

Beginning in the mid-19th century, about 1.3 million Indian contract labourers were exported to Mauritius, Jamaica, British Guiana, Trinidad, St Lucia, Granada and Natal to satisfy the demand for labour that was both cheap and docile (Meer 1980: 3). Who were the indentured that landed in Port Natal in 1860? For the most part their history has been captured by a meticulous checking of ship lists to reveal the different castes of the indentured and the villages they originated from (Bhana 1991).

Building on this painstaking and valuable foundation we sought to fill out the picture of the life and times of the indentured. We sought to understand their motivations for coming, the way they reconstituted life in an alien environment and, in particular, the position of women, especially single women. To achieve this we sought to reconstruct life stories, revisit the story of indenture and present a more nuanced picture. Sourcing material, especially searching for the voices of the subalterns, is difficult by the lack of 'their' perspective, and the overwhelming voice of the ruling classes. We followed Edward Said's pointer of searching in the direction of 'unconventional or neglected sources', of trawling the 'official' archives, while simultaneously 'listening' to the voices of the indentured through letters, newspaper reports, and anecdotes handed down , and by matching them with stories of the indentured in different locations (Said 1993: vi).

This approach helped to recover biographies and voices of some of whom history has largely ignored. This includes in particular omissions of gender, a difficult task for, as Verene Shepherd reminds us, 'colonialist historiography has tended to mute the voices of exploited people, and the subaltern, as female, was even more invisible' (Shepherd 2002: 7). Our approach underscores the fact that the indentured were not mere prisoners of the 'system', but they were often imaginative, creative beings who found all manner of means to survive, challenge, even 'escape' the strictures of indenture. Many of the indentured marched to their own tunes using a myriad of tactics to escape the gaze of the colonial masters.

Another theme that runs through the story of indenture is the indenture-as-slavery thesis. Hugh Tinker classified indenture as a new form of slavery (Tinker 1974). It was at Kendra Hall in Durban in February 2010 that one of the first meetings was held to constitute a committee to organise the commemoration of the 150th anniversary of the arrival of the first indentured in Natal. We attended the meeting and the most heated discussion centred on this very debate. Many in the audience equated indenture with slavery, even rejecting a suggestion that the wording be changed to 'indenture was akin to slavery' or any words that sought to differentiate the two. As the debate unfolded the intentions of those insisting on the word 'slavery' was two-fold. First, they were wary of the fact that by differentiating between the two the brutality of indenture would be muted. Second, operating as a subtext it indicated a desire that those who came as indentured should be distinguished from passenger Indians whose history and accomplishments had been fore-grounded at the expense of those who came from indentured stock. The overwhelming majority adopted the word 'slavery' in the statement read out at the end of the meeting. This article responds to this debate by arguing that notwithstanding the brutality of the system of indenture, one cannot distort the past for the exigencies of more immediate political purposes.

Origins

The introduction of Indian indentured labour into Natal was a direct result of the British annexation of Natal in 1843. British settlers were attracted to the colony whose white population doubled from around 8,000 in 1857 to 17,821 in 1869 (Thomson 1952: 3). Settlers experimented with a variety of crops but it was sugar that accounted for the bulk of the total gross value of arable farming. Farmers, frustrated by the lack of capital and the absence of cheap and malleable labour, turned to Britain to solve the problem of capital and to India to ease the labour crisis. The indigenous Zulu were 'unreliable' because they had access to land and were unwilling to enter into a subservient labour relationship. Some lived on locations established by colonial officials who utilised the existing distribution of power in Zulu society to achieve control, others lived on Protestant missions where converts to Christianity responded with great vigour to market incentives, while some also rented land from the government as well as land speculators who were waiting for an increase in immigration and a rise in land prices (Marks 1990: 26–29).

The arrival of 342 Indians aboard the Truro on 16 November 1860 ended a decade-long struggle for cheap labour. The majority of the 152,641 migrants who arrived between 1860 and 1911 were young males in the 18–30 age group. The average male:female ratio was approximately 64:28, while fewer than 20 per cent of the indentured comprised families (Bhana 1991: 20). The list of immigrants included many castes. Although the majority of migrants were middle-to-low caste, there were some upper-to-middle level castes such as Moodley (traders), Brahmins (priests) and Rajput (landowners). However, caste was a malleable category because sometimes the indenture 'up-casted' to gain status and at other times 'down-casted' to overcome reservations about higher-caste migrants. The authorities actively discouraged the recruitment of Brahmins and Muslims. Two-thirds of the migrants were from Tamil Nadu and Andhra Pradesh in the south-east, and the rest from Bihar and Uttar Pradesh in the north-east of India. Migrants from south India spoke Tamil and Telugu; northerners spoke dialects of Hindi which came to form a South African Hindi (Mesthrie 1992: 7).

On the Move

The decision to emigrate was forced on most by demographic and economic dislocation which resulted from the wars that shattered the Mughal Empire, the administrative reorganisation of India under the British Empire, and natural disasters. Under the zamindari system, absentee landlords charged exorbitant rents and demanded it in cash rather than kind. The 1882 Famine Commission reported that two-thirds of the peasants were in debt. Poverty and landlessness forced many to migrate to cities where some were enticed by recruiting agents who promised wages several times higher than those current in India (Clarke 1986: 10). While the majority of the indentured migrants were most likely from among this mass of uprooted peasants it would be wrong to see them merely as 'victims'. Most would have given thought to their decision to emigrate, even if they knew little of their destinations be it Trinidad, Natal or Mauritius.

George Mutukistna told the Wragg Commission of 1885 that he 'came out as an indentured Indian ... finding India too crowded: I could not find employment there.' He knew, he said, that 'I should be bound to hoe the fields if required, but I came [because] I thought that, in the long run, I should be able to better my positions' (Meer 1980: 397). Goordeen Bhagoo and his wife Golaba Lalsa arrived in Natal on the *Warora* in April 1890. The ship's list has them as 'resident of [French] Guadeloupe', which is located in the eastern Caribbean Sea. Born in Lucknow in 1865, Goordeen moved to Guadeloupe in 1881. After five years he returned to Lucknow, married Golaba and emigrated to Natal. He served his indenture with the railway department, and thereafter opened stores in Charlestown, Newcastle and Ingangane. He was prominent in the 1913 strike and was sent by Gandhi from Volksrust to Newcastle to help organise strikers. He also built a temple in Newcastle and was a renowned wrestler (NAB, MSCE 35615/1942). The stories of Goordeen and Mutukistna, and the many other similar narratives in the archives illustrate that migrants were not always 'plucked' from villages. Such individuals weighed their options and were probably swayed by the lack of economic opportunities at 'home'.

The Plantation

Indenture was governed by the 'agreement' which specified the conditions of work, housing, pay, medical treatment and so on. While the contract provided guarantees on paper, in practice indenture was a period of brutality, poverty and moral disintegration for many as employers failed to fulfil their end of the bargain. Appalling servitude defined the indentured system, with many narratives of brutality on the plantations. Take the story of Mungi, for example. She had arrived with her husband Halhori from Shahabad in July 1881. She was in an advanced stage of pregnancy and, according to Dr Lindsay Bonnar, gave birth to a stillborn child in Durban on 12 August. The following day, still weak, she was forced to go by rail to Isipingo with a group of Indian migrants and from there, made to walk 40 miles to Umzinto on a 'cold and rainy day' because 'there was no wagon or means of shelter, the want of which was doubtless the cause of the poor young woman's untimely death … When the woman complained of poor health no attempt was made to obtain any sort of accommodation for her … No carriage was provided for her either' (Desai and Vahed 2010).

Attorney-General Gallwey reported on 7 November 1881 that 'the woman's death resulted from her being moved too soon after her confinement. The Protector should inform Mr. Reynolds that the woman's death was caused by the improper and undue haste by which she was conveyed to the estate'. The recommendation by Dr Charles Garland, chairman of the Medical Board, that 'no woman ought to be required to work for 14 days after a miscarriage or a confinement', was disregarded because planters did not want 'idle' labour (Desai and Vahed 2010: 130). The treatment of Mungi was not isolated. According to Maureen Swan:

> Plantation labourers were overworked [as much as a 17- or an 18-hour day during the overlapping crushing and planting seasons], malnourished and very poorly housed, usually in barracks arranged in rows of back-to-back rooms without window or chimney. This resulted in abnormally high disease and death rates … There is a solid weight of evidence in the Protector's files to suggest [that] degrading conditions formed the pattern of daily life throughout much of agriculture (Swan 1991: 121).

The indentured did not simply submit. Many resisted in a variety of ways, mostly individually, and usually on a small scale. The story of one woman is quite remarkable.

Votti Veeramah Somayya

Indentured women were paid lower wages and received less food rations but their burdens stretched beyond issues of sustenance and labour. Some were subject to sexual violence. Votti's story draws our attention to ways in which some women fought the multiple oppressions. Votti arrived in Natal in May 1890. The 18-year-old, described as a 'woman of prepossessing appearance' in one document, fought to be allocated to Gavin Caldwell of Ifafa with her shipmates Govindsamy Naik and Bappu Ponnusami. She lived with Naik as 'man and wife' and when Naik committed suicide in November 1890, became Bappu's partner. Caldwell complained to Protector Mason on 19 December 1891 that Votti was constantly 'running off' to adjoining estates and refused to work. However, no one was prepared to employ Votti because, in the Protector's opinion, her 'conduct and character were too well known in the neighbourhood'.

In March 1892, Caldwell again sent Votti to the Protector with instructions that he effect a transfer. The Protector succeeded in transferring her to Charlie Nulliah, the son of indentured migrants. Bappu sought to follow but Votti told the Protector that she had 'no husband in the colony although I have been living with Bappu … I do not wish to live any longer with Bappu.' Within a few months Votti submitted several petitions for another transfer, including one to the Administrator of Natal, Francis Seymour Haden, in April 1893. Amongst her complaints was that Nulliah made 'indecent overtures to me'. The Protector refused to accede to her request and instead she spent seven months in prison. Each time, she said, 'They used to bring me into court and ask if I would go back to my master and then they sent me to [jail]. I will not go back. You can cut my throat but I will not go back …' Votti asked to be 'transferred to some respectable European person'.

Attorney-General Gallwey petitioned the Colonial Secretary on 11 April 1893 to transfer Votti, highlighting 'the rather unprecedented action of the Protector in transferring to another Indian the services of an unmarried Indian woman'. Votti's seven months in prison and 'her readiness to undergo the same again, implies the existence of some good reason such as the main one stated by her for her determination never to return to him'. Mason countered in a letter to Colonial Secretary Bird on 1 May 1893 that Votti had trumped up the charges to annul her contract. Gallwey responded to the Colonial Secretary on 18 May 1893 that 'the presumption of immorality in the case of Indian men and women is very great; [though] the proof in individual instances may be difficult to establish'. Mason was forced to cancel Votti's contract on 31 May 1893.

Votti was transferred to Deane Anthony (40211), who owned a 'respectable Indian eating house and was known as of good character', to complete her five-year term. Ironically, she was assigned to another single Indian male employer without objection from the authorities. She married Rangasami in October 1893 while still under indenture. Theirs was a violent six-year marriage. Rangasami was fined for assaulting Votti in June 1898. The following year, on 23 August 1899, he stabbed Votti with a knife and was imprisoned for three years. In March 1900 Votti instituted proceedings against Rangasami for a juridical separation 'on grounds of cruelty'; and successfully sued for a half share of his assets and the cost of the suit.

Votti disappears from the archives at this point but her narrative is one of confronting the system of indenture, even though it meant consecutive terms of imprisonment; the perils of being a single woman; and adeptly using the legal system for protection. Votti emerges as a courageous woman who was held down by no man, economically, socially or sexually. Such stories restore the status of women from that of Hugh Tinker's 'sorry sisterhood' of single, broken creatures' into historical pioneers (Mehta 2006: 22).

Weapons of the Weak?

While Votti's 'resistance' was singular, there were rare instances of collective action by the indentured. Dubar, Brijmohan, Nagishar and Sarju, were charged for the murder of their employer Alexander Arnold on 25 July 1905. Alexander and his brother Charles owned the adjoining farms of Bellevue and Springfield in Pietermaritzburg. Alexander was murdered shortly before midnight while making his way from Bellevue to Springfield. The men were tried in September 1905. A reconstruction of events revealed that on the day of the murder while they were preparing supper Alexander instructed Dubar to cut the grass. He refused because he had completed his work for the day. An angry Alexander kicked him in the testicles and pushed him to the ground. Brijmohan confronted Alexander who struck him with a stick on his head. Alexander again instructed them to cut the grass. This time it was Budhri who refused and he was struck on the face. They killed him that night by beating him on the head with a stone. The jury returned a guilty verdict on 25 September 1905 and the men were sentenced to hang (Natal Archives Repository, Records of the Supreme Court 1/1/85, 35/1905).

The murder of employers was rare, but these individual acts were interspersed with less frequent forms of collective response.

The most spectacular collective action of the indentured was the 1913 strike, which involved thousands of indentured Indians as it spread out of the coalmines in Northern Natal to the city centres of Pietermaritzburg and Durban, and outwards down the south and north coasts (Desai and Vahed 2010: 371–98). Generally, however, collective resistance was rare. Unable to get redress through a collective withdrawal of labour and the use of the legal system, many indentured resorted to individual acts of resistance that ranged from absenteeism to suicide, while others consistently courted imprisonment or deserted. Workers 'act in their daily life in small ways, resisting pressures as well as submitting to demands, being silent at times and vocal at others, conforming to rules as well as negotiating them, and through small acts of self-assertion seeking to retain a sense of dignity' (Joshi 2005: 12).

Inside the 'Hidden Abode'

Violence was not only a feature of the relationship between employer and employee, but also present within the intimacy of families, due largely to the imbalance in gender ratios and degrading living conditions. The plantation system undermined stable family life, with women often on the receiving end. Wootme was murdered at Blackburn Estate in Inanda on 5 April 1890, her head smashed with an axe by her husband Mulwa. The couple had shared a hut with two unmarried men, Sahebdeen and Moorgasen. Mulwa testified in court:

> I and the woman lay down. The woman said 'go to work now'. I did not go. Then I killed the woman. That is all. We lived with Sahebdeen and Moorgasen who said if the woman would cook for them they would give her clothing and give us rations. The woman cooked food and took it to the field for the men. She did not bring me food. I went to Mr. Townsend for a house. He did not give us a house. I killed the woman because she went with other men and I said 'I was not sufficient for you.'

Mulwa was sentenced to be hanged by the neck until he was dead. Asked to plead in mitigation, he told the judge, 'You can do as you please.' The jury did, however, ' … express their condemnation of the system by which both sexes, married and unmarried, are mingled together in living and sleeping in the same hut, thus leading to most disastrous results, both in prostitution and criminality' (NAR, II, I/ 56, PMP 3839/1890). Unhealthy living conditions, coupled with the gender imbalance between men and women exacerbated sexual tensions and jealousies. There was tension too between the new possibilities that the act of migration opened for women, and the desire of men to continue to assert patriarchal roles.

The Race Question

There are no substantial records of individual social relations between Africans and Indians. The introduction of indentured labour, Fatima Meer wrote, undermined the negotiating power of the Zulu vis-à-vis white settlers. Thus, whatever African 'perceptions of Indian indentured workers was in 1860, included in it must have been the suspicion, if not the knowledge, that they had been brought in ... to be used against them in ways perhaps not immediately understood' (Meer 1985: 54). Racial stereotypes formed almost as soon as the indentured arrived. The *Natal Mercury* reported within a few days of the arrival of Indians: 'Our "poor Zulus" hardly know what to make of these nondescript newcomers ... there is evidently no love lost between the two races ... No, Mongolian and Negro will never intermingle, at least not in Natal' (*Natal Mercury*, 22 November 1860).

Settlers exacerbated tensions by placing Africans in positions of authority over Indians, as overseers and policemen, and often used them to punish Indians. Telucksing, a storekeeper in Verulam, told the Wragg Commission that 'the *kafir* constables here treat the Indians like dogs and sometimes arrest us for doing nothing wrong at all, saying that we have been drinking; they tyrannise over us in every way imaginable'(in Meer 1980: 388). In 1877, 86 of the 'Delta coolies all armed with large sticks and bludgeons' marched towards the Albion Estate in Isipingo, 'shrieking vengeance against four *kafirs*' who had been hired to prevent Indians from passing through the estate's mill (NAR, II, I/2, 209/1877, 19 May 1877).

Gandhi challenged the afflictions facing the diverse group of Indians by calling on them to unite. He saw the struggles in South Africa as linked to those in 'the Motherland'. In the process he did not pursue an 'alliance' with Africans. The crucial question then, to paraphrase Madhavi Kale, is to what extent Indians were 'victims and unwilling instruments' and to what extent they were 'cannily complicit' in the creation of a racially inflected society in colonial Natal (1999: 110–11).

Muharram

While indenture was dislocating, the indentured sought to reconstruct aspects of the lives and the institutions that they had left behind. They also created spaces for various acts of recreation and leisure. Wrestling, the smoking of *dagga*, music and the singing of religious songs were all popular but nothing exemplified the attempt of the indentured to reclaim personhood than Muharram, ostensibly a religious occasion, but turned into a carnival of exuberance, exhibitionism and 'noise' as the indentured, once a year, streamed out of the plantations and the barracks and took over the streets. In examining police reports, 'eyewitness' accounts, newspaper articles and photographs, there were street scenes reminiscent of Mikhail Bakhtin's description of the medieval carnival as 'the second life of the people, who for a time entered the utopian realm of community, freedom and abundance ... Carnival celebrated a temporary liberation from the ... established order; it marked the suspension of all hierarchical rank, privileges and norms of prohibitions' (Bakhtin 1968: 44). Muharram became a transgressive space, albeit a celebration permitted by law. As the indentured mocked each other during the processions, they also mocked the morals and 'rules' of the ruling class. The imaginary homeland that the indentured reconstructed in Natal allowed them to not simply become victims of race and class oppression, but to create spaces of refuge as they struggled against the worst excesses of white rule.

The Myth of Return

Most migrants probably saw emigration as a short-term measure and intended to return. Maistry was a Telugu of the dhobi (washer man) caste born in a small village near Madras [now Chennai]. As a young man he was employed as a dhobi by the Royal Battery. When the Royal Battery moved off, 'there was nothing' for him to do and after consulting with his wife and parents, he indentured for five years. Maistry and 11 others from the same village, eight waiters and three cooks, made the voyage to Natal where Maistry took over washing duties at a local hotel. Maistry took a second wife in Durban and they had two children. With a new life forming around him in Natal, Maistry did not return to India after completing his indenture. During the First World War, he volunteered as a stretcher-bearer in East Africa. When he returned from the war he joined Addington Hospital as a dhobi, eventually becoming head laundryman.

Maistry retired after 28 years of service and in 1947 decided to return to his homeland. 'I had half a mind to settle in India,' he told Hilda Kuper. Yet the nostalgic ideal of what awaited him was shattered when he found that the village and villagers had moved on without him. His first wife and most of his close friends and relatives were dead. The infant daughter that he had left behind was married and barely remembered him. Maistry returned to Natal when he realised that a life lived so far away had stolen from him his sense of 'home' (Kuper 1960: 11).

Maistry's story is not unique. Back on what they thought was 'home' soil, returnees slowly realised that indenture had changed them and also set them apart as the 'other'. Their hallowed 'motherland' had all the appearance of a 'foreign' country. Reintegration proved difficult because of the loss of caste and social and cultural rejection by villagers. One particularly tragic story is that of Munigadu who, finding life untenable in India, returned to South Africa by walking 2,000 miles from Dar es Salaam to the Zululand border where he was apprehended and deported back to India in 1924 after a number of unsuccessful legal wrangles (Desai and Vahed 2010: 426–29).

The End of Indenture

The termination of indenture in 1911 was generally welcomed by white South Africa. The *Cape Times* (4 January 1911) saw it 'as the first solution of the Asiatic problem. If anything were needed to stimulate this frame of mind it has been General Smuts' patriotic declaration … that South Africa as a young country should be thrown open to White immigrants, regardless of education or language.' It was African labour that whites were keen to lay their hands on and it was in their dispossession that the future contours of 20th-century South African political economy can be glimpsed. Slowly at first, and then with greater intensity after the defeat of the Bambatha Rebellion of 1906, the African dispossessed were turned into cheap labour that began to replace Indians in the colonial workforce. The availability of African labour rendered Indians superfluous in the farming, mining and the public sectors. As the 'cheap bodies' of indenture left the plantation, so the 'cheapened bodies' of the Zulu took their places in most economic sectors.

Conclusion

Many migrants were destroyed by what the system of indenture allowed employers to get away with. The rampant diseases on plantations, the horrible living conditions and social dislocation have been recorded (Desai and Vahed 2010). But this is only part of a complex story. How the indentured responded to the system makes for fascinating reading. Biographies provide a glimpse into the shadows and ambiguities of a world that was left behind and a new life that was to be made. Indenture was not slavery. It was for a limited time and was not passed on to one's descendents, the system underwent changes over time, the plantation was not a 'total' system of control and migration was a liberating experience for some who may have sought an escape from India.

Boodha Dulel Sing (8726), a Rajput, arrived in Natal in September 1874. After serving his indenture with Glasgow Natal Sugar Co. in New Guelderland on the north coast, he bought a few acres of land in Nonoti and began planting sugar cane, tobacco and vegetables. In 1880 he married Lukhia, the colonial-born daughter of Subnath Bissoonoth Roy and Beemby Keenoo. They had five sons and three daughters. By the time Boodha Sing died on 15 November 1919, his farm 'Hyde Park' measured almost 5,000 acres, and employed over 100 Indian workers (NAB, Master of the Supreme Court Estates 4800/1919). Sheochand Ragoo of Shahabad arrived in Natal as a 20-year-old in May 1892. After serving his indenture with John Swales of Verulam, he became a farmer in the area, acquired wealth and was a strong supporter of Gandhi. His son Ramgobin was educated at Gandhi's Phoenix Settlement, stayed at the Phoenix Settlement during the 1913 strike, and in later years ran a bus service, was chairman of the Indian Bus Owners' Association and started the Inanda Government Aided School (NAB, MSCE 2290/1956).

As we write in the agency of the likes of Boodha Sing and Raghoo, and challenge the idea of the colonised as simply victims, we must not ignore the fact that 'Europe did colonise, not the other way around, and in so doing perpetrated and provoked a great deal of violence, both physical and cultural. To acknowledge this fact, the fact that imperialism had real effects, is not to remove agency. It is merely to refuse to trivialise it' (Comaroff and Comaroff 1997: 117). In seeking to go beyond the names on ship lists, their village and caste origin and the plantations they were allocated to, we argue that a richer and more complex history of indenture is uncovered. It allows for research agendas that go beyond the local and address the nature and kind of relationships that the indentured had with India. It provides a more substantial foundation for comparisons with the indentured who went to other countries and indeed to those who were indentured within India itself. It creates a fertile ground for challenging meta-narratives like colonialism as a catch-all. For example it begs to compare the local consequences of dispossession of the Zulu people with the impact of British insurgency in India.

References

Bakhtin, M. M. 1968. *Rabelais and His World*. Cambridge, Mass: MIT Press.

Bhana, S. 1991. *Indentured Indian Emigrants to Natal 1860–1902: A Study Based on Ships Lists*. New Delhi: Promilla.

Clarke C. G. 1986. *East Indians in a West Indian town: San Fernando, Trinidad, 1930–1970*. London: Allen & Unwin.

Comaroff, John and Jean Comaroff. 1997. *The Dialectics of Modernity on a South African Frontier*. Chicago: University of Chicago Press.

Desai, A. and G. Vahed. 2010. *Inside Indian Indenture. A South African Story, 1860–1914*. Cape Town: HSRC Press.

Guha, R. and G. C. Spivak (eds). 1988. *Selected Subaltern Studies*. Oxford: Oxford University Press.

Joshi, C. 2005. *Lost Worlds: Indian Labour and its Forgotten Histories*. London: Anthem Press.

Kale, M. 1999. *Fragments of Empire: Capital, Slavery, and Indian Indentured Labor Migration in the British Caribbean*. Philadelphia: University of Pennsylvania Press.

Kuper, H. 1960. *Indian People in South Africa*. Maritzburg: University of Natal Press.

Lal, B. V. 1980. 'Approaches to the Study of Indian Emigration with Special Reference to Fiji', *Journal of Pacific History*, 15 (1): 52–70.

Marks, S. 1990. *The Ambiguities of Dependence in South Africa*. Baltimore: The Johns Hopkins University Press.

Meer, F. 1985. 'Indentured Labour and Group Formation in Apartheid Society', *Race and Class*, 26 (4): 45–60.

Meer, Y. S. 1980. *Documents of Indentured Labour in Natal, 1851–1917*. Durban: Institute for Black Research.

Mehta, B. J. 2006. 'Engendering History: A Poetics of the Kala Pani in Ramabai Espinet's The Swinging Bridge', *Small Axe,* 11 (1): 19–36.

Mesthrie, R. 1992. *English in Language Shift: The History, Structure and Sociolinguistics of SAIE.* Cambridge: Cambridge University Press.

Said, E. W. 1993. *Culture and Imperialism.* New York: Alfred Knopf.

Shepherd, V. 2002. 'Constructing Visibility. Indian Women in the Jamaican Segment of the Indian Diaspora', in P. Mohammed (ed.), *Gendered Realities: Essays in Caribbean Feminist Thought,* pp. 107–28. Kingston: University of West Indies Press.

Swan, M. 1991. 'Indentured Indians: Accommodation and Resistance, 1890–1913', in S. Bhana (ed.), *Essays on Indentured Indians,* pp. 117–36. Leeds: Peepal Tree Press.

Thomson, L. M. 1952. *Indian Immigration into Natal, 1860–1872.* Pretoria: Union Government Archives.

Tinker, H. 1974. *A New system of Slavery: The Export of Indian Labour Overseas, 1830–1920.* London: Oxford University Press.

3

Tracing the Journey of South African Indian Women from 1860

Mariam Seedat-Khan

On Thursday, 4 October 1860 men, women and children boarded the Belvedere in Calcutta and set sail for the shores of Natal. Eight days later the Truro left Madras and both ships arrived at the port of Natal in November 1860. Within a period of six months 1,029 Indian labourers comprising men, women and children arrived in South Africa in search of a better life. They were going to work under what they thought would be ideal conditions. They arrived filled with dreams and hopes for the future. The dream was short-lived. The barracks that they were accommodated in while waiting to board the ships were far from adequate. The conditions on the Belvedere, Truro and other ships were inhuman. Death and disease saw families lose loved ones. Women were raped and subjected to hard labour. Conflict ensued and violence was common on the ship. The harsh experiences endured contributed to the development and building of strong ties among the women and their families. Women were instrumental in maintaining and promoting a familiar environment. It is these experiences that strengthened their role in South Africa and within the Indian community. Women were determined to maintain a sense of family, community, religion and identity. Based on existing scholarship and 20 qualitative interviews conducted with Indian women in South Africa, this article provides a sociological story of indentured women's experiences.

This article is an attempt to understand (a) the journey of Indian women from their arrival in South Africa in 1860 and their lived experiences; (b) the unique gender and cultural challenges faced by Indian women in South Africa; and (c) the social construction of their gender identity in this continuum.

The British Empire pauperised Indians in India, and found new systems to further exploit them by offering them a 'free ticket' out of poverty to a land of opportunity (Desai and Vahed 2008: 9). The advertisement painted a romantic version of what life would be like in Natal. It read like a tropical holiday, a conflated version of the reality. 'You will find a house rent free ... care is taken not to separate friends and relatives ... there is an abundance of good water and vegetables ... varieties of work are available for women and children ... you will receive generous food rations ... *women are paid half wages ...*' (ibid.: 97). They were promised an idyllic life on the sugar cane fields of Natal in South Africa. The Sudra (labourer) classes were Tamils from Madras; they were among the first group of Indians to respond to the call for indentured labourers prompted by their need for survival and escape from poverty. The promises made by the British never materialised. The living and working conditions were harsh. Stories of abuse, exploitation, poor medical care, diets and tragedy abound. The struggle would prove to be part of a never-ending politically, socially and economically binding relationship between South Africa and India that continues to this day at multiple levels. Colonialism, the caste system, apartheid and the indentured labour system are among the key features that created and reproduced social, political and economic cleavages between people of different race, caste and gender both in South Africa and India. These exploitative practices were instrumental in the subjugation of women on both continents. Oppressive measures by women and men against women and toward women continue to be socially reproduced on both continents. Interviews conducted with 20 South African Indian women between 2009 and 2010 reveal that Indians continue to grade their fellow Indians based on the shade of their skin and caste. Fairness or whiteness is still favoured by South African Indians; this is a remnant of the institutionalisation of 'apartheid', as well as a deep-rooted caste system imported from India into South Africa. Through colonisation the British had 'civilised the heathens' with the use of religion, war, pillage and theft. India and South Africa both suffered at the hands of colonisers; the colonisers proudly displayed their flags on the shores of the two continents, exploiting local resources and deepening poverty. Women in the colonies occupied the lowest rungs on the economic ladder; patriarchal traditions and gendered policies rendered them vulnerable.

Arrival of Indians

Between 1860–1911, 152,184 indentured labourers arrived in Natal; of them 'one-third of immigrants were female' (Vahed 2002: 78). Indians made South Africa their permanent home, despite the hardships they faced under indenture. Women were instrumental in recreating a familiar environment. Through religion, culture and diet women reproduced the Indian way of life in Natal. The contract for indentured workers was to be five years. Once this period ended, they were free to re-indenture, return home on a free passage or seek work elsewhere in Natal. 'Approximately 60 per cent of indentured workers were allocated to sugar estates; the rest were employed by municipalities of Durban and Pietermaritzburg, the Natal Government Railways and as "special servants" such as cooks, waiters, policemen, clerks and interpreters' (ibid.). However, the indentured labourers were overworked and lived in poor conditions. They were not allowed to refuse any work, demand higher wages or leave the employer. All acts of desertion and other offences were viewed as criminal acts (ibid.). The Indian state had insisted that a minimum quota of women, '40 per cent of the indentured workers were women' (Freund 1991: 419). This group not only consisted of wives, but also independently indentured women.

The Indian Woman

M. K. Gandhi, a respected lawyer and passive resistance campaigner, claimed both South Africa and India as his home. Traditional in his beliefs, he argued that both

> Men and women are equal in status but are not identical, man is supreme in the outward activities of a married couple, and home life is entirely the sphere of the woman. The care of the children and the upkeep of the household are quite enough to fully engage all her energy. In a well ordered society the additional burden of maintaining the family ought not to fall on her. The man should look to the maintenance of the family, the woman to household management, the two thus supplementing and complementing each other's labours (Gandhi in Meer 1991: 14).

Gandhi's complementary form of labour between man and woman becomes problematic when the Indian woman moves out of the domestic sphere, when husbands abandon their wives in India and remarry in South Africa. 'The good woman is the virtuous woman, patient, suffering, venerating the tradition of the past and sacrificing her entire being to her husband, her children and her family'(Meer 1972: 37). When single, widowed and unmarried women began to enter the workforce in large numbers traditional roles began to change. Adary Venkiah, a female indentured labourer, number 117677, arrived in South Africa with her two children in January 1906. She was searching for her husband Ramsamy, indentured labourer number 112027. Ramsamy was found in Dundee, Northern Natal; he was remarried to Mahalatchmy, indentured labourer number 112028. They had met aboard the ship on their way to South Africa. Ramsamy had no intention of returning to his wife Adary and his children in India. He had deliberately left his family in India to be with Mahalatchmy; they were from the same village of Anakpally in India. Ramsamy and his second wife had never imagined the arrival of Adary. This was a bold step that Adary took to reunite her family. She learnt that polygamy was illegal in South Africa and Ramsamy was ordered to annul his second marriage and register his marriage to her. Her brave action resulted in changes at a policy level. Polygamy was conditionally recognised in 1907 (Desai and Vahed 2008: 193–94). Other women were left behind in India never to see their husbands again. 'They faced the prejudice and opprobrium of tight-knit communities as married but not really' (ibid.: 193). Angel, indentured labourer 105829, represented the strength and resilience of Indian indentured woman. She arrived in South Africa as a 24-year-old, single Christian woman. She fought the system and defied tradition. She refused to engage in sexual relations with her master while she was also accused of taking on a series of sexual partners. She demanded what was promised to her under the contract that she signed in India. Angel returned to India after her contract ended (ibid.: 197).

The Indian Indentured Women

The *Truro*, *Belvedere*, *Umtata*, *Pongola*, *Umvoti* and *Congella* were among the first ships to leave the shores of India (Desai and Vahed 2008). The human cargo included women. They were single, married, orphaned, outcast, mothers, sisters, daughters and wives. Their journey was a difficult one, filled with violence, oppression, deprivation and suffering. Some suffered in silence while others challenged the system to the bitter end. The Captain's log of the *Umvoti*, that left Madras on the 25 August 1888, tells a story of poor doctors with poor values. The Indian women were the objects of sexual gratification and were forced to take on multiple sexual partners on their journey to the port of Natal. Women who challenged the sexual violation were punished and often jumped ship to escape suffering. The captain reports that the women were 'anything but compliant and submissive ... last night a [single] Indian woman assaulted several other women and threatened to assault ...' (ibid.: 37–38). Challenging the way in which Indian families function and live, and the role that women play in the social construction of what it means to be an Indian woman in South Africa today needs to begin with the stories of the women who sailed on the ships from India. Such a study addresses a series of broad sociological areas such as Indian culture, gender, identity and religion. These intersected for the indentured women and continue to be important areas of debate and discussion for both academics and Indian women themselves. These factors intersect along critical areas within the South Indian community; it forms a pivotal part of their identity as Indians, as women and as South Africans. The diluted nature of Indian culture in South Africa continues to determine gender relations among the men and women among Indian families in South Africa. The task is a challenging one with racial, cultural, religious and gender identity questions that will require exploration at multiple levels.

Religion

The three religious groups that arrived in South Africa as indentured labourers were Muslims, Hindus and Christians. Although each religion provides evidence for the equal treatment of men and women, it is the practice of patriarchy that keeps Indian women 'subservient' (Meer 1991: 22). 'While the Quran specifies the common origin and equivalent social status of male and female, Islamic law subordinates women' (ibid.). The Indian patriarch in the family skilfully used religion as a form of oppression. Limitations were placed on women, which confined them to the domestic sphere and forced them to turn to religion as a form of comfort and solace.

The laws of Manu and the Quranic tradition conspired to change and reduce the status of Hindu and Muslim women and to make them completely subservient to men. Their roles were redefined so that they became objects of male sexual passion, household drudges and, among the leisured, means of expanding the masculine ego (Meer 1972: 34).

This continued feature of the gendered relationships between Indian men and Indian women, and husband and wife within Indian families confined women to roles with predetermined rules that could not be challenged without severe consequences (ibid.: 37).

The tragedy of this conspiracy was that she herself was never aware of it. So intense were the social strictures conditioning her role ... that she accepted her designation as sacred and extolled it and revered every part of it. ... The system was generated and sustained by its victims, and each generation of women guarded it zealously and prepared the next to be imprisoned within it (ibid.: 35).

The Transition of Indian Women in South Africa

'Identity marks the conjuncture of our past with the social, cultural, and economic relations we live in. Each individual is the synthesis not only of existing relations but of the history of these relations: he is a précis of the past' (Rutherford 1990: 19). The history of Indian women and their lived experiences has contributed to their social, political and economic position in South African society. The notion of a single woman being employed on sugar-cane farms in and around Natal did not appeal to the colonial farm owners.

I came from India with a man and we were indentured to Umzinto. He is dead. He committed suicide by hanging himself. I don't know why he did it. He was not my husband. I was only living with him. Six months after that man hanged himself I left. My master [Caldwell] said that I was a single woman he did not want to keep me unless I got a husband and I said I did not want a husband and my master became disagreeable (Desai and Vahed 2008: 19).

The extract tells a story of Indian indentured women who defied the norms of a traditional Indian woman. Leaving behind family, friends and everything familiar is also not an act that any man or woman embarks on without good reason. The indentured Indian women whether, single or married, made choices. These choices led them to the Port of Natal as indentured labourers. During the period 1860 to 1911, 'a heterogeneous collection of indentured workers were imported'. The difficulties faced by Indians, could be the reason that they sought to recreate their culture and religion in Durban (Vahed 2002: 77). The shared experiences of the indentured labourers brought them together in the spirit of community, family, religion and culture. N. Yuval-Davis' 'multi-tiered construct' (1997: 16) of citizenship is an important construct that can be referred to in order to fully understand Indian women. The Indian woman in South Africa today is a 'multi-tiered construct' which can be applied to integral structures of the individual's membership in a variety of settings, such as the family, the home, the community, the workplace and the political and economic arenas.

Why Indian Women?

Interviews with Indian women reflect that they have historically played a supportive role to their husbands, families, community, religious organisations and the South African liberation movement so much so that 'Indian women in South Africa have been nurtured in an even more oppressed atmosphere than their sisters in India' (Meer 1972: 35). Indian women arrived in South Africa as appendages to their male counterparts, the family's primary breadwinner and because 'the law stipulated that each group of male workers should be accompanied by a minimum proportion of women' (ibid.: 37). When these women became employed they earned half the rations of their male counterparts. Often one woman was forced to live with several men. The women lived under the rule of the estate owners and were not allowed to leave the estate without their children. They became objects of sexual gratification for multiple men. The children that were born out of these sexual encounters became the responsibility of the indentured women. This further reinforced their subjugation and oppression. These conditions heightened the tenuous circumstances which Indian women found themselves in, and conspired to inform and develop their own and new identity. An identity that would prove to be unique: this would be the identity of the South African Indian woman.

The women who accompanied their merchant husbands were confined to the homes, closeted and fearful of going out on to the streets. Those families that lived in rural areas enjoyed greater liberties and worked with their husbands taking care of businesses although 'labour is not conventionally part of the familiar definition of the lives of Indian women'. Popular representations in South Africa of the Indian women projected by Indians themselves generally emphasised delicacy and dependency. 'Prestige resides in an idealised household where the woman's role is domestic and secluded' (Freund 1991: 415). This notion of delicacy and dependency is only one type of Indian woman that is visible in South Africa today.

Indian women themselves have been responsible for socially constructing new roles and identities. They have begun to pave the road for other Indian women who will follow in their paths. The likes of Fatima Meer, sociologist, mother and activist, challenged Indian women in Durban, throughout South Africa and the world. Her leadership role and commitment to transformation for all women was a catalyst for the broader community of all women both rich and poor, black and white. Women like Meer, whose father arrived as a merchant in Natal, is representative of a family who took the lead in maintaining a South African notion of the Indian women while embracing South African society with both hands as citizens of their new home. Meer's journey echoes the struggles of her predecessors: 'the indentured Indian women'. The story is a familiar one with new twists, different hardships and sacrifice of family, country, community and religious groups. Her funeral in 2010 in Durban bore testimony to her struggle throughout her life. Her separation from her family, her absence from her children and her responsibility to the pursuit of justice forced her into challenging positions. Her situation was far from normal and her role in South African society was multifaceted.

The Indian Family

The abnormal structure of the Indian family in South Africa, created in 1860 by the low proportion of women and the restrictions of indenture, was rectified in the second decade of the twentieth century when Indian family life in South Africa settled into traditional conservatism, and women assumed full responsibility for maintaining that conservatism. The home was the bastion of

Indian life struggling against a foreign environment; surrounded by the strong forces ... it depended upon its trustees, the women (Meer 1972: 37).

Women themselves needed to take responsibility then, and now in the role they play in reproducing the Indian family and the Indian women's position in South Africa. If it is good or bad, powerful or powerless we need to fully understand the strengths and weaknesses of a group of Indian women who arrived as indentured labourers and how the past has moved along a continuum from one generation to the next socially reproducing the Indian women. 'In an atmosphere of hostility and rampant discrimination where the "brown skinned Indian" was caught between the native African and the domineering Afrikaner, the Indians' only mooring for identity and self-respect was religion and culture' (Ratnam 2000). The social pressures of culture, religion, class and caste on Indian women are instrumental in confining them in a variety of ways to a subordinate position within the family. The primary role of the Indian indentured women was to be a good wife, mother, cheap labourer, object of male pleasure, in addition to meeting gender quotas.

A few Indian women entered wage employment post the First World War. Women preoccupied with activities outside the home focused on 'cultural and charitable work' (Hiralal 2003: 1). In the 1930s the status of Indian women reflected their isolation, poor education and found them largely dependent on their families for social and economic support (ibid.: 2). The impact of the Second World War had specific consequences for Indians in Durban during the late 1930s and 1940s. Women were engaged in wage labour; self-employed women were hawkers, domestic workers, cooks and market gardeners. They occupied low-paying jobs at the bottom rung of the economic ladder (ibid.: 3). The socioeconomic circumstances were not at all promising for the Indian women during this period. Indian families were faced with frequent rent increases and restriction to specific trading areas. This was a mechanism that was met with great success under apartheid in South Africa. The income earned from these occupations was meagre. Indian families were sometimes forced to draw on child labour to supplement the family income. The Social and Economic Planning Council report refers that 70.6 per cent of Indians in Durban were living below the poverty datum line and 40.5 per cent were destitute. The 1930s and 1940s were characterised by rising costs of living, periodic food shortages and general economic insecurity among Indians (ibid.: 2). Although Indian women were poor, their resourcefulness and familial responsibility strengthened their resolve to find solutions to these persistent problems. Their perseverance, resilience and courage passed down from generation to generation of Indian women, 'As Indian family life developed outside the indenture system, Indian social, cultural and familial life in South Africa was recreated along new creolised lines in rural areas and in the urban periphery' (Freund 1991: 414). The role that the Indian women socially constructed in the 1860s and early 1900s remains an important part of the role of Indian women in South Africa today. Remnants of conservatism still remain under the guardianship of Indian women in South Africa 150 years later. It is this conservatism that lends itself largely to the notion of today's Indian women in South Africa.

Socially Constructing the Indian Women

The Indian woman is a visible role player in South Africa today. (She is) part of an Indian community in South Africa that represents one of the 'highest concentrations of Indian diasporas in the world, outside India' (Radhakrishnan 2003: 2). The uniqueness of her character, culture, religion and practice has to a large degree contributed to her isolation from the wider South African society. But her experiences of oppression and suffering have also fostered a strong sense of comradeship with women across the colour line. This was visible during the apartheid years. Women as mothers, sisters and daughters provided the mechanisms for their families and each other to effect change in an apartheid state. The combination of their isolation as Indian women and their strong sense of comradeship were critical in creating enduring and strong economic, political and social bonds between Indian women and other women in South Africa who were equally oppressed under apartheid. Their similar and shared experiences bonded them together with ties that would last a lifetime. When Winnie Mandela spoke at the funeral of Fatima Meer in 2010, she referred to her as 'my sister, my friend and a mother to my children, during the difficult times of apartheid I could depend on her to take care of my children when I was away, arrested or in hiding. She understood me and we shared a similar goal'.

While Indian women are beginning to integrate into South African society, they maintain a degree of separateness in living, working, socialising, schooling and, in general, a way of life that Indians have socially constructed for themselves: a legacy of the principles and values of separate development and segregation popularised by apartheid in South Africa and the caste system in India. South African Indian women have perpetuated a culture of separateness within a society from which they also feel somewhat alienated.

Indian women can be understood from two perspectives: their journey and accumulated experiences in South Africa have been constructed by their social experiences, and the experiences of those that came before them. Their stories of pain and suffering under indenture and apartheid continually shape and reshape what it means to be an Indian woman in South Africa today. Her religion, culture, customs and traditions have not only survived but recreated in new ways over the last 150 years. As S. Hall says, the identity of Indian woman in South Africa is '… far from being externally fixed in some essentialised past … [it is] subject to the continuous play of history, culture and power' (1993: 394).

Indian women began their journey in 1860 and have managed in varying degrees to integrate into South African society while retaining their own fluid identity as Indian women. They continue to make a lasting impact and they have always been and will continue to be an integral part of South African society. The Indian woman in South Africa is a complex subject of investigation, her journey is by far the most valuable in understanding her today. She is an Indian woman in her current form largely because of her 'identity as being', her sense of unity and commonality is a product of the way she is positioned by the narratives of the past (Hall 1993: 13). Her 'identity as becoming', is indicative of the fluidity and reflects the way she positions herself within the narratives of the past. The lessons that she internalises and the practices that she engages in informs 'the Indian woman'.

The Gender and Cultural Challenges faced by Indian Women: Then and Now

How do we define Indian women? 'Not only had they been cultivated to venerate, obey, and follow but they had been so protected from outside influences that they alone could be expected to nurture and protect the conservatism of Indian culture and retain its purity' (Meer 1972: 38).

Indian indentured women carried their traditions, religion, identity and a way of life and culture to South Africa. The traditions, good or bad for these women, were closely guarded by them because of the familiarity and comfort they represented. The practice of Indian traditions in a foreign land provided a sense of normality, security, belonging, comfort and a link with the homeland. Understanding the Indian woman in the context of her everyday life, home, family, work and community environment is not without its challenges.

Conclusion

'Patterns created by an encysted culture, that of the Indians of South Africa, and the ways in which it has determined the structural conservatism of the Indian family in its treatment of women' (Meer 1972: 33). It is these patterns that continue to resurface in the historical journey of Indian women from 1860 to today. The critical aspect of this article was to understand the image of the Indian woman and how it is interpreted by Indian women in a South African society today. The contextualisation of the Indian women cannot be understood in isolation. It needs to be explored against the backdrop and history of her journey. Indian women can be seen as a separate and unique group of women. They have gone on to achieve global recognition, they can be found in the fields of medicine, science, law, business and academia. They continue to enter the labour market at its lowest rungs. The 'encysted culture' has evolved to a small degree; Indian women have evolved at multiple levels, however has it really changed the expectations of Indian women? '... while the traditions, values and practices of migrants were important, community and identity were forged in the interaction of actual historical circumstances, political policies, social experiences and the meanings afforded to these in daily practice and discourse in Natal' (Vahed 2002: 77). Have culture, religion and the collective experience of their 150-year journey from indentured labour to 2010 strengthened them and contributed to the Indian women we see today, or have these experiences boxed them into age-old gender practices? The history of oppression suffered by Indian women has been extensive both in South Africa and around the world.

While Indians might wish to maintain their unique traditional identity based on their rich cultural heritage, it will ultimately be their interaction with broader South African society that will determine their future in the country. In this regard, Indians need to reflect changing times and challenge the stereotypes about the Indian community, acknowledging that the Indian community is as much a part of South Africa as any other group.

References

Desai, A. and G. Vahed. 2008. *Inside Indenture: A South African Story, 1860–1914*, (2nd edn). Durban: Madiba Publishers.

Freund, B. 1991. 'Indian Women and the Changing Character of the Working Class Indian Household in Natal 1860–1990', *Journal of Southern African Studies*, 17 (3): 414–29.

Hall, S. 1993. 'Cultural Identity and Diaspora', in P. Williams and L. Chrisman (eds), *Colonial Discourse and Postcolonial Theory: A Reader*. London: Harvester Whaetsheaf.

Hiralal, K. 2003. 'We shall Resist,' The Role of Indian Women in the Passive Resistance Campaign 1946–1948', unpublished paper presented at 'Workshop on South Africa in the 1940s'. Kingston: Southern African Research Centre.

Meer, F. 1972. 'Women and the Family in the Indian Enclave in South Africa', *Feminist Studies*, 1 (2): 33–47.

———. 1991. *Black Women Worker* (2nd edn). Durban: Madiba Publishers.

Radhakrishnan, S. 2003. '"Not Everything's Black and White": Gender and Power in Post-Apartheid South Africa', unpublished paper presented at the American Sociological Association Annual Meeting. Atlanta, Washington, DC.

Ratnam, A. 2000. 'Observations about Diaspora'.

Rutherford, J. 1990. 'A Place Called Home: Identity and the Culture Politics of Difference', in J. Rutherford (ed.), *Identity: Community, Culture, Difference*. London: Lawrence and Wishart.

Vahed, G. 2002. 'Constructions of Community and Identity among Indians in Colonial Natal, 1860–1910: The Role of the Muharram Festival', *Journal of African History*, 43 (1): 77–93.

Venkata Ratnam, C. S. 1996. *Industrial Relations in Indian States*. New Delhi: Global Business Press.

Yuval-Davis, N. 1997. 'Women, Citizenship and Difference', *Feminist Review*, (57): 4–27.

Walker, M. 1998. 'Academic Identities: Women on a South African Landscape', *British Journal of Sociology of Education*, 19 (3): 335–54.

4

In a Faraway Sugar Cane Field: Imagining Indentured Labour in Colonial India

V. Geetha

The practice amongst Brahmins and other upper-caste groups in southern India to marry their daughters off when they were barely eight or nine years old continued until the mid-20th century. Colonial legislation attempted to remedy this, but social practice prevailed. Young brides came to reside with their husbands on the onset of puberty — this experience often proved tragic if not calamitous for many of them.

Subbalakshmi, a Brahmin child, too endured this fate. But her life turned out to be different; married at 11 and a mother at 14, she sustained an inner life through reading, keeping a diary, bird watching and, at least until her middle years, through an engagement with political causes. She grew up at the time of Gandhi's astonishing advent into the Indian political scene (1920s). Of the many things that remained with her from this period of her life was one image that troubled her in old age and in her dreams: a Tamil woman labourer from South Africa, beseeching her for help. Mythily Sivaraman, her granddaughter and biographer, notes that even when she had sunk into depression and madness, Subbalakshmi was obsessed by this image (Sivaraman 2006). Why was this lonely woman, who never quite came to terms with her assigned social roles of wife and mother, obsessed by another woman's fate?

It is possible to read her dream in terms of a more generalised national-political desire that animated her times. Of the many instances that fashioned early nationalist angst and desire, indentured labour was one of the most eloquent — in fact it was central to the nationalist project in the first two decades of the

20th century, and 'imagined' in rather particular ways, and equally through eloquent silences. This article is about 'imaginings' of indentured labour, in the context of South Africa, and to a lesser extent in other places where Tamil labour travelled.

Coolie and Untouchable: The Strategic Silences of Indian Nationalism

From 1894, Indian nationalists had debated the problem of Indians in South Africa. At the annual session of the Indian National Congress, a delegate from Natal persuaded the Congress to pass a resolution asking the British government to veto a law (the Natal Act of 1894) disenfranchising Indians in South Africa. In 1895 the National Congress passed a resolution objecting to the harsh treatment meted out to Indians in South Africa. In the 1896 session of the Congress, held in Calcutta, the South African problem was discussed at length. South Africa became a fixture in the petitions put forth by the Indian National Congress, more so with Gandhi's entry into South African political life.

The Indians who thus attracted nationalist empathy were traders and professionals — not that the plight of labourers was not discussed, but such discussion was almost always initiated to show up the moral pretensions of an Empire that claimed had to have abolished slavery, rather than substantive issues to do with labour.

Nationalist anxiety over the South African question was prominent in the Tamil press. *Swadesamitran* and *India*, two Tamil news weeklies, carried news on South Africa on a fairly regular basis. The press covered important historical developments, the views of leaders of the Indian National Congress, the various resolutions that it tabled on the South African question; Mohandas Gandhi's views; stories of hardship narrated by returnees; and finally opinions on the lessons South Africa held out for Indian nationalism.

The views of Subramania Bharathi, the greatest of the modern Tamil poets, and editor of the weekly, *India*, while broadly endorsing the nationalist position on the South African question, sounded another and more critical note. Commenting on Indian demands for freedom of mobility in the Transvaal, he wondered about men agitating for something so routinely denied to Indians in their own land by colonial political restrictions (Bharathi in Viswanathan vol. 6, 2005: 239). He was also embarrassed about Indian complaints regarding racial discrimination. In a short story dedicated to the so-called untouchable and working castes of India his protagonist, engaged in famine relief work, is anguished by the humiliation and privation endured by untouchables:

> What we do of a day comes back to haunt us the very next day. Whatever we do unto paraiahs and pallas, others do unto us. If our Sringeri Shankaracharya and the Vanamamalai Jeer (revered religious leaders — author) were to visit Natal and the Transvaal they would have to reside in ghettos outside the city. They may not walk in roads where other men walk. ... They cannot dream of what they have now — palanquins, coaches ... We consider one part of our society low and despicable and now the world considers us lowest of all nations. We consider a segment of our own to be untouchable ... Now, the world considers us, both Hindus and Muslims untouchable (Bharathi, in Viswanathan vol. 7, 2006: 149–50).

In another story, Bharathi's female protagonist recalls the so-called South African Indian's plight, as described in the 1896 session of the Congress, only to offer this astonishing comparison:

> In 1896 when the Indian National Congress gathered in Calcutta ... G. Parameswaran Pillay spoke, supporting a resolution (on South Africa): 'There our people cannot move about without a pass. They cannot go out at night. They ... have to live in ghettos specially built for us. We are allowed only to take third class coaches in trains. ... thrown out of tramcars ... not allowed to enter restaurants ... They spit on us, say abusive words to us ...' Sisters, is our situation in Tamil Nadu ... all that better? Think about it ... We cannot move about on our own. We are not shut away in ghettos, but are nevertheless under lock and key. They have a special coach for us on the railway. ... Men dislike us, scold us, beat us. They prevent us from speaking freely ... they sell us to the highest bidder ... (Bharathi in Viswanathan vol.: 9, 2008: 534–36).

These reflections notwithstanding, Bharathi was moved and inspired by events in South Africa and wrote about how the Indians courageously and persistently proved themselves worthy of their 'Aryan' heritage. This racial pride was evident too in Bharathi's rueful sense of what Indians, especially the Tamils in the Transvaal, had to endure, caught as they were between 'mlecchas (the white men) and savages (the Africans)' (Bharathi in Viswanathan vol. 6: 257). Importantly, this sense of being of a 'superior' race was accentuated by the fact that Indians were expected to and had to perform menial tasks in South Africa, such as cleaning toilets which in India was a task imposed upon untouchables. South African Indians felt both aggrieved and indignant at being asked to perform 'untouchable' tasks, and Bharathi registered their sense of distinction and status.

Interestingly, this aggrieved tone is present in Indian petitioning in South Africa as well and in disparate contexts. A 1909 petition to the Protector of Emigrants by 29 people in Natal complained of 'two Indians here of the pariah caste named Anjuru, and Munsamy brothers, who are appointed as constables' and were insolent towards their caste superiors, daring even to touch them.

> We do not complain of the writs being served and attachments' made or of our houses being searched, but what we wish to point out is that if a pariah touches our things or makes an arrest we [are] polluted. They also put on airs and in many ways behave in an objectionable manner, when they are discharging their duty. ... (Bhana and Pachai).

A similar, though more muffled and guarded tone is present in the petitions of non-indentured Indians, complaining against discrimination. In such instances the petitioners, including Gandhi, note that they are not to be confused with indentured Indians who are not genteel or refined enough to avail of equal rights. They would of course attain such a state eventually, but meanwhile their status cannot be used as an index of Indian culture or morality. Today this is a critical truism, that neither the Natal Indian Congress nor the Passive Resistance movement paid attention to workers' lives or needs — except by way of moral concern, expressed most anxiously by Gandhi — until 1913. Yet, indentured labourers were discursively useful and helped to mark the venality of the planters as well as to distinguish appropriate from inappropriate political action — Gandhi referred to them consistently, if only to call attention to British claims to fair play and to render credible the denial of rights to Indians.

Claims advanced in the name of freedom, equality and justice in India and against discrimination by Indians in South Africa constituted the claim makers as particular kinds of political subjects. Indian nationalists underscored this subjectivity by insisting that there existed a putative unity amongst all Indians in spite of differences in class, creed and the persistence of caste and gender inequities. Acknowledging that these problems existed, they yet noted that they had a right to self-government and would on their own attend to these contradictions once they had the political authority and right to do so. Bharathi resorted to angry rhetoric in this regard and claimed that no outsider had the right to point to the 1,000 castes that were, for different though they may be, the men and women of these castes were 'children of one mother'. Indians in South Africa during this period marked their political subjectivity by calling attention to their 'difference'; in doing so they constituted those they distinguished themselves from the labouring class as an inevitable supplement to their claims, both in a discursive and political sense.

I turn now to the views of Pandit Iyothee Thass, a Dalit-Buddhist writer and journalist, who wrote consistently on the South African situation, but from a radically different and anti-nationalist point of view. A *siddha* doctor, writer and publicist, Thass had followed nationalist deliberations from the beginning of the formation of The Indian National Congress. He petitioned nationalists in 1891 on the plight of the untouchables, the need for them to be educated to be gainfully employed, but no one listened. Subsequently, he set up the Dravida Mahajana Sangam and appealed to the British government to address civil disabilities imposed on untouchables. He befriended Colonel Olcott of the Theosophical Society in Madras, who was sympathetic to the untouchable question and had set up special schools for children from the community. He accompanied Olcott to Sri Lanka, and accepted *diksha* from a Buddhist monk in Colombo. Thereafter, he renounced his Hindu identity, proclaimed himself a Buddhist and founded the Sakhya Buddhist Society.

Thass founded a Tamil weekly, *Tamizhan*, and utilised its columns to draw attention to nationalist prevarication on questions of social inequity and the need for social reform, and the social plight of untouchables. He believed that untouchables, or at least the pariah caste to which he belonged, were former Buddhists who had been degraded by caste Hindus and pushed into untouchable ghettos. He wrote on Buddhism's metaphysics and counselled an overarching philosophy of *jeevakarunya*, or compassion, as a counter to Vedanta and other modern-day avatars of Hinduism. His example proved attractive to educated and politically and socially conscious untouchables across southern India, and also to Tamil labourers and others who had migrated to different parts of the British empire. His son Rajaram migrated to Natal and set himself up as a waiter and through him lower-caste Hindus in South Africa came to know of the activities of the Sakhya Buddhist Society, and soon a branch emerged in Natal (Van Loon 1995: 211). This complex historical and cultural context structured and informed Iyothee Thass' responses to the South African problem.

Discussing a report in *Swadesamitran* that objected to all Indians being called 'coolies' and disallowed the use of transport in certain places, he wondered at the effrontery of those who would speak of this, and yet not countenance the name-calling of untouchables in India; or the disabilities endured by them (Thass in Aloysius vol. I, 1999: 19–20). What perhaps irritated and proved most galling to Iyothee Thass was nationalist sanctimoniousness — that they could actually speak of the cruelty of the white man and not confront the cruelty black men showed other black men; that they could wax eloquent about coolies they had never seen, but not dare to challenge the cruel practice of denying untouchables water and fair wages in India. He noted: 'Bharat Mata cannot help her children in Johannesburg because she accepts an unjust norm as just in India, even as she protests its injustice in South Africa.' He wondered at those who would feign to forget caste differences while on board the ship to South Africa because they were all poor and caught in a common fate, but would begin to elaborate such differences once they had a bit of money (ibid.: 211–12).

Thass was also not against indentured labour. Responding to the nationalist Gopal Krishna Gokhale's plea for an end to indentured labour on the grounds that it constituted traffic in human beings and led to cruel labour practices, he observed that he was not sure this was entirely true. For one, reports from South Africa were for the most part about traders and their problems and not really about coolies. Even if it was the case that coolies were being overworked, this need not be construed as such a terrible thing for work never hurt anyone. Nationalists would do well to remember that labourers in India were scarcely better treated. Besides, a Natal coolie back from serving indenture was invariably better off than his counterpart here. A returnee, even if an untouchable, typically came back with money with which he often bought himself a small house or a piece of land, a situation far better than when he was a half-starving coolie in India. He opined that Gokhale and others should talk to returnees to find out the true story of indentured labour and then decide whether it ought to be continued. But then nationalists would not indeed, could not do so for there were no men of the working classes in their ranks. And 'just as a poor man's child is Charity's child and a poor man's wife everyone's wife, the poor man's voice is also not his own' (Thass in Aloysius vol. I, 1999: 236–37).

Further, the nationalists objected to indentured labour because many of them belonged to the Hindu upper classes and castes and were afraid of losing field labour to migration (Thass in Aloysius vol. I, 1999: 346–47). Thass did not agree with the argument which claimed indentured labour deprives Indian industry of ready workers. Such workers as industry needed had to be skilled somewhat and untouchable labourers were rarely that, having almost no access to technical education or to even government service (ibid.: 238–39).

Even as Thass protested nationalist self-righteousness, he did not entirely deny the privations that Indians were subjected to — he acknowledged the coolie protests of 1913, but did not think it was a good idea to oppose the state or to ask for it to change its laws, since states are not likely to take kindly to such demands (Thass in Aloysius vol. I, 1999: 497). Thass was not sure about the extent of coolie unrest, though, and drawing on a set of figures published as news, he suggested that perhaps the coolies were not as large a number as they were thought to be. Many former coolies had set themselves up as small traders and farmers, and some had returned to India. Those who were left behind could not be more than 30,000, he argued, and it might be the case that they were the ones subject to violence in the mines and on plantations. But the fact remains that they were paid well, and that the British did heed their demands. Thass argued that those who were ill-treated and abused could not hope to find succour with the nationalist Congress or the better-off Indians in South Africa. As far as governments were concerned a protesting coolie was like a beggar seeking to command. If workers were dissatisfied, they could always leave (ibid.: 499–504).

Thass's responses are startling, to say the least. That he did not make much of coolie tragedies, as they were being spoken of in the wake of Gokhale's return from South Africa, is not surprising. An emergent historiography of caste relations in colonial India clarifies that in some contexts the cruel contradictions of colonial rule were seen as liberating by untouchables. Thass was convinced of the bountiful and just nature of the British rule, and considered nationalists absolutely seditious — arguing that British rule was inherently more fair and just than rule by Hindu kings and priests. On the other hand, he was uneasy with the question of labour in that faraway continent, and conceded that workers could desert their place of work, if it came to that.

It is clear that the nationalists did not recognise the link between the conditions in rural India and those that beckoned to labourers from across the seas; when they did, they highlighted the ruinous effect of colonial land and revenue policies and did not interrogate the social landscape of rural India which compounded the disastrous consequences of colonial interventions in agriculture and land transactions. Thus, it seems fair to say that in Thass' contemporary responses to the problem of indenture, the labourer is pushed to the foreground in a manner that was unusual for the times.

Scholarship on indentured labour from South Africa has since established the problem of indenture as not always germane to the famous struggles associated with Gandhi. There have been excellent accounts of class politics in Natal during that period — witness Maureen Swan's work on the miners' and sugar plantation workers' strike, and U. S. Mesthrie's work on the period 1924–1927 when the doctrine of assisted emigration back to India was proposed and accepted without taking into account what that meant for returnee workers (Mesthrie 1985). Thass's views allow us to complicate that understanding. In turn, work on class lets us annotate Thass's observations differently to mark their partial usefulness for an understanding of the life of the labourers.

In this sense, Subbalakshmi's lonely woman labourer remains a figure in search of a history that needs to be pieced together from different trans-oceanic sources. In this context, it is important to consider the peculiar gendering of indentured labour in the Indian nationalist context since it is this that rendered it a morally vicious condition.

Beloved Sisters and Accursed Mothers: Labour, Gender and National Honour

A Tamil nationalist newspaper angrily wrote, in 1919, that 'our beloved sisters that have gone to the (Fiji) islands as indentured labourers ... are compelled to lose their chastity ... indentured women labour there has at times to be the wife of six or seven labourers ... No civilised nation can give room to such disgraceful practices ...' (quoted in Sivaraman op. cit.: 147). Annie Besant echoed this moral horror and castigated Christian England for promoting polyandry and encouraging promiscuity. Sarojini Naidu, poet and nationalist leader, berated the British for bringing dishonour upon Indian men and women by pushing them into terrible living conditions, where their labour fed the very earth and was manure for its produce (quoted in Sivaraman op. cit.: 147–48).

The moral status of the indentured labouring woman alarmed colonialists as much as it bothered nationalists. This alarm was central to the recruitment process itself, as Essop Sheik has shown. Wanting to assure the world that indentured labour was not enslavement and would not compromise the domestic and therefore moral life of labourers, plantation owners and their agents wished to have wives migrate along with their husbands, and if that could not be done, preferred that single women found mates as soon as they landed on distant shores (Sheik 2005: 21–56). As colonial secretary Gladstone put it, '... the separation of the men from every natural and domestic relation of life' could only prove disastrous (Northrup 1995: 76).

While it was not easy to find wives willing to migrate with husbands, the fiction of marital respectability as a virtue that could — and must — be sustained in new worlds was assiduously cultivated by recruiters. This was done by drawing distinctions between different kinds of women. Labouring women, or at least those who were capable of labouring, were preferred over and above 'beggars, devotees or dancing girls' (quoted in Metcalf 2007: 148). By thus mapping labour and sexual virtue onto each other, recruiters made a case for securing female labour that would be both productive as well as docile.

But matters did not work out quite as they were intended to. For one, single rather than married women migrated, often feigning marital status. Second even in instances where man and wife migrated, the conditions of migration rendered marriage unstable (Bhana and Pachai op. cit.). Further, there were many who contracted marriages of convenience, or in a spirit of caprice, often across caste boundaries. Such unions could not be expected to have the solidity of ties cemented by lineage, kin and caste ties. Ashwin Desai and Goolam Vahed record the story of 16-year-old Muniyammah who agreed to wife and bed Chinan even while on board the ship to South Africa and how, as she arranged this passage into conjugality, she became suspect in the eyes of both her 'betrothed' as well as the ship's officers. Ultimately, she committed suicide (Desai and Vahed 2010: 19–22). But the absence of kin and caste networks that regulated one's life choices could also prove enabling. The story of Votti — also recorded by Desai and Vahed — is a case in point. Intrepid, stubborn and self-possessed, she negotiated her way through several liaisons, work contexts and employers and held her own, before dropping out of history (ibid.: 6–10).

It was as if by crossing the waters they not only left behind home but also a social and cultural map with its emotional and moral directions. In some cases this proved tragic; in others, it opened up a world of possibilities. In other migratory contexts too this has been noted: that sexual — and emotional — ethics could not be policed once the waters were crossed. Contemporary Tamil fiction featuring Tamil diaspora labour worlds hints of 'loose' women abroad, different from women at home. Pa Singaram's *Puyalil Oru Dhoni* (Storm-tossed Boat, 2005), centres around the lives of Indian migrant labourers and others who are drawn to various kinds of public women — including those who cross the seas from India as performers and women of pleasure. Sexual confusion beset the lives of those left behind as well. *Allam* (The Salt Pans, 2002) features the hard life that was the lot of a labouring peasant woman whose husband left for the Straits settlements and never returned. The novel explores her sense of hopelessness and difficulties in raising their three daughters on her own. Though remarried, her life is constantly clouded by uncertainty of her husband's possible return and the stability of her new marriage.

In South Africa, the sexual anomie that followed sea crossings had an additional edge to it: women who migrated as 'wives' or who became 'attached' to a man on migration were seldom seen as labourers, and employers were reluctant to pay for their upkeep while they were keen on extracting labour from them. Women migrants for their part could and did desert their work stations for both personal and professional reasons. Employers could not hold them to a contract, since they were 'dependent' wives and were not contractually bound to labour. The greatest problem, though, had to do with the ostensibly unsettling impact they had on labouring men — sexual rivalry, violence and suicide were endemic in the colony and this worried officials, planters and, of course, nationalists in India who were concerned about the fundamental immorality of indentured labour (Sheik op. cit.: 42–55, 71–80).

Not surprisingly, sexual instability to do with indentured labour was coded as moral sorrow and fear in nationalist discourse. Recruiters of labourers in the early 20th century complained that nationalist pamphleteering prevented their work. These pamphlets labelled them as abductors of women whose sole intention was to introduce them to immoral life (Carter and Torabully 2002: 33–34).

Nationalist rhetoric became shrill in the wake of Gandhi's agitation over orders that insisted women take out registration certificates on their own, and later the declaration of Indian marriages as non-legal, both of which he insisted imposed immorality on women. The one cast doubts on their conjugal status while the other rendered women who were wives to be nothing but 'concubines' (CD-Rom Edition, *Collected Works of Mahatma Gandhi*, vol. 5, 2000: 212; Gandhi 1928: 169).

However, the hapless woman labourer became a haunting presence outside the context of nationalist ire as well — and not the least because the figure possessed affective value. Thus, writers whatever their political leanings repositioned the labourer in literature and song. Bharathi wrote a lovely poem on sugar cane cutters in Fiji, based on a report filed by Gandhi's friend and confidant, C. F. Andrews. Bharathi's poem does not dwell merely on the woman's sexual vulnerability but also on her loneliness, her loss of home (Bharathi 1987: 255–56). Echoing Wordsworth's *Solitary Reaper* and Keats' poignant vignette of 'Ruth among the alien corn' the poem paints an unforgettable picture of displacement, sorrow and a fate that one cannot control.

Before I end this section, I would like to draw attention to two images of the female labourer, the one from a well-known and iconic short story titled '*Thunbakeni*' (Well of Sorrow) by Pudumaipithan, Tamil fiction writer and an early literary modernist, and the other from a deliberately construed origin myth from Sri Lanka.

Thunbakeni, published in the 1930s, tells the story of an untouchable woman, Marudi, who is recruited to work in a tea estate in Ceylon. Her husband is wrongfully imprisoned and she has to earn a livelihood. She realises very soon that her sexuality is a commodity that she may be coerced to trade in, and learns to negotiate that situation. Her daughter, growing up on the estate, too is subject to a similar fate. The story is an unforgettable portrait of the female estate labourer, not entirely a duped victim but an essentially tragic historical figure of sorrow and shame, an eloquent symbol of an unequal, exploitative and unjust society (Pudumaipithan in Venkatachalapathy 2000: 285–310).

The second image is from C. V. Velu Pillay, a union organiser amongst Tamil plantation workers in Sri Lanka. When asked by the anthropologist Valentine Daniel to envisage the future that possibly awaits the struggling labour population, he narrated this origin myth:

> Tamil Tai who is Siva's daughter, the apple of his eye, Sivamani, when thirsty drinks from the paarkadal, the ocean churned by Vishnu and promptly gets pregnant. Her father is angry with her, and cursed her to go into painful labour. And her children and their children's children were also cursed to labour all their lives.

> After much anguish and pain, she gave birth to a daughter and then died as many of women die during labour to this day. Sivaperuman was deeply saddened. He held out to his granddaughter one of the spears left behind by his son, Murugan and told her to give it to her sons. 'It belongs to your mother's brother (tai maman). Tell your sons to follow him to the land that he has gone to. And let your daughters follow your sons. In that land there will be a bush. It will have spread so as to cover much of that land. Tell your sons to use this ayutam and your daughters their bare hands to harvest every last leaf from this bush and thereby make that land prosperous. After the last leaf has been harvested, my son Murugan will come to claim his ayutam. Then your curse shall be lifted.' As soon as his grand daughter received the spear, its tip bent and one of its sides became the sharpest of blades, changing the whole into a kavvattukkatai (the curved knife used for pruning tea bushes). This is our symbol: a kavvattukkkatti and the koluntu (two leaves and a bud) ...

... there is that curse where the pain of labour in childbirth continues
in the pain of labour among the bushes on the mountains of the tea
estates. But that as Sivaperuman said, will end only when every last
tea leaf has been plucked. But the more one prunes a bush the more
luxuriantly leaves grow. This is the crux of our life's problem. How
will this end? How will this curse be lifted? How will every last leaf
be nipped off? That is our secret. It will happen. And when it does,
we will go to Kadirgamam. And there we will give Murugan his knife.
And what do you think will happen? (Daniel 1996: 39–40)

The story ends here, with Velu Pillay asking the anthropologist a
question. Expecting Siva's boon to be fulfilled, according to plan,
E. Valentine Daniel suggested that 'It will turn back into a spear!'
(ibid.: 40). Velu Pillay, however, did not agree. As Daniel noted,
'He sketched over the outlines of the knife extending it into the
shape of a sickle in whose arc remained three leaves and a bud'
(ibid.).

Pillay's story, that gestures towards revolution, belongs to a
genre of Tamil folktales, featuring avenging women, either sisters
of mothers who seek to settle scores for acts of dishonour they
have been subject to, and the avengers are usually sons. There is a
twist in the tale here, since the spear — the stand-in object for the
communist sickle — has to be presented to the god Murugan, the
maternal uncle of the avengers. The maternal uncle is central to
several rites of passage to do with women across many Tamil castes
and that he would spearhead a revolution is significant. Tamil
kinship and religious faith are thus made to do duty to an imagined
future. It is equally significant that Pillay links reproductive and
productive labour, and his tale suggests that the cycle of birth
may not ever end and so labourers will continue to be born and
recruited, unless this process is interrupted by revolution.

These stories engender labour in rather distinctive ways — the
one indicts the conditions of labour and the other draws attention
to the existence of a cursed working class through an enabling
myth. The one lets us view a private tragedy that is actually a public
shame, while the other goes beyond the question of indenture
and forced recruitment and hints at redemption and an end to
class war. Both tell the story of the woman labourer from non-
nationalist points of view and in fact return the figure that haunted
Subbalakshmi's dreams to a history that is far more complex and
mediated than nationalists wished to admit, and which turns the

gaze back on the larger cultures of subordination and exploitation that produced her.

Lesser Histories and Labour Sub-cultures: What Indian Nationalists did not Imagine

The criss-crossing histories of colonial South Africa and India helped leverage political gains for Indians in South Africa and Indian nationalists. The South African experience was worn by Indian nationalists as a sort of badge and the symbolic importance granted to that experience precluded them from addressing the question of diasporic Indian labour elsewhere, especially in the Straits settlements and Sri Lanka.

From the 1840s to 1860s, during the first and second phase of migration to Sri Lanka, 70,000 labourers died, and of those who survived several returned home (Nadesan 1993: 22). In Malaysia, moral conditions that bothered nationalists in the case of South Africa were widely prevalent and considered given and normal. A colonial official remarked that 'no Tamil woman can go to the federated Malay States and return with a rag of reputation left' (quoted in Adapa 2001: 11). Almost everyone, including officials and planters, knew that a certain number of women were regularly received into prostitution as soon as new labour camps were set up (quoted in Adapa 2001).

Yet, lower-caste labouring Tamils and Telugus did not attract nationalist angst in quite the same way that Gujarati Hindu and Muslim traders did. The reasons are worth speculating: I will restrict myself to Sri Lanka. For one, recruitment to Sri Lanka was through a *kangany*, a village or rural migrant who worked his kin and caste networks to bring workers to plantations. Even when indentured labour was in practice, the *kangany* carried out a form of 'assisted' migration, offering to settle debts of prospective labourers, lending them money to make the passage, and being available on the plantation as a purveyor of their affairs. His presence effectively mediated colonial authority, both on the plantation and outside of it. The *kangany* became the focal point of discussions about the conditions of labour and their reform: planters in Ceylon as well as the government of Madras pointed to his complicity in making life difficult for labourers, while evading their own responsibility (Peebles 2001: 21–79). Significantly, the *kangany* features rather differently in the common memory of labourers: as a paternalistic figure, given to cruelty and violence, and yet an intimate rather than distant enemy (Mayilvahanan 1982: 22–25; Nadan 1993: 38–43).

Indian nationalists protested general labour conditions but these protests did not possess moral indignation which accompanied the campaign against indenture. Ironically, the interests of labourers were often defined and represented by agents appointed by the government of India and this ensured that the conditions of labour were discussed in terms of rules, ordinances and concessions that may be wrung from the planters and the government of Ceylon (Peebles 2001: 129–51). Therefore, it did not acquire the imaginative resonance that representations of labour in other contexts did. Gandhi for South Africa and Andrews for Fiji worked on the hearts and minds of Indian nationalists in a way that government agents, however scrupulous, could not.

In Sri Lanka, unlike in South Africa and even Fiji, former labourers did not become modest farmers who had leased land or even bought their own — and this and the very limited prospects for mobility in the plantations, either by way of education or a new livelihood prevented the emergence of a medial English speaking class that could represent its grievances in the language and register of political liberalism. The bilingual Tamil intellectuals of Jaffna, Hindus and Christians, did address the question of labour sympathetically in the early period but the workers remained, in their eyes, 'Indian' coolies. Left-inspired trade union politics in the plantations in the 1930s and the Ceylon Indian Congress around the same time set the labour question in Sri Lanka on a path that did not intersect all the time with the distinctive nationalist direction that Jaffna Tamils had set for themselves and this history haunts it to this day.

Conclusion

The early Indian nationalist imagining of indentured labour was premised on significant and profound silences to do with caste and gender on the one hand, and the national subject on the other. These silences have been examined intensely in the South African context, and we in India need to take our cues from that work; this article is a very modest attempt to do so. It is clear that the scholarship from South Africa alerts us to rethink our own refiguring of the gender and caste questions in the early 20th century.

Note

All excerpts from Bharathi and Iyothee Thass are translated from Tamil into English by V. Geetha.

References

Adapa, Satyanarayana. 2001. '"Birds of Passage" — Migration of South Indian Labour Communities to South-East Asia; 19–20th Centuries, AD', CLARA Working Paper, No. 11. Amsterdam.

Aloysius, Gnana (ed.). 1999. *Iyotheethasar Sintanaigal* (The Thought of Iyothee Thass), vol. I, Folklore Resources and Research Centre, Palayamkottai.

Bhana, Surendra and Bridglal Pachai. *A Documentary History of South African Indians*, online edition. http://www.sahistory.org.za/pages/library-resources/online%20books/bhana. Accessed 27 June 2010.

———. 'Pariah Constables Pollute Hindus'. http://www.sahistory.org.za/pages/library-resources/online%20books/bhana/part01-A-21.htm. Accessed 27 June 2010.

———. 'Moothen Pleads for his Wife to be Returned'. http://www.sahistory.org.za/pages/library-resources/online%20books/bhana/part01-A-02.htm. Accessed 27 June 2010.

———. 'Wife Lays Bigamy Charge'. http://www.sahistory.org.za/pages/library-resources/online%20books/bhana/part01-A-13.htm. Accessed 27 June 2010.

Bharathi, Subramania. 1987. *Kavitaigal* (Poems). Manivasagar Pathipagam.

Carter, Marina and Khal Torabully. 2002. *Coolitude: An Anthology of the Indian Labour Diaspora*. London: Anthem Press.

Daniel, E. Valentine. 1996. *Charred Lullabies: Chapters in an Anthropology of Violence*. Princeton: Princeton University Press.

Desai, Ashwin and Goolam Vahed. 2010. *Inside Indian Indenture: A South African Story, 1860–1914*. Cape Town: HSRC Press.

Gandhi, M. K. 1928. *Satyagraha in South Africa*. Ahmedabad: Navajivan Publishing House.

———. 2000. *Collected Works*, vol. 5, CD-Rom Edition. Government of India.

Mayilvahanan, Vijayalakshmi.1982. *Malayaga Naatu Patalgal* (Folksongs from the Upcountry), BA thesis. Kandy: Peredeniya University.

Metcalf, Thomas. 2007. *Imperial Connections: India in the Indian Ocean Arena 1860–1920*. University of California Press.

Mesthrie, U. S. 1985. 'Reducing the Indian Population to a Manageable Compass: A Study of the South African Assisted Emigration Scheme of 1927', *Natalia*, No.15, November.

Nadesan, S. A. 1993. *History of the Upcountry Tamil People*. Sri Lanka: A Nandalala Publication.

Northrup, David. 1995. *Indentured Labour in the Age of Imperialism, 1834–1922*. Cambridge: Cambridge University Press.

Peebles, Patrick. 2001. *The Plantation Tamils of Ceylon*. London: Leicester University Press.

Nadan, Saral. 1991. *Malayaga Vaaimozhi Ilakkiyam* (Oral Literature from the Upcountry). Chennai: South Asian Books.

Sheik, Nafisa Essop. 2005. *Labouring under the Law: Gender and the Legal Administration of Indian Immigrants under Indenture in Colonial Natal, 1860–1907*, MA thesis. Howard College, University of KwaZulu-Natal. http://indenturedindian.files.wordpress.com/2008/08/essop-sheik-ma.pdf. Accessed 27 June 2008.

Singaram, Pa. 2005. *Puyalil Oru Dhoni*. Tamizhini, Chennai.

Sivaraman, Mythili. 2006. *Fragments of a Life: A Family Archive*, New Delhi: Zubaan.

Swan, Maureen. 1984. 'The 1913 Natal Indian Strike', *Journal of Southern African Studies*, 10 (2): 239–58.

Tamizhselvi. 2002. *Allam*. Trichy: Maruda.

Van Loon, Louis. 1995. 'Buddhism in South Africa', in Prozesky Martin and John W. de Gruchy (eds), *Living Faiths in South Africa*. London: C. Hurst and Co.

Venkatachalapathy, A. R. (ed.). 2000. *Pudumaipithan Kathaigal* (Pudumaipithan's Stories), Nagercoil: Kalachuvadu Pathipagam.

Viswanathan, Seeni (ed.). Subramania C. Bharathi, vols 6 (2005), 7 (2007), 9 (2008). *Collected Works Chronologically Arranged.*

5

Made in India, Proudly South African: Commemorating 150 Years of Indian Presence in South Africa

Rehana Vally

In 2010 South Africans of Indian origin celebrated 150 years of their presence in the country. It was the first time in 150 years that they could celebrate an event specific to them as equal citizens on a countrywide scale and as part of the national events of 2010. It was the first time that people of Indian origin in South Africa could create an official opportunity to make their experiences an integral part of South African history. The events of 150 years ago are part of history.

The year 2010 was a remarkable year for South Africa. The country was the first African country to host the prestigious FIFA World Cup which generated feelings of national pride in ordinary South Africans. At the national level, the 150-year anniversary of the arrival of Indians in South Africa was dwarfed by the soccer World Cup. At a local level, it was mired in controversy. This event was meant to celebrate a past. Whose past? The past did not unfold as a homogeneous set of events and held different meanings for different people. The two waves of Indian immigration for example, implied two different pasts and different experiences of setting down roots. There was hardly any consensus about the past and what they remembered thereof.

Many understood the political significance of this celebration but could not agree on its meanings. They needed to agree on how to celebrate the past and what to celebrate from the past. Was it about the Indian contribution to the struggle against apartheid? Critics of this view were concerned that a focus on Indians detracted from the nation-building project. Moreover, they could not celebrate the event in isolation, as things they remembered from the past influenced their perspectives. In fact, fieldwork showed that the meanings they attached to past events were not found in the past but in their present. Much of the controversy around the 150th-year celebrations arose from diverse interpretations of the past. In addition to the two waves of Indian immigration each linguistic and/or religious community also had its own past.[1] Nonetheless they all agreed that their past in South Africa began with the docking of the first ship bringing in indentured labourers at the Durban harbour on 16 November 1860.

I was initially interested in the way local communities organised and celebrated this event, in the meanings they attributed to 150 years of their presence in South Africa. I wanted to understand how they used the past to make sense of the present and how they negotiated the diverse narratives. I conducted fieldwork in Laudium, the erstwhile Indian township of Pretoria. In July 2010, I attended the three-day function organised to celebrate the 150 years of presence in South Africa. It was done under the banner of 'The 1860 Legacy Foundation: The Pretoria Chapter'. The organisers scheduled the event after the World Cup and before the month of Ramadan to ensure maximum participation. I recorded the speeches and was given an uncut visual recording of the three-day celebrations. In the hall and its surrounding areas, I interviewed participants and members in the audience. After the event, I interviewed members of the organising committees.

Divided Pasts, Common Future

The first Indian migrants probably had the intention to return to India but as Rosaldo (1989: 102–3) points out *people's actions alter the conditions of their existence, often in ways they never intend or foresee.* The Indian migrants acted according to their needs and searched for ways to cope with unfamiliar South Africa. They became what A. Appadurai calls *deterritorialised people* living in two seemingly disconnected worlds. Theirs was a creatively imagined world constructed from their deterritorialised experience. Their coping intentions were culturally shaped as they searched for ways to combine their desire for cultural continuity with the demands of the new space. Over time, the Indian immigrants in South Africa set down roots and, with each new generation, India gradually retreated as the quintessential home or space of origin.

But memories of India as the land of their ancestors remain. They are visible in the social stratifications that divide South Africans of Indian origin into different caste-type and religious communities, which also inform the degree of compatibility and interaction among them. In the everyday life context, food and the different styles of regional cooking and religious rituals as cultural markers are perhaps the only tangible vestiges of their origins in India. Though these identity markers provide a sense of cultural continuity they have changed considerably and their validity is increasingly contested. Yet, they help maintain a sense of Indianness (Ebr-Vally 2001).

These cultural markers play a role in consolidating group identity and the shifts in meaning demonstrate the vicissitude of their life experiences. As identity markers they also convey and sustain the memory of the different groups. Knowledge of who they are is expressed through these cultural identity markers. The strength of these cultural markers lies in their ability to connect South African Indians to India and each other to the group they identify with. These groups are represented in different ways. The first distinction is made between north and south Indians. The south Indian group can be further divided into Tamil-speaking, Telugu-speaking and Hindi-speaking groups. They can then be further subdivided into religious groups. The scenario for north Indians is not very different. They too can be subdivided into different linguistic and religious groups. Their stratification includes the village layer which is largely absent among south Indians who for the most part are regarded as descendents of indentured labourers.

The varied experiences of each group set them aside from each other. Though they were recognised throughout history as a homogeneous group of Indians by the state and other South Africans, it was not the case among them. Each group had its own memories of India. Their origins were located in different parts of India, they came in different waves, or they came from different classes and castes. Their memories set them apart for what they wished to remember and so maintain their social and cultural differences.

South Africa Indians were affected by the strict immigration laws and they often could not arrange suitable spouses for their children. They thus reimagined their social structures in ways that transformed incompatibility rules. What mattered was religion, which provided the basis to bring caste-type and linguistic groups under one banner. Such shifts happened within the north and south Indian groups but, as a rule, north Indians and south Indians were deemed incompatible.

In 2010 South Africa was a different place. Apartheid had ended 16 years before. South Africa hosted the football World Cup, occupied a non-permanent seat on the UN Security Council and hoped to join Brazil, Russia, India and China as emerging powers known as the BRIC countries. Diplomatic relations between South Africa and India were re-established. All South Africans were subjected to the same visa rules. This was a change for people of Indian origin who previously benefited from a special status to visit the land of their origin. These changes once again required people of Indian origin to reimagine their place in post-apartheid South Africa.

The 150-year celebration of Indian presence in South Africa provided them with the opportunity to address these issues. They could voice them publicly and it was an opportunity to revisit the past. Celebrating their arrival was an excellent moment to say who they are and where they belong. How did residents of Laudium use the commemoration of 150 years of living in South Africa to address issues of social and religious stratification?

The 1860 Legacy Foundation: The Pretoria Chapter

Zaynab and Mariam are middle-aged women, well respected and very active in the local Laudium community. They are involved in different community organisations like health, frail care or women's issues. They are respected for their communal engagements and as far as possible try to convince Laudium residents to militate against class and religious divisions. They played a key role in organising the Pretoria Chapter of the 1860 commemoration.

It was early in 2010 at a photographic exhibition on Marabastad that Zaynab and Mariam perchance learnt about plans to commemorate the arrival of Indians into South Africa. They recognised the scope of this event as a potential turning moment in the local politics of communal life in Laudium. Zaynab collected as much information on the 1860 commemoration idea and from the vision statement of the 1860 Legacy Foundation, understood that 1860 was basically highlighted as the moment of first substantial contact with South Africa and the contribution of South African Indians to politics and nation building. The 1860 Legacy Foundation invited South African Indian communities to consider celebrating this event and use their imagination in deciding on the form and meanings of their event. This may have been a carte blanche to organise something around the 150 years of Indian presence in South Africa but the openness of the invitation actually pointed to the difficulties in constructing an event that would be acceptable to all. The South African Indian community is not homogeneous and the event could not be either.

Finding Common Ground

In Laudium, the organisers of the event needed to locate their event into a more substantial and acceptable context for all participants. As a space India was already too far removed from the psyche and ordinary imagination of Laudium residents. It still held meaning for an older generation but to the youth it was a space from the past that had very little relevance in their lives.

India is history, matters little and no longer has the force to bring people together. South Africa is where they live. It is their space and their histories and memories are anchored here. The organisers of the Laudium event understood that they could not make Indian origins the central point of their event. They all agreed that the event was to affirm their presence in South Africa and their con-tribution to it. Politics and the struggle against apartheid was an option but how far back in history should they go? Should they continue to emphasise the Gandhian connections of some Pretoria residents and their involvement in the Passive Resistance? Highlighting the contribution of Passive Resisters was anchoring the experiences of Pretoria Indians in a past when they were fighting for their South African citizenship. This was part of history with very little influence on their present circumstances. Moreover, Zaynab explained that it has no meaning for the youth, that they needed something that could involve young people.

Choosing heroes to adorn the event was a generational question. Heroes like Maulvi Cachalia, Nana Sita or even Mahatma Gandhi were not known to a vast number of Laudium residents. Some of the young people I spoke with during the three-day event knew of Mahatma Gandhi from school projects but were not particularly interested in his life and experiences in South Africa and did not relate to him in any communal way. The organisers were aware of this and sought ways to bring young people into the celebration. They accepted that knowledge of local heroes was a question of different memories for different generations. Only the present provided them with the common social framework in which to locate experiences relevant to them.

Indians moved to Laudium about 50 years ago from Marabastad which was an area set aside for black occupation. Black Africans, Coloured and Indians lived side by side. Eski'a Mphalele in *Down Second Avenue* (2008) and Jay Naidoo in *Coolie Location* (1990) have written about their experiences of growing up in Marabastad and both have remarked on the tensions and conflict surrounding cross-racial relations and linguistic and religious interactions. Yet, residents of Laudium needed the idea of Marabastad to construct an appropriate post-apartheid socio-cultural and political image of South African Indian experiences in Pretoria.

The organisers recognised the 150-year celebration as an opportunity to make Pretoria Indian experiences under the apartheid state a part of South African history. This was the fitting moment to demonstrate the common experiences of Laudium residents in Marabastad. Despite the social and religious distinctions that mark Laudium society, the Marabastad experiences and their forced removal to Laudium created a common fount of memories that all could identify with. Furthermore, the embedding of their common experiences in Marabastad allowed them to connect their history to that of Black peoples who were forcibly removed from their locations.

Enacting a New Communal Space

For the organisers, and especially social activists like Zaynab and Mariam, the 150-year commemoration provided an excellent social alternative to the present Laudium society that was weighed down by an unwillingness to interact with people from other religious and linguistic groups and across racial lines. The 150-year commemoration was an opportunity to raise questions about social life in Laudium in a public forum and subtly ask Laudium residents to consider the disadvantages of living in such enclaves. Caste and caste-type structures that defined the core of Indian identity in South Africa had, according to Zaynab and Mariam, become a threat to Indians in post-apartheid South Africa.

Laudium residents, they held, needed to take stock and change the status quo to create a new, consensual, more inclusive communal space which would transcend past divisions and mobilise around an acceptable form of sub-national identity.

The commemoration thus provided a legitimate reason to examine afresh the weight and contribution of knowledge from the past for the present. Intertwining the Marabastad experience with the 150-year commemoration was an attempt to establish a different social and spatial framework within which to locate their memories. Their memories of living in South Africa now found a space of origin, Marabastad. Their forced removal to Laudium authenticated their belonging to South Africa. Amarlal explained that Marabastad is the District Six of Pretoria. Whether this resulted in the romanticising of Marabastad is beside the point as the emphasis on the loss of communal life through forced removals was a potent metaphor that made them less Indian and more South African. Marabastad — 'city of many colours' in a mixture of Setswana and Afrikaans — forms part of a living memory. It still stands, although decrepit and as such forms a *lieu de memoire* as described by Pierre Nora. Many residents of Laudium still have businesses there. The challenge for the organisers was rallying the different Laudium groups and organisations around this idea.

Many Organisations, One Platform

The challenge for Zaynab and Mariam was to create a platform of representation for the diverse religious and cultural organisations in Laudium. This required some ingenious planning and intimate knowledge of local dynamics. From past experiences they knew that consensus ranked high in the public arena of Laudium. Very often individuals and organisations in Laudium used consensus and horizontal representation to either thwart or support public initiatives. As much as Zaynab and Mariam wished to bypass these unspoken rules based on 'consent', they understood their importance as they were attempting to organise a successful event and worked hard at it.

The success of the three-day event was built on a carefully negotiated consensus. They proceeded by getting an organising committee together which was tasked to present and coordinate the event with the different organisations and the Laudium public. As far as possible, they wished to create a forum for ordinary people to participate. This was also a tactic to prevent any organisation from trying to dominate the project.

The logical way of tackling issues of representation in Laudium was to ensure a broad base representation. Zaynab and Mariam voiced the opinions of many Laudium residents, that Laudium is a township divided into different religious organisations that dominate public life in Laudium. Zaynab's observation, that the quickest and affirmative way to organise this function was to involve all possible organisations, echoed the sentiments of most organisers interviewed. They dealt with delicate issues like that of Muslim over-representation skilfully by emphasising equal participation over the right to be represented. The mix of organisations and independent individuals worked well as some informants remarked that culture is not an individual aspect and further argued that culture as a collective identity called for collective action. This meant that even organisations had to put Laudium above their groups.

There was no money. The national body had no funds to disburse. This was an opportunity to 'test' the collective good in Laudium. The organisers involved individuals who were active in community affairs, local politics and in business. People gave generously of their time, money and resources. Wealthy businessmen donated funds. Young technicians donated their skills and technical know-how. The organisers were unanimous in their praise for the young people who helped decorate the hall, set up the sound system, organised the stage lighting, the giant TV screens and visual recordings of the three-day events. Mariam captured this very well when she exclaimed, 'You know this could not have happened without the assistance of the young people. Ya Allah, without them we were finished.'

The 150-year celebration of Indian presence in South Africa provided the platform to display their African identity in public. It was the forum within which they could reflect on the social and cultural constructions of their diverse identities. Each group had its own memories to affirm which also marked the limits of compatibility and interaction among groups. The demands in post-apartheid South Africa required them to use their memories differently: where it was used to justify social distinctions, it now was used to find commonality.

Commemorations and celebrations are collective and ritualised activities where people participating create a social significance for what is taking place. The next section develops P. Connerton's idea that societies remember through ritual activity.

Ritual and Performance of Memory

Whether we draw inspiration from Maurice Halbwachs on collective memory (1925) 1992 or from Connerton's more recent discussion on 'social memory' (1989), the environment in which South African Indians lived has had a significant influence on what they remember about their past. Until 2010 the question of publicly displaying their Indianness did not arise. For 150 years it was an internal issue for South Africans of Indian origin. The transformation to political equality brought its own demands. Only this time, public recognition and promotion of cultural differences required South African Indians to deconstruct and 'display' the key parameters of what makes them Indian. After some reflection, the organisers of the Pretoria Chapter decided on holding a three-day public event that underlined Halbwachs (1992) and Connerton's theory that commemoration and rituals are a form of collective remembering. Their reasoning that a performance would allow individuals and organisations to participate was in accordance with Rimé et al. (1998) that participation in rituals and social sharing helps to enhance social integration and restore self-concept and self-esteem. Further explanation is provided by Richard Schechner (1995) who aptly observed that public performance is a true reflection of social and cultural reality. The organisers of the Pretoria Chapter saw this as an opportunity to showcase Indian culture. The use of the term 'showcase' brings to mind presentation, enactment and performance and in the classic sense of ritual theory, it was about presenting a window into who we are. The three-day commemorative events in Laudium were thus social rituals and performances that displayed a mélange of their perceptions of memory and identity.

Made in India — Proudly South African

Nalini Padyachee was born in Durban and moved to Laudium in 2000 as a newly qualified school teacher. She is married, lives in Laudium, has two daughters aged 15 and 12 and teaches at one of the local primary schools. She attended all the events and the

Sunday event was special because she could show everybody in Laudium that she was very South African and a wee bit Indian. She walked through the streets of Laudium together with children from her school and other colleagues. She wore a sari over her jeans and used a tee shirt as a blouse. To Nalini, the sari is normally a formal and ceremonial garment worn at weddings and temples and at formal occasions as ethnic wear. On this day she wore it over jeans because it was more practical to walk and run in and explained it as part of my Indian culture. She carried a banner with the slogan 'Made in India Proudly South African' and in detail explained how comfortable she is in straddling the two worlds. She expressed the sentiments of many Laudium residents who defined themselves in the same way.

To the organisers this was an opportunity to bring people of Laudium together: to give them the platform to affirm their ties with South Africa; to publicly voice their concerns about feelings of alienation within the South African nation and also display their Indian 'wee bits'. The challenge was to bring different communities that had grown distant from each other together and create a dialogue among them. The answer lay in their use of memories; in combining memories of Marabastad, their common Indian origins and 150 years of living experience in South Africa as a backdrop for the events. Theatrical performance was the ideal medium to use. This allowed organisations and individuals to prepare their acts and present them to the public. Amarlal expressed the feelings of the organisers that the function was about 'showing ... Indian heritage, showcasing their culture and who they are ... Only people could show this. So, they let everybody show this.'

This was an astute choice as people and cultural and religious organisations searched their memory archives for acts that showed the magnanimity of their culture. The coordination and planning of these acts was left to the women who used to meet in the mornings to practice. For the first time, the organisers were proud to note in the memory of Laudium, Hindu and Muslim women were together organising the Saturday entertainment programme. Women from the Hindu Seva Semaj put together an act that detailed the history and religion of north Indians in South Africa. They put young children in costumes to represent first immigrants, Gandhi and Kastoorbha and deities from Hinduism. Gandhi was a Gujarati and they were proud to 'own' him. The choice of cultural representation was more difficult for Muslims. Aunty Julie and Zohra who organised Muslim events lamented the absence of dance and music as cultural expressions among Muslims in Laudium. They had to find something in Islam and these had to be uniformly acceptable to all the Muslim organisations. They proceeded by elimination, cutting out *quawwali* best described as gospel music of Islam or *qasidah*s which are poems recited mainly by women. They were left with the Qur'an and chose texts from it that were appropriate for the occasion. They chose texts with a universal message of peace that were interdenominational and praised humanity. Muslim woman of 70 and older, who watched Gujarati women perform dances on the stage, bemoaned the absence of dance and music as part of the Muslim display. She reminisced her youth in Marabastad when *rasra*, a wedding dance performed by women, was part of Muslim weddings. It was in a thick voice that Hanifa Masi, a 74-year-old woman, remarked: 'It's all gone. Maybe they still do it in India, but here nothing. Now there are girl parties, they put *mehndi* but they only know how to eat and talk about clothes. Us, we had *geet* and *rasra*.'

Performers looked hard to find ways of combining their South African and Indian cultural identities in positive ways. Their messages conveyed a mixture of religiosity, culture and compassion. A group of ladies who wished to sing '*Vande Mataram*' as part of their sketch 'A Passage to India' met with objections from Muslims who saw it as anti-Muslim. The organisers together with the ladies reached a compromise where in the presentation; the elderly ladies did not wear white saris, did not carry the Indian flag and agreed to sing only the refrain of '*Vande Mataram*' as they marched onto the stage in their slacks and T-shirts. Their main message was reflected in an old South African song which recalled Pretoria but which they had adapted. The lyrics were changed from 'We are marching to Pretoria' to 'We all march unitedly and sing our song whole heartedly. We salute, we salute, we salute South Africa, the land of milk and honey. Hindu Muslims all South Africans, all are humans in this world. When we reach the gates of heaven, we all pray to one and only God.'

This commemoration is an illustration of the fact that social memories are not fixed. They are fluid and relational. In Laudium, social memories were used to construct fields of relations within groups as well as determine the degree of interconnectedness between groups (Barth 1992). The demise of apartheid demanded a repositioning of Indianness and the 150-year commemoration provided the public context within which to reimagine this. Participants at the three-day event delved into their Indian past and used relevant practices and identity markers to make their point. The context for this was provided by the euphoria of nationalist fervour which accompanied all public events in 2010. It provided the scope for Laudium residents of Indian origin to affirm their South African identity: 'We are culturally Indian but our hearts are South African'. The message was abundantly clear. Their attachment to India is of a symbolic nature. Their *lieu de memoire* in the sense of Pierre Nora is South Africa.

Note

1. The terms 'groups' and 'community' are used interchangeably and in a capacious manner.

References

Appadurai, A. 1991. 'Global Ethnoscapes. Notes and Queries for a Transnational Anthropology', in R. G. Fox (ed.), *Recapturing Anthropology. Working in the Present*. Santa Fe. School of American Research Press.

Barth, F. 1992. 'Towards Greater Naturalism in Conceptualizing Societies', in A. Kuper, *Conceptualizing Societies*. London: Routledge.

Connerton, P. 1989. *How Societies Remember*. Cambridge: Cambridge University Press.

Ebr-Vally, R. 2001. *Kala Pani: Caste and Colour in South Africa*. Cape Town: Kwela Books.

Halbwachs, M. (1925) 1992. *On Collective Memory*. Chicago: University of Chicago Press.

Jelin, E. 2003. 'Contested Memories in the Southern Cone: Commemorations in a Comparative Perspective', in P. Gready, *Political Transition: Politics and Culture*. London: Pluto Press.

Mphahlele, E. 1971. *Down Second Avenue*. Garden City: Anchor Books.

Naidoo, J. 1990. *Coolie Location*. London: SA Writers Series.

Nora, P. (ed.). 1997. *Les Lieux de Mémoire. La Republique. La Nation. Les France T*. Paris: Gallimard Quarto.

Ricoeur, P. 2004. *Memory, History, Forgetting*. Chicago: University of Chicago Press.

Rimé, B., C. Finkenauer, O. Luminet, E. Zech and P. Philippot. 1998. 'Social Sharing of Emotion. New Evidence and New Questions', *European Review of Social Psychology*, 9: 145–89.

Rosaldo, R. 1989. *Culture and Truth: The Remaking of Social Analysis*. Boston: Beacon Press.

Schechmer, Richard. 1995. *Future of Ritual*. London: Routledge.

6

Commemoration, Celebration or Commiseration? 150th Anniversary of Indentured Labourers in South Africa

Brij Maharaj*

In 1860 the *Truro* and the *Belvedere* anchored on the shores of Port Natal. Out of its holds emerged a human cargo of indentured labourers from the Indian subcontinent. The journey had replaced their names with numbers and their future was to be cogs in the white man's machine. Hardly had they landed on *terra firma*, they were separated and bundled off to sugar plantations to labour under conditions of near slavery. As historian P. S. Joshi argues, the indentured labour system was introduced by the British as a substitute for 'forced labour and slavery'. The indentured coolies were half slaves, bound body and soul by a hundred and one inhuman regulations' (Joshi 1942: 4).

Reflecting on the history of indentured Indians on the occasion of the visit of the Indian President Abdul Kalam in September 2004, the then Premier of KwaZulu-Natal, S'bu Ndebele, said:

> I wonder what it must have been like to be wrenched from your small village in India, hounded into a compound in Calcutta and forced onto a ship. How difficult it is to comprehend the horror of the pain inflicted on young men and women. And once here to have to labour under slave-like conditions for a pittance[1] ...

The 150th anniversary of the arrival of indentured labourers in South Africa provides a vantage point and an opportunity to reflect critically on the past, as well as to analyse the present as a basis for future projections.

The Indian question in South Africa featured prominently on the national agenda for the greater part of the last century. Politicians from diverse white parties were unanimous on one issue — the Indian population in South Africa should be reduced to the minimum possible. The main mechanisms to achieve this were denial of political rights, limited employment opportunities, restrictions on their ownership and occupation of land, and repatriation. Indians managed to survive the economic and political onslaught primarily because of their rich cultural and religious heritage, community survival strategies and the importance they attached to education. Furthermore, compared to the indigenous population, there was differential incorporation into the economic system. For example, there was space for the merchant class, albeit circumscribed, to own buses, and to own land in the city, while Africans were 'temporary sojourners' in terms of the Urban Areas Act of 1923.

Traditionally, South African Indians have been viewed as a homogeneous community, because they were herded together as one race group, and they organised and mobilised against apartheid from this base. There was always two kinds of responses, one broadly collaborationist and one not. Furthermore, there were various divisions and tensions related to class, religion, language, geographic origins and associated changes with the passage of time and remoteness from India. The post-apartheid, democratic era has witnessed the resurgence of ethnic and sub-ethnic identities. It would appear that some are trying to reinvent the divisions of 1860. These issues came to the fore in discussions and debates to observe the 150th anniversary of the arrival of indentured labourers in South Africa. Political matters permeated the discussions and the following issues were at the forefront, and will be the focus of this chapter which is divided into five sections: post-apartheid anxieties; purpose of celebrations; who represents the 'Indian'; the Indian Government and the Pravasi; and the ANC Government response.

Post-apartheid Anxieties

Given the atrocities of apartheid, the ANC leadership was astounded when two-thirds of the South African Indians voted for the National Party in the first democratic elections in 1994. While the disappointment in the ANC leadership was understandable, the party has failed to engage with issues affecting the community, and this has exacerbated the vulnerability of Indians. The contradictions of apartheid and the complexities of a fractured society played an important role in influencing political affiliations. Local Government Deputy Minister, Yunus Carrim emphasised that the

> ... presence of Indians poses interesting challenges for the tasks of nation-building and non-racial, democratic transformation in South Africa. The ways in which and the degree to which Indians are integrated into the post-apartheid society will be a not unimportant measure of how successful a non-racial democracy South Africa has become (Carrim 1994: 19).

Ethnic minorities throughout the world have fears about majority domination. Indians constitute the most vulnerable ethnic minority in the country, and have been 'sandwiched' between the economically dominant whites and the African majority. As racism, ethnic chauvinism, xenophobia, cronyism and the celebration of mediocrity become more pronounced in the new South Africa, and the ruling elite blatantly flout democratic principles forged on the anvil of struggle, the descendents of indentured labourers increasingly feel disillusioned, marginalised and excluded from the rainbow nation, and anxiously retreat into their religious and cultural cocoons which is sometimes interpreted as a form of racism.

However, racism is clearly not the preserve of one community. If Indians are prone to withdraw into their own culture, other communities are just as much swayed by racial considerations. The nascent tensions and conflict between Africans and Indians have resurfaced periodically (especially during the Mbeki era when the non-racial project was betrayed), and have increased the vulnerability of the minority group, who also believed that they were being sidelined in affirmative action and black economic empowerment schemes. While those in the business and professional sectors thrived in the post-apartheid era and jostled with the political elites for power, privilege, patronage and position, working-class Indians increasingly feel disillusioned, marginalised and excluded from the rainbow nation.

The new-generation Indian elite, with a few exceptions, like their other South African counterparts, selfishly pursue mindless material accumulation and conspicuous consumption, which is quite often accompanied by social and moral degeneration (e.g., as victims and perpetrators of crime). Simultaneously, there has been a retreat from a proud tradition of self-help, sacrifice and community upliftment.

What, Why and How?

There were robust public debates in the media, as well as in political and civil society circles, about the need to recognise the 150th anniversary as a significant milestone in the history of South African Indians, how this event should be observed, and the nature of connections with India. Professor Goolam Vahed raised the following concerns:

> What is it that we should remember, celebrate, and commemorate? Memory and identity are selective and subjective representations and the challenge is to stitch together a collective memory of the past without ostracising anyone. What does this (ethnic/racial) commemoration mean in a country whose constitution is committed to non-racialism? ... Post-apartheid South Africa has seen the mushrooming of religious, language and ethnic identities among Indians. Speaking in the collective about a common 'Indian' experience goes against the grain of the historical and contemporary experience.[2]

There were some discussions about whether the focus should be on commemoration or celebration. There was a view that it would be inappropriate to celebrate 'enslavement and oppression': 'In as much as we are proud of what has been achieved we must not let the brutal oppression of our forbears be forgotten. In my mind this would be a tragic erasure of history'(Ismail 2010).

Inevitably, there were concerns over divided loyalties, and the associated implications (Ismail, 26 May 2010). In this regard, Ahmed Kathrada, who spent 25 years with Nelson Mandela on Robben Island, was very clear: 'We are first and foremost South Africans and owe our loyalty to our national flag and national anthem. We may be of Indian origin and have cultural and other ties with India, but we are all South Africans'(Subramoney, 4 April 2010: 3).

Former Head of the South African Human Rights Commission, and Chairperson of the 1860 Gauteng Legacy Foundation,

Jody Kollapen, maintained that the celebration should reflect the South African diversity (Moodley 2010). In a similar vein, Cyril Ramaphosa, member of the National Executive Committee of the ANC, maintained that there should be a South African celebration, 'given the centrality of the South African Indian community in the body politic of our nation, it is distinctively a celebration by South Africans, for South Africans and about South Africans'. Pravin Gordhan, Minister of Finance, also argued for a non-racial South African celebration: 'It is not a generation of Indians we are celebrating, but a single democracy of non-racial, non-sexist South Africa' (Naidoo 2010).

Political scientist and activist Lubna Nadvi contended that the purpose of the commemoration was 'to remember both the suffering/trials and successes of the indentured labourers, as well as to locate the current generation of Indian South Africans in a contemporary African context with a sense of place and purpose' (Nadvi 2010). The chairperson of the Eastern Cape Legacy Foundation similarly contended that 'we need to also emphasise the role that Indians have and will continue to play in the development of our young democracy'.[3]

Eastern Mosaic, a weekly national television programme which has an Indian lifestyle focus, summarised the issues and challenges pertaining to the 150th anniversary:

> How does one do justice in recollecting, and honoring, the journey through one and a half centuries of an Indian community who has been viewed, for the greatest part of that period, as a minority and as insignificant to the country they've adopted as home–a country far removed from their motherland, and alien to their culture, religion and ways of life? How does one not only commemorate but also empower the memory of such a people, and address their unique contribution to such a country, in the most solicitous and worthy of terms?[4]

A related issue was about representation, and whether it was possible for the South African Indian community to organise and mobilise as a collective.

Who Represents the 'Indian'?

Linked to debates about whether there should be 'celebration' or 'commemoration', a major issue was who legitimately represented the 'Indian'. There was a view that the demise of the Natal Indian Congress (established by Mahatma Gandhi in 1894) was premature, and that it should be revived. Fortunately, this suggestion was rejected, and a return to cabal politics avoided. Former Secretary of the NIC, Dr Farouk Meer, said:

> While understanding the feelings of marginalisation being experienced by Indians and the need among sections of the community for a progressive home outside the ANC ... it would not, at this stage, be appropriate to revive the NIC. We feel it is important that the specific concerns of Indians be taken up with the ANC and that Indians become more active within the structures of the ANC. It is the ANC as the governing party that has the power to address the concerns, needs and interests of Indian South Africans, and it is to the ANC that we must turn for help (Naran 2008).

A major problem has been a dearth of astute, credible leadership in the community, which can genuinely represent the working class and the poor, and this was succinctly captured by journalist Ami Nanackchand:

> A community which never had a homogenous political base since the curtain came down on the Natal Indian Congress, suddenly finds itself trying to acquire one; a community with a rich history of political thought and leadership, is now in search of a savior from the trauma of multi-faceted attacks, abuse and internal dissension; a community that bonded with other exploited fellow countrymen in passive and in militant consciousness across racial, ethnic, religious and a mélange of divisions; now finds itself designated once again with that familiar '*coolie girmitiya*' identity ... and like an *amakwerekwere*[5] should return to its native 'Bombay'... Indo-South Africans are confronting the search for leadership (Nanackchand 2009).

Three organisations focused on the 150th anniversary: a major issue was legitimacy and representation. The 1860 Heritage Foundation was basically a 'family' organisation that had no sustained record of public accountability and transparency, with some controversial links with India, especially with the RSS and the VHP:

> The Antar Rashtriya (Sahayog Parishad) with which Mr Gokool wants to co-celebrate has very close links to the RSS. We will gladly provide the research should anyone want to check but any Google

search will show you the strong links. We respectfully submit that any such co-celebration with a RSS linked group will be very detrimental to the harmony and long term vision of the LF (Legacy Foundation) and the manner with which we have come together and request that the 1860 LF rejects this (Sulaiman 2010).

The 1860 Commemoration Council had been in existence for about 10 years but not much is known about its modus operandi. There was a view that there was a need for a new, representative, democratic organisation to focus on the 150th anniversary. Since the beginning of 2009 several public meetings were held to establish such a structure. The leaders of the Heritage Foundation and Commemoration Council participated in these meetings. The new organisation that emerged was the 1860 Legacy Foundation which was officially launched on 23 March 2009 in Durban.

The process followed to establish the 1860 Legacy Foundation was democratic, transparent and public. The mission statement, aims and objectives of the committee were in the public domain for two months for scrutiny and critical comment. The mission of the Foundations was:

> To co-ordinate a structured and integrated programme of local, provincial, national and international events and, to mobilise all South Africans, irrespective of race, creed, linguistic, religious, social or any other affiliation into a united effort that acknowledges the Indian contribution while enhancing the building of a non-racial society in South Africa (1860 Legacy Foundation launch presentation 2009).

The vision of the 1860 Legacy Foundation was to coordinate the 150th year commemoration and celebration of the arrival of people of Indian origin to South Africa in a manner that:

(a) acknowledges the contribution, sacrifice and commitment of these early settlers;
(b) represents the current interests and aspirations of all stakeholders wishing to commemorate this auspicious milestone; and
(c) advocates for the continued involvement of people of Indian origin in all facets of South African Society with the emphasis on nation building (1860 Legacy Foundation launch presentation 2009).

The meeting to elect the 150th anniversary committee was the largest and most representative gathering held in the South African Indian community in the post-apartheid era. While there was no deliberate 'social engineering', the committee elected reflected the class, religious and linguistic diversity of the community, with a healthy blend of experienced and emerging leaders (Table 6.1).

Table 6.1: Members of the 1860 Legacy Foundation (May 2009)

Ashwin Trikamjee	President of South African Hindu Maha Sabha
Mickey Chetty	President of South African Tamil Federation
Shireen Moonsamy	Author and Immediate Past President of Gopio
A.V.Mohamed	Chairman of the Juma Masjid
Vasugi Singh	Educator, Bharatha Natyam Scholar and Arts Patron
Usha Desai	Gujeratji Hindu Sanskruthi Kendra and Arya Samaj
Lubna Nadvi	Academic, University of Kwa Zulu Natal
Orlean Naidoo	Women's Rights Activist
Kishore Morar	Sports Administrator
Sushie Moodley	South African Andhra Maha Sabha
Satish Dhupelia	1860 Commemoration Council
Roshan Ramdin	School Principal, Community Activist
Aslam Ismail	South African Muslim Networking Forum
Faisal Suleiman	South African Muslim Networking Forum
Brij Maharaj	Academic, President: Shree Sanathan Dharma Sabha of South Africa
Faisel Khan	Lecturer, Media
Sindhu Bhogal	Youth Leader, Arya Samaj South Africa
Seelan Archery	1860 Commemoration Council
Brandon Pillay	Youth Leader and Activist
Krish Gokool	1860 Heritage Foundation
Dasrath Chetty	President Gopio
Solly Pillay	Gopio
Lazarus Pillay	Representing the S. A. Christian Community

Source: 1860 Legacy Foundation, KZN Funding Proposal, 16 February 2010, p. 3.

Initially there was a Durban bias, and this was stressed by ANC member Dr Farouk Meer:

> ... the 1860 Legacy Foundation was democratically elected to represent Durban. To create the impression that it is now a body that represents the province and the nation is not true. Clearly, there is (a) problem with the structure of the body (Dorasamy 2010).

This imbalance was addressed as committees were subsequently established in other provinces (including Eastern Cape, Western

Cape, Gauteng and Free State). A KwaZulu Natal branch was also established in which the ANC had more influence. A national weekly newspaper, the *Post*, which focuses on the South African Indian community, described the optimistic mood as follows:

> The countdown has commenced for the 150th anniversary of the arrival of indentured labourers in South Africa ... To this end, national, regional and local organizations have been established, to ensure that this event is observed across the length and breadth of South Africa, culminating with the grand finale in November 2010. Religious, sporting, cultural and welfare organizations have been galvanised into action ... There have been robust debates about the links between Africa and India, too, which, no doubt, will be explored further.[6]

Sensitive to divisions in the community, the *Post* also emphasised the need for unity:

> Leaders and those aspiring to such positions need to take a leaf from the books of our ancestors. When the 100th anniversary of the indentured arrival on these shores was observed in 1960, leaders from across the political, ideological, language and religious spectrum, straddled the divisions and forged a sense of unity of purpose, at the height of brutal apartheid oppression. There is no reason to believe that this cannot be achieved again 50 years later. Let's avoid reports of 50 years later that today's leaders had failed this community in 2010.[7]

There was agreement that the commemoration of the arrival of indentured labourers should be rooted in an African context. In this regard, it was necessary to heed Goolam Vahed's warning that honouring the past should not 'lead to ghettoisation and isolation from historical relationships with other 'racial' groups in post-apartheid South Africa'.[8] The establishment of the 1860 Legacy Foundation had been endorsed by the South African and Indian governments, with the latter arranging a regional or 'mini' Pravasi Bharatiya Divas.

Pravasi Bharatiya Divas

The Indian Government supported the 1860 Legacy Foundation. However, it went ahead and organised a regional Pravasi Bharatiya

Divas (PBD) on 1–2 October 2010 at the International Convention Centre in Durban, independently of the 1860 Legacy Foundation. According to the Indian Government, the Pravasi Bharatiya Divas

> ... will provide an opportunity for the global Indian community living in the African continent to learn more about each other and how their strengths could be leveraged for greater economic and other benefits. The exchange of ideas, success stories and best practices, will generate enthusiasm and synergies which will benefit not only the Indian community but also their countries (Sharan 2010).[9]

The conception of the Durban Pravasi was not clear, and the nature of local consultation was limited, selective and confined to the compliant elite. Regardless of how honourable the intentions might have been, the majority of the descendents of the indentured labourers would not benefit in any way whatsoever from the PBD, and the registration fee of between R400–800 for the event determined that most could not attend. It would appear that any connection with the 150th anniversary and the PBD was actually a veneer, an expensive public-relations exercise, ostensibly in the name of indentured labourers, and at great cost to the South African and Indian taxpayers, and commercial sponsors.

The PBD was not concerned about the South African Indian masses in Chatsworth, Phoenix or Lenasia, nor the African masses in Inanda, Umlazi or Alexandra. An 'Indian' event that is perceived to exclude the majority is doomed to fail, and possibly increase tensions for the descendents of indentured labourers in South Africa. Responding to such criticism, the Indian Consul-General in Durban contended:

> We are a foreign government and we are here to form a relationship with South Africans, and that includes cultural events, business and academics. We have always maintained that everything was open to the public (Pillay 2010).

When the BJP Government introduced the PBD in 2003, the intention was to attract those with dollars, pounds and Euros to invest in India (a proportion of which went into the coffers of the Sangh Parivar). There was no interest in the descendents of indentured labourers in countries like Malaysia, Fiji, Trinidad, Surinam, Mauritius and South Africa (who possibly remind India of its less sophisticated past). The majority of South Africans have no direct links with India except as an abstract, spiritual motherland (which many pilgrims find disappointing as the faith has been commodified, and religion betrays the poor and disadvantaged).

The High Commission of India contended that 'overseas Indians have emerged as important constituents of their adopted countries and are playing a strategically important role in shaping the future course of development in India'.[10] How do the descendants of the indentured influence events in India? This statement is far-fetched and can only be read as hyperbole. As fully fledged citizens, South African Indians owe no allegiance to India. What is more important is to begin to ascertain the influence of the India connection on South African Indians. Already attempts, albeit unsuccessful, have been made to introduce the religious and violent communal divisions of India into South Africa, through right-wing Hindu organisations which are virulently anti-Muslim and Christian. The relationships between religions are fairly harmonious in South Africa and this has been significantly influenced by the way in which Indians participated in the struggle for democracy.

An associated development has been subtle attempts to reintroduce the abominable caste system which had virtually disappeared in South Africa. More specifically, for thousands of NRIs pursuing dollar-based incomes in South Africa, caste is the only basis for engagement with anyone of Indian descent. And they pejoratively refer to the descendants of indentured labourers as '*yah gana katne wale log kya jante hai*' (What do these cane cutters know?). The local indigenous population is viewed literally as evil characters from the scriptures. Interestingly, the motherland could benefit from the indentured diaspora:

> When you come to think of it, we of the Indian indentured diaspora ... have a lesson to teach the world, especially Mother India. We have demonstrated how, in certain circumstances and under certain conditions, apparently divinely ordained social and cultural institutions and practices deemed immutable can, in fact, change. The way the caste system has broken down in the Indian indentured diaspora is a good example. Religious tolerance is another (Lal 2008).

What makes this orgy of extravagance and elitism all the more disturbing is that both India and South Africa have witnessed heightening inequality and poverty. It bears remembering that the poorest 20 per cent of South Africans receive 1.6 per cent of the total income while the richest 20 per cent receive 70 per cent. The Indian Planning Commission recently reported: 'As the responsibility of the State for providing equal social rights recedes in the sphere of policymaking, we have two worlds of education, two worlds of health, two worlds of transport and two worlds of housing, with a gaping divide in between' (Report of an Expert Group to Planning Commission 2008).

The 150th-year commemoration represented a historic opportunity to raise crucial issues affecting both countries in an era where globalisation has favoured the few and brought untold misery to the majority, for example, the dire state of rural poverty in both countries. The extravagant expenditure incurred for the Pravasi could have been far better spent on urgent social priorities relating to health, welfare and education for the poor who comprise at least more than two-thirds of the total population in both countries. Rather, the local Indian Consulate used the moment to host a dinner (paid for by our government) and create a platform for business links. The intellectual side of the PBD is simply a sop, a cover for the meeting of elites.

The minority new elite in India and South Africa (beneficiaries of neoliberalism) selfishly pursue mindless material accumulation and conspicuous consumption, and will benefit from the new economic and trade agreements negotiated at the Durban PBD, while hundreds of millions in the former (caste-riddled society) and millions in the latter barely subsist (victims of neoliberalism). This is a violation of the ideals of Mahatma Gandhi to which the governments of both countries pay politically expedient lip service. For example, in his keynote address at the closing banquet of the PBD, President Zuma said:

> Gandhi walks through our histories leaving imprints that still direct the paths of both India and South Africa. Gandhi's philosophies remain as relevant today as they were during his lifetime. It is these beliefs that have ensured the continuity of our relations over the years and led to the strengthening of political, economic and social ties between our two nations. His ideology of empathy, respect for one another irrespective of race, appreciation of one another's and understanding have been the foundation of most countries' constitutions (Hassen 2010).

ANC Government Response

It was evident that the South African Government was keen to support some form of celebration/commemoration, and this is perhaps best encapsulated by the following statement by President Zuma on his state visit to India in June 2010:

> When we celebrate the 150 years of the arrival of Indians in South Africa we do so fully conscious of the value that our compatriots of Indian descent add to the diversity and unique character of our beloved country, South Africa. In those 150 years, we have seen Indians who were brought to the country as slaves in the sugar plantations toil their way out of the dehumanizing and demeaning garments of slavery, to excellence in different fields. These have impacted positively in South Africa's development programmes.

> This long, hazardous yet worthy journey has unleashed many heroes and heroines who have left an indelible mark in the collective memory of the nation, also at a political level. Many outstanding freedom fighters of Indian ancestry in our country continue to inspire us because of their bravery and commitment. Like many of us, these giants of the struggle for justice and peace were inspired by the giant extraordinary, Mohandas Karamchand Gandhi ... When we cite names of prominent Indian South Africans, the tendency is to focus only on those who are politically inclined. As we celebrate the 150th anniversary this year, we will also celebrate the achievements and contribution in the fields such as sports, commerce, cricket, legal, social cohesion and others.[11]

The ANC Government supported the establishment of the 1860 Legacy Foundation for several reasons. The Government had been inundated with requests for financial assistance from various organisations across the country to support 150th commemoration events. It envisaged that the Foundation could play a major role in co-coordinating events as well as serving as a fiduciary agent for public funds. By the end of January 2010, the Foundation had received funding applications totalling R75m for projects such as documentary films, monuments, museums, art displays, feeding schemes, books, websites and cultural programmes. The Foundation revised the budgets of the different projects and the total was reduced to R45m and this was submitted to the KwaZulu-Natal Government.

A major tension was that the ANC appeared to be keen to use 150th anniversary events as a platform to mobilise the Indian community to support the party. An issue of concern was whether the 1860 Legacy Foundation could become a surrogate of the ANC. The majority of the members of the Legacy Foundation with progressive credentials, and who were leaders and activists in civil society (Table 6.1), were more independent and critical in terms of public political affiliations.

KwaZulu-Natal Premier, Dr Zweli Mkhize, was quick to dispel that the ANC support for the 150th anniversary was a vote catching ruse; acknowledged the Indian economic, social and cultural contribution to the country; and affirmed financial support for commemoration events:

> We are supporting the 1860 celebrations not to buy votes or curry favour but to support the legacy if Indians in South Africa (which) should not be viewed strictly as an Indian affair. It will be inclusive, embracing all people of the province ... Economically, Indians have helped build and maintain our economy. From a social and cultural perspective, mosques, temples and churches have provided stability to our country ... A final amount has not been decided, but we plan to help fund the individual celebrations throughout the province (Saib 2010).

However, at a public meeting convened by the Premier's office on 28 August 2010, community and civic organisations were informed that the KZN Government did not have funds for disbursement for 1860 Legacy events:

> The Premier apologised profusely ... for not acknowledging receipt of funding applications from the 1860 Legacy Foundation ... and admitted that this was an error ... but not intentional. He reassured us that the 1860 Legacy Foundation was recognized ... as the central organisation co-coordinating the commemoration of the 150 years and that if funds were available then this body would be the recipients (Brief Report 2010).

It was possible that the failure or reluctance to provide funding was related to a deliberate marginalisation of the1860 Legacy Foundation because it adopted a critical public position on matters affecting the descendants of indentured labourers which often conflicted with ANC policy. For example, the Legacy Foundation hosted two public meetings to oppose the Durban Metro's plans to destroy the historic Warwick Early Morning Market (EMM) which was intrinsically linked to the descendents of indentured labourers, displace poor traders and deny them their livelihoods. The Indian leadership in the ANC had endorsed the destruction of the EMM. A mass meeting convened by the Legacy Foundation on 28 July 2009 resolved:

> That the historical and cultural legacy of the Early Morning Market building and surrounds must be preserved as a tribute to the struggle and courage of indentured labourers and all other oppressed people who made a living of the land and who sustained themselves through the EMM ... That the livelihood of all traders, irrespective of race, creed or political persuasion must be protected.[12]

The reaction from the different organisations that had applied for government funding via the Legacy Foundation was one of dismay and disappointment, and is encapsulated by the following response:

> It is sad to see that once again the Indians are ignored. This has reared its ugly head time and time again. We fought for freedom side by side with the blacks of this country. Our people lost so much. Yet when freedom came the very oppressors become the brothers and kinsmen to the blacks. How quickly they forget. ... Indians are resilient and will prosper as we always did in the face of exceptional odds. The Government must not feel that by withdrawing funding for this event will faze us. Remember this (is) just another month in the thousands of years that Indians have walked the earth. In as much as this date is significant for Indians in South Africa it will pale in comparison to time. I am saddened but not fazed ... this for me is a realisation as I am sure it is for many South Africans of Indian descent that we need to claim back our dignity (Timmal 2010).

Sensitive to such sentiments, the central and provincial government agreed to fund one national event in Durban, in partnership with the 1860 Legacy Foundation and other civil society formations on 4 December 2010. By all accounts, this national event was very successful and well supported, and the opening ceremony was broadcast on radio and television. In his keynote address at the function the national Minister of Arts and Culture, Paul Mashatile, paid tribute to the contribution of Indians in the economic and education sectors, as well as in the struggle against apartheid, and affirmed their status as South African citizens:

> On this important occasion, we wish to reiterate once more that the South African Indian community, whose fore-fathers came from India to work as indentured labourers, 150 years ago, are today as South African as any other citizen of our country. As we mark this anniversary we do so to remember not just the arrival of those brave Indian labourers, but also to celebrate the contribution of the South African Indian community to the overall development of our society. ... We honour the courage, the spirit of sacrifice, hard work and love for our country that was demonstrated by those early Indian labourers, who had to endure harsh working conditions that were reminiscent of slavery. Like their fellow African brothers and sisters, they faced multiple forms of exclusion, denial, discrimination and even humiliation ... As we today celebrate the proud legacy of the Indian community in South Africa, and their triumph against slavery, oppression and discrimination, we must recommit ourselves to the ideal of united, non racial, non sexist, democratic and prosperous South Africa.[13]

Conclusion

Notwithstanding the politics, the 1860 commemoration and celebrations served to galvanise and mobilise a vulnerable minority community. While those in the business and professional sectors thrive in the post-apartheid era, working-class Indians increasingly feel isolated. A significant outcome of commemoration events was an affirmation of their status as South African citizens at the highest level. Cynics may well argue that this was largely rhetorical.

The sobering thing is like Shaka's Day, the 150-year commemoration, became an Indian event. It points to the fact that we are still divided and the danger, despite the best intentions of the organisers, is that these kinds of commemorations can rebound by reinforcing rather than sundering boundaries. It is interesting to note that many local Indians preached by day the need to use the 150th anniversary to build Indo-African relations and ensure that the events are accessible to the poor, while at night they cavorted with those who seek to build an insular Indian identity of the privileged and the connected.

Professor Goolam Vahed warned ominously that the

commemorations should not become a tool of the political elites to curry favour with the powers that be, but consideration should be given to measures that can be instituted to improve the lot of the thousands who face a bleak future and for whom the commemoration will have a very different meaning (1860 Legacy Foundation launch presentation 2009).

From a diaspora perspective, the connection with the motherland, India, was weak.

A silent, unspoken question was whether it was possible to build a democratic, progressive platform from the grassroots level that could articulate the problems and challenges facing the South African community, without harking back to the ethnic politics and feuding of the tri-cameral era, or becoming the surrogate of any political party? It would appear that the national strategies to coordinate the commemoration of the 150th anniversary of the arrival of indentured labourers in South Africa could provide the catalyst to establish such an organisation. Regardless of what form it may take, a challenge for the new organisation would be build a national monument dedicated to the memory, history and culture of the indentured Indians—a long overdue project. After all, 'South Africa at the present moment is living through a time of memory' (Govinden 2008).

Notes

*The author is a founder member of the 1860 Legacy Foundation.

1. http://saiva-sithantha-sungum.org/pg037.html. Accessed 1 October 2010.
2. http://www.1860legacygauteng.co.za/index. Accessed 10 December 2010.
3. Press Release: South African Indian Cultural Day on 12 May 2010 at the Nelson Mandela Metropolitan University.
4. Eastern Mosaic commemorates 150 years since the first indentured Indian labourers arrived in South Africa. http://www.easternmosaic.net/pdf/150_Years_2.pdf. Accessed 10 October 2010.
5. Disparaging term for migrants to South Africa from other parts of Africa.
6. Post editorial, 'Let there be Unity of Purpose over 1860', 11–15 November 2009, p. 16.
7. Ibid.
8. Presentation made at the launch of the 1860 Legacy Foundation, 23 March 2009.

9. A.K. Sharan, Consul-General of India, 'Celebrating India's Years of Freedom', *Post*, 11–15 August 2010.
10. Press Release, High Commission of India Cape Town, Pravasi Bharatiya Divas Africa, Durban, 1–2 October 2010.
11. Issued by The Presidency, 2 June 2010. http://www.thepresidency.gov. za. Accessed 10 June 2010.
12. Resolutions adopted at the Mass Meeting convened by the 1860 Legacy Foundation, 28 July 2009.
13. http://www.dac.gov.za/speeches/minister/2010/4_12_2010.html.

References

Brief Report. 2010. Meeting at Premier's Office. Durban. 6 September.
Carrim, Y. 1994. 'Changing Ethnic, Racial and National Identities of Indian South Africans in the Transition to a Post-Apartheid South Africa', paper presented at 'The Nature of Community and its impact on Inter-State Relations at the End of the Twentieth Century' conference. p. 19. Trinidad.
Dorasamy, A. 2010. '1860 Bodies Bicker', *Tribune Herald*, p. 1. 2 May.
E-mail from Aslam Ismail. Legacy Foundation member. 30 March 2010.
E-mail from Aslam Ismail. Legacy Foundation member. 26 May 2010.
E-mail from Lubna Nadvi. 'Some Thoughts on the 1860 LF'. 23 December 2010.
E-mail from Dr Faisal Sulaiman. 20 August 2010.
E-mail from Kammal Timmal. 'Everything Indian'. 21 October 2010.
Govinden, B. 2008. A Time of Memory—Reflections on Recent South African Writings. Durban: Solo Collective.
Hassen, F. 2010. 'Zuma Praises India-SA Bond', *Post*, p. 14. 6–10 October 2010.
Joshi, P. S. 1942. *The Tyranny of Colour—A Study of the Indian Problem in South Africa*, p. 4. Durban.
Lal, Brij V. 2008. 'Marking the 135th Anniversary of the Arrival of Indian People in Suriname', The Hague Immigration Lecture, p. 7.
Moodley, A. 2010. 'Country Celebrates Indian Contribution' *Citizen*, p. 8. 18 May.
Nanackchand, A. 2009. 'Emerging Leaders could be Saviours', *Post*, p. 16. 5–9 August.
Naidoo, T. 2010. 'Let All SA Celebrate this Indian Landmark', *Sunday Times*, p. 3. 8 August.
Naran, J. 2008. 'ANC is Political Home of Indians, Says Former NIC Executive', *Tribune Herald*, p. 3. 21 September.
Pillay, S. 2010. 'Academic Slams Diaspora Event as "for the Elite"', *Sunday Times*, p. 3. 3 October.
Presentation made at the launch of the 1860 Legacy Foundation, 2009. 23 March.

Report of an Expert Group to Planning Commission. 2008. 'Development Challenges in Extremist Affected Areas'. New Delhi, Government of India. p. 1. April.

Saib, A. 2010. 'Premier Says 1860 Support No Vote Ploy', *Tribune Herald*, p. 2. 20 June.

Sharan, A. K. 2010. 'Celebrating India's Years of Freedom', *Post*, p. 16. 11–15 August.

Subramoney, M. 2010. 'Promoting Culture, but SA Comes First', *Tribune Herald*, p. 3. 4 April.

7

The Legacy of Indentured Indians in South Africa: The Politics of Saving the Early Morning Market in Durban

Lubna Nadvi

We must protect the market ... we must not let them take one screw
away. It does not just belong to the traders and barrow boys. Let us
save our heritage. They will have to demolish us first.
—Fatima Meer, sociologist and anti-apartheid activist, 2009

This article attempts to reflect on the broader economic and political
legacy of the indentured Indian workers who, having arrived in
South Africa in 1860, began to establish a very significant presence
in what was at the time the colony of Natal, today known as
Kwa-Zulu Natal. 150 years later, their descendants commemorate
their arrival on the shores of Natal: to remember the multi-faceted
legacy that their forefathers and mothers have left them. The
history of that legacy has manifested itself in a variety of ways, but
it has arguably remained very much a working-class legacy shaped
by political strife and struggle pitted against continuing forms of
imperialism and neoliberal agendas.

A key aspect of that legacy has come to define itself in terms of
how the descendants of the early indentured labourers have sought
to protect and preserve the constituent economic foundations
their forefathers and mothers have left them, as well as engage
with the post-apartheid state which has, since 1994, increasingly
attempted to marginalise many historically disadvantaged communities through strategies such as evictions, electricity and
water cutoffs, a consequence of the shift towards the adoption of
a neoliberal economic policy such as Growth Employment and

Redistribution — GEAR (Bond 2002, 2006).[1] These new forms of state repression have led to the emergence of new sites of struggle, and in Durban (eThekwini), historically Indian townships such as Chatsworth have become areas of contestation between local residents and the Municipality which continuously attempts to marginalise and punish poor communities who are unable to pay rents or afford water and electricity (Desai 2000, 2002).[2] While some of the contested issues have been addressed through engagement between the communities and the Municipality, there are nevertheless battles between people living in these communities such as subsistence farmers, fishermen and street traders and the local Municipality over the rights of such people to earn a subsistence livelihood in areas which the city deems as being municipal or even private property, and hence off limits to poor people.

One such struggle that has emerged since the beginning of 2009, that has captured the attention and imagination of Durban's civil society and indeed that of the national and international media, is the struggle waged by the traders located within the Early Morning Market (EMM) community in the Warwick Junction precinct in the city of Durban, to preserve their market from being demolished by the city council in order to build a mall in its place. Caught totally by surprise at the sudden announcement by the city's authorities in February 2009, the trading community has (together with concerned members of broader civil society) embarked on a sustained campaign to fight the Municipality and do everything in its power to protect the market. This struggle is a very significant one within the context of the legacy of the indentured Indian labourers as the majority of the traders who own stalls in the market are the descendants of those indentured workers who arrived in South Africa in 1860 and thereafter, and who, through their entrepreneurial initiatives, managed to secure the building of a fresh-produce market where they could sell fruits and vegetables, once their period of indenture had ended. This market, while originally called the Victoria Street Early Morning Market, is now popularly known as the Early Morning Market.

This article seeks to explore the contestation between expressing forms of citizenship in relation to the preservation of historical legacies and subsistence livelihoods (through informal economies) in a modern, urban context, versus the top-down imposition of decisions by a city council which does not seem to value these core democratic ideals and has effectively reneged on practising good governance in the case of the EMM. Locating the analysis within the framework of a very significant historical landmark, such as that of the 150th commemoration of the arrival of Indian indentured workers, enables the interrogatation of themes such as imperialism and the oppression of the working classes as ongoing social challenges that have evolved over centuries, and have never quite been eradicated.

History and Profile of the Early Morning Market and Warwick Junction

The history of the EMM began shortly after the arrival of the first indentured Indian workers from India to the shores of Natal. The indentured labourers, who, many historians have argued, arrived and worked in conditions akin to slavery, were meant to serve an initial period of five years as indentured workers, mostly on the sugar cane plantations of Natal (Desai and Vahed 2007; Henning 1993). Once their period of indenture ended, they were to return to India. However, many opted to stay and make a living in Natal, either through renting land and farming or some other form of trade.

Many of those that stayed and were able to lease land from the British landowners, or eventually purchase land, effectively took up market gardening, growing a variety of fresh produce. This meant that the former indentured workers were now able to earn their living through largely self-sustainable means, even though they were still subjected to various taxes such as the infamous three-pound tax. Regardless of these economic constraints, the farmers sought to find innovative ways to sell their produce. From about 1890, the trustees of the Grey Street Mosque in Durban (the largest mosque in the Southern hemisphere) allowed farmers to sell their fruits and vegetables on the mosque premises. A new fresh-produce market was opened in the Grey Street precinct in August 1910.

Sadly, due to communal disputes between Hindus and Muslims, Hindu farmers boycotted the new market. In response to this, the then city authority, the Durban Town Council opened a street market in Victoria Street, called the Victoria Street Early Morning Market. This became a place that encountered the wrath of a number of the city's residents who complained about the street carts, boxes and other items that blocked the street where the traders sold their goods. In addition, many traders ended up sleeping under their carts with their families. There were also concerns relating to hygiene, unsightliness and safety issues. In response to these complaints, the Market Master proposed that the market be moved to another site, namely Warwick Avenue. The new market was opened in January 1934, and has since then been functioning as the Early Morning Market.

Over the past 100 years, the Warwick Junction area, in which the EMM is located, has become the centre of informal trade, and a commercial district for the working classes where they can ply their trade and sell their goods as street traders, hawkers and stall holders. Given that the junction also serves as the Municipality's core transportation hub with commuter taxis, buses and trains all converging in this area, there are approximately 450,000 people who pass through the junction daily. Since 1994, the deregulation of street trading saw a flood of informal traders enter the economic arena. The land on which the EMM operates is classified as municipal property, hence the Municipality has often been involved in controlling and manipulating the economic activities of the market traders, often in a somewhat arbitrary manner.

Development plans for Warwick Junction and Emerging Contestations

The Warwick junction, while an economic hub, has also been a development challenge for the city of Durban. In an evolving post-apartheid context and the fact that the informal economy of the city began to flourish after 1994, a critical upgrade to the area was called for and implemented in the early years at the turn of the 21st century. This involved putting into place infrastructure and regulatory systems (such as by-laws) for the smooth functioning of the informal trading activities in the area and improvement of the physical condition of the junction (eThekwini Municipality undated brochure).

Once the initial process of upgradation to the Warwick Junction was completed in the early 2000s, the Municipality began to focus on a new phase of restructuring and development for the area. This was meant to address transportation rationalisation, improve public spaces, upgrade housing and increase opportunities for formal and informal trade. In 2006, the eThekwini Municipality hired a team of consultants to prepare a status report for Warwick Junction. The recommendations of the consultants suggested a major overhaul of the Warwick area, but without mentioning the building of a mall. The proposals appeared to be more trader-orientated than supporting formal business. It was also assumed that the plan to overhaul the precinct would not detract from previous projects in the area and therefore, one of the core principles guiding the project proposal was to ensure the integration of relevant previous studies and development proposals (Warwick Development Consortium Report for eThekwini Municipality 2006).[3] In assessing and preparing an evaluation report of the Warwick Junction region in 2006, the Warwick Development Consortium acknowledged that several challenges existed in the area. These included the issue of declining sales by traders, racial demographics, multiple site ownership and the fact that big businesses were increasingly developing controlling interests in the area.[4]

In the processes leading up to the implementation of the new proposed development plan, the Municipality organised a few meetings and invited communities to share their views on the proposals. In these initial meetings, it appeared that the traders and other communities consulted were satisfied with the plans as they did not seem to in any way appear to impact negatively on them. They were, however, under the impression that these new building projects would take place over the Berea railways lines and at the station (in close proximity to), rather than at the EMM site.[5] Given that an environmental impact assessment (EIA) had been conducted for the Berea Station site, which had been a participatory process, it did not occur to the trading community that there was anything endangering their community.

At two meetings held on 18 February 2009, the eThekwini Municipality publicly announced its plans to demolish the EMM structure and build a mall in its place. It was effectively announcing that the development site had now been moved from the original Berea Station area to the EMM site. The traders were also informed that they would be temporarily 'relocated' to another site a short distance from the current EMM, and that they could supposedly continue trading. This was the first time that the EMM traders had heard of such development plans. They were justifiably outraged and a huge uproar followed, with the traders demanding answers from the Municipality about the lack of consultation around a decision that appeared to be a fait accompli. A number of letters were written by the traders to the Municipality seeking clarity on these announcements. The EMM traders were not prepared to accept these 'new' proposed arrangements.

It subsequently emerged through further investigation and probing by the EMM traders and press reports, that the city Municipality had agreed to award a development contract to a private developer listed as Warwick Mall (Pty) Limited, associated with a property development company called Isolenu, without following the proper public consultation processes. Given that the land on which the EMM is located is classified as municipal/council property, the City Council had in 2008 authorised the city manager, Dr Mike Sutcliffe, to explore the possibility of granting a lease to a private developer to build a mall, in response to a report drafted by the city manager, where he made a proposal to this effect.[6] There were also some suggestions by the property developer that the mall could be built by June 2010, giving the impression that the project was linked to possible profit-making schemes associated with the 2010 FIFA World Cup.

However, despite taking this decision, the City Council was subsequently legally bound to abide by a policy process which demanded that it engage in a process of public consultation with regard to granting leases of council property. The Asset Transfer Regulations Act of 2008 required that the City engage in a public participation process in respect of the proposed lease.[7] The Municipality committed itself to doing so.

In May 2009, the Municipality approached the AMAFA, the Provincial Heritage Conservation Agency, to obtain approval for the development plans for Warwick Mall. The AMAFA, however, refused to grant it permission to proceed, citing concerns that

> there was no real public buy-in to the scheme and that conservation principles had not been considered. In addition they argued that the removal of the market and the destruction of some of the fabric, removal of the primary element (the gates) and the domination of the remaining fabric, was effectively in contradiction with internationally accepted conservation principles (AMAFA 2009).

Between April and August 2009, a series of public meetings and workshops were held to discuss the issue; however, these became increasingly unpleasant as the contestation between the EMM traders and the city Municipality grew even more intense.

Unfortunately, the process turned uglier as it went along, provoking the establishment of a number of court cases between the Municipality and different groups of traders from the Warwick Junction and the EMM. Relations between the city and those who opposed the Warwick Development Project reached a point where the city manager alleged that a number of 'liars' had been spreading misinformation about the development and where others claimed that people need to listen to the side of the Municipality rather than to reports from trader leadership, street trader committees and organisations (Report from Public Meeting on Warwick Mall Development held at ICC, 2009).

One of the meetings at which the eThekwini Municipality attempted to 'convince' the public of the necessity of the Warwick Development Project, is instructive. At a public meeting in July 2009, the city Municipality presented its plans for the Warwick Development Project. It argued that the development would achieve the following objectives:

(a) optimise the road-based system by rationalising and consolidating public transport including buses and taxis;
(b) reduce traffic accidents in the area;
(c) create a predominantly pedestrian preference corridor;
(d) consolidate and develop land uses for commercial, social and heritage activities;
(e) eventually establish a single-ticket system which would enable commuters to travel on any mode of transport using a single ticket; and
(f) create a space for commuters for shopping and leisure through the building of a mall.

While the argument from the city 'seemed' appealing, the traders as well as members of broader civil society questioned the necessity of having to demolish the historic EMM building in order to achieve these objectives. They argued that all these could be achieved by 'upgrading' the area, without demolishing a historic building which was the economic lifeblood of thousands of traders. Effectively, those who were opposed to the destruction of the EMM were not opposed to the general upgrading of the area (KZN Provincial Government 2009).

Political Mobilisation by the EMM Traders and the EMM Support Group: 'Saving the Market'

Upon being informed of the proposed demolition of the EMM in February 2009, the EMM Traders Association held a series of meetings with the city to object. However, the Municipality remained adamant that it was going ahead with its plans. Apart from the EMM group, there were the street traders and the bovine head cookers who would also be affected by the development and proposed relocation of the traders, as they plied their trade directly outside the EMM building. However, the street traders and bovine head cookers eventually agreed to being relocated while the development was taking place, as they were promised that they would be given space and upgraded facilities in the new mall space to trade. The EMM traders did not agree to the idea of either being removed or having the EMM structure demolished. They eventually sought the assistance of the public and broader civil society.

The city authorities continued to harass the EMM traders during the period between February 2009 and early 2010, confiscating the goods of some traders, conducting spot checks of stalls and during confrontations at the market site, police fired at traders, including elderly women. In May 2009 the Municipality refused to grant the traders permission to march in peaceful protest, a right which is guaranteed by the South African Constitution. In May and June 2009, the EMM traders arranged solidarity meetings at the market, where they were confronted by the city police, shot at and physically assaulted. The police used teargas and rubber bullets in an attempt to disperse the crowd. Following these onslaughts by the city authorities, a major public campaign to save the Early Morning Market was started by the traders, activists, academics, civic and religious groups and trade unions. A series of public meetings were held, driven initially by the 1860 Legacy Foundation, a body launched in 2009, and then jointly with the EMM Support group (comprising a cross-section of civil society including academics and various civic groups), where people publicly pledged to stop the EMM structure from being demolished, and to boycott the retail outlets based in the mall. At one of these meetings, a KZN provincial government-level task team was set up to take submissions on the matter and report back to the public.

The eThekwini Municipality called its own meetings where it did its best to argue that the development was in the best interests of the city, and to give the impression that most people were in agreement with the project. In July, at one such meeting called by the city authorities, there were racial remarks made from the floor which implied that Indian people were benefiting from the market, and it was time that things changed. The city authorities, however, remained silent and did not condemn such remarks. In the aftermath of this meeting, there was a huge public outcry in the media at the attitude of the city management, and ongoing tension between city authorities and those who opposed the demolition of the market.

The EMM traders also engaged in legal action to get an interdict from the Durban High Court to stop the demolition as well as deal with other aspects of the city's harassment of them. They were successful on some levels and not on others. In November 2009, a civil case that tried to get the city to legalise traders that it deemed 'illegal' was postponed to early 2010. In December 2009, the EMM filed papers with the Durban High court to stop the city from evicting traders that it deemed 'illegal'. The city Municipality, apart from harassing the EMM traders, was also harassing the barrow boys, who assist in moving fresh produce around the market and who are a huge support network for the traders. One of the legal court actions found in favour of allowing the barrow boys to continue working. In addition, many traders were not allowed to trade by the Municipality as they were called illegal traders, given that they did not have individual permits. However, many of the traders have had their businesses passed down to them from previous generations and at the point of transfer of ownership did not necessarily obtain the documentation the city now demanded that they have. This did not necessarily (according to most civil-society arguments) make them illegal. As a result of this so-called 'illegal' status, the city started clamping down on such stall holders within the EMM, and many trading spots ended up vacant as traders left their places.

The KZN Provincial Task Team reported back to the public in August 2009 on its findings and made recommendations based on the various submissions made by a range of stakeholders. The report reflected broadly a summary of wide-ranging views, including those who supported the development to those who opposed it.

It is important to note that most people who opposed the building of the mall did not necessarily oppose the improvements to the transport infrastructure, as outlined earlier in this article.

In its report, the Provincial Task Team argued that 'The benefits of the development must be recognized ... as it will contribute to the significant upgrading of the area ... and that there will be an economic development to the city as a whole'. It further emphasises that 'this fact should not be minimalised or glossed over due to the atmosphere of high emotions and mistrust' (KZN Provincial Government 2009).

It becomes clear, from the above statement, that the KZN provincial government appeared to be in cahoots with the eThekwini city Municipality, in favouring the development process moving forward, even though there was widespread public opposition to it. The provincial task team also recommended that the consultative process (which was at the time seriously flawed) must be reopened but the process must come to a close by 30 September 2009. It also argued that the environmental assessment process must also be concluded by 31 October 2009.

The Struggle Continues ...

Since the end of 2009, there has been a pending legal case between the EMM traders and the city Municipality, which at the time of writing this article had not been concluded. However, the EMM Traders Association and the traders (who have been allowed to trade with their legal permits) have continued trading. In addition, in 2010 they marked two very significant historical milestones. This included the 100th birthday of the EMM as well as commemorating 150 years since the arrival of indentured Indians in South Africa. At the 100th birthday event, various members of the public as well as government officials such as Ravi Pillay, the Chief Whip of the ANC in the KZN Legislature, and politicians such as Amichand Rajbansi, Head of the Minority Front political party, affirmed their commitment to the struggle to save the market. The Councillor for the ward (municipal area) in which the EMM is situated, Vusi Khoza, committed himself to ensuring that the market structure would not be demolished to build a mall. At the 150-year celebrations the Deputy Mayor of the eThekwini Municipality, Logie Naidoo, conceded that the EMM matter could have been handled differently by the city Municipality, and that hopefully there would be a 'win–win' conclusion to the issue.

It becomes clear from all these declarations from public officials that they have finally tapped into and understood wider public sentiment that the EMM is off limits, at least for now. Having attended events where the public mood was very clearly in favour of keeping the market structure, the politicians have not been able to do much else but to go along with this public mandate. It is clearly in their political interests to do so, at least until the outcome of the pending court case. However, this does not mean that sinister and untoward activities do not continue to happen within the market. For example the day before the market community was to celebrate their 100-year birthday they were informed by the Municipality that they could not do so, as the event contravened city by-laws. They obtained a last minute court interdict and the event went ahead and was a success. On the morning of the 150-year commemoration it was discovered that the plaque that had been revealed on the 100th birthday had 'mysteriously' disappeared and had been stolen. It is clear that such underhand activities were carried out in an ongoing attempt to 'undermine' the morale of the market community.

However, the EMM traders and their supporters are certainly not in any way intimidated. In August 2010, they observed Heritage Day by staging a play called 'Marketeers' which told the story of the arrival of the indentured workers, the building of the EMM and the current struggles which traders face in terms of the still looming threat to the market. The play was jointly staged and produced by a civic group called Women in Action (part of the EMM support group) and the traders themselves. Traders who had never acted, danced or performed on stage before took on the challenge of participating in the play.

In the final analysis, what the struggle to save the market illustrates is that civil society and active citizenship mobilising around an issue which is deemed to be of public interest, in post-apartheid South Africa, is clearly as powerful today as it was during the anti-apartheid struggle era. While the city authorities had intended to remove the market traders from the market in early 2009 and demolish the structure, the building still stood at the time of writing this article. This is certainly a testament to a powerful collective civic battle waged vigorously despite facing the full onslaught of the city authorities and indeed the state. The fact that this has been a largely non-racial struggle, bringing together the descendants of the indentured labourers as well as the broader EMM community on a common platform around preserving subsistence livelihoods, has ensured that the city officials, despite their best efforts to, in some instances racialise and divide the market community, have not succeeded. While the final fate of the EMM is still unclear, it appears, however, that the struggle to save it may be an ongoing one. At the time of writing, the eThekwini Municipality had withdrawn its plans for the development and were not going ahead with the building of the proposed Warwick Mall. The campaign to 'save the market' has nevertheless been an important period in the city's history, bringing the public together on a matter which affects the most vulnerable residents of the city. One could arguably conclude that the benefits of 'urban development' (being pushed by the city Municipality) have been seriously challenged by the EMM traders and their supporters, who have argued that any development that seeks to destroy livelihoods is effectively not really development, but rather a violation of basic human and constitutional rights in order to advance neoliberal agendas (Amin 1990; Desai 2002). The struggle continues.

Notes

1. Development specialists such as Patrick Bond have written extensively on the post-apartheid government's neoliberal economic policies which have further marginalised previously disadvantaged communities in South Africa.
2. See A. Desai for an analysis of the post-apartheid struggles being waged by historically disadvantaged communities.
3. Acknowledgements to Andrea Tirone, MA candidate in the School of Politics, UKZN, for assistance with collating fieldwork documentation.
4. See eThekwini Municipality, Documents filed in KZN High Court Case No. 11559/2009 (2008a, 2008b, 2008c).
5. Information obtained from informal conversations with members of the EMM Traders association, including Harry Ramlal and Romilla Chetty and Chair of the EMM Support Group, Roy Chetty.
6. Information obtained from informal conversations and interviews with members of EMM Traders association and various press reports.
7. See eThekwini Municipality, report dated 24 February 2009 (2009a).

References

AMAFA. 2009. *eThekwini/coast built environment committee minutes – 05/05/2009.* C20 Chetty Affidavit, Case No. 11559/2009, KwaZulu-Natal High Court, Durban. Filed on 13 August 2009.

Amin, S. 1990. *Maldevelopment: Anatomy of a Global Failure.* Tokyo: UN University Press.

Ballard, R., A. Habib and I. Valodia (eds.). 2006. *Voices of Protest: Social Movements in Post-Apartheid South Africa.* Scottsville: UKZN Press.

Barsamian, D. 2004. *The Checkbook and the Cruise Missile: Interviews with Arundhati Roy.* Cambridge: South End Press.

Bond, P. 2002. *Elite Transition: From Apartheid to Neo-Liberalism in South Africa.* London: Pluto Press.

———. 2006. *Looting Africa: The Economics of Exploitation.* Scottsville: UKZN Press.

Desai, A. 2000. *The Poors of Chatsworth.* Durban: Madiba Publishers.

———. 2002. *We are the Poors: Community Struggles in Post-Apartheid South Africa.* New York: Monthly Review Press.

Desai, A. and G. Vahed. 2007. *Inside Indenture: A South African Story. 1860–1914.* Durban: Madiba Publishers.

Dobson, R. 2007. 'iTrump [inner Thekwini regeneration and urban management programme] area based contribution towards managing the informal economy'. Report submitted to eThekwini Municipality. http://www.durban.gov.za/durban/government/abms/studies/Itrump. pdf/view. Accessed 10 January 2008.

Dobson R., C. Skinner and J. Nicholson. 2009. *Working in Warwick: Including Street Traders in Urban Plans.* Durban: School of Development Studies, University of KwaZulu-Natal.

eThekwini Council. 2006. '2010 and Beyond: eThekwini's IDP'. http://www. durban.gov.za/durban/Council/council_news/idps. Accessed 10 July 2007.

eThekwini Municipality. N. d. 'Business Support Unit: Informal Trade Information Brochure'.

eThekwini Municipality. 2008a. *Confidential minutes of meeting of the Executive Committee eThekwini Municipality*, pp. 330–31. Meeting held 22 September 2009. Retrieved from: The Record filed by the eThekwini Municipality in Case No. 11559/2009, KZN High Court, Durban.

———. 2008b. *Minutes of street traders' imbizo.* Meeting held on 04/11/2008. C6 Chetty Affidavit. Case No. 11559/2009, KwaZulu-Natal High Court, Durban. Filed on 13 August 2009.

———. 2008c. *Proposed Warwick mall development: Confidential report to committee,* pp. 323–27. 18 September 2008. Retrieved from The Record filed by the eThekwini Municipality in Case No. 11559/2009, KZN High Court, Durban.

———. 2009a. *Proposed Warwick mall development,* pp. 352–54. Report dated 24 February 2009. Retrieved from: The Record filed by the eThekwini Municipality in Case No. 11559/2009, KZN High Court, Durban.

Ganpath, K., J. Wicks and Sapa. 2007. 'Durban Police Arrest 500 Street Traders', Mercury. 20 June.

Govender, B. G. and T. P. Naidoo. 2010. *The Settler: Tribulations, Trials, Triumph.* Durban: Barlow Govender Foundation.

Henning, C. 1993. *The Indentured Indian in Natal (1860–1917)*. New Delhi: Promilla & Co.

Klein, N. 2007. *The Shock Doctrine: the Rise of Disaster Capitalism*. London: Penguin Books.

KZN Legislature. 2007. *The Elimination and Prevention of the Re-emergence of Slums* (Act No 6 of 2007).

KZN Provincial Government. 2009. *Report of the Provincial Task Team on the eThekwini Early Morning Market and the Warwick Avenue Mall Development*. Durban: KZN Provincial Government.

Nadvi, L. 2008. 'The Ugly Side of the Beautiful Game: The Socio-Economic Impact of the 2010 FIFA World Cup on the City of eThekwini and its Poors', *World Journal of Managing Events*, 2 (1).

Robbins, G. et al. 2005. Consolidated Report: Durban Inner City Economic Environment, Durban: iTrump/Inner City Spatial Development Framework Project.

Report of National Strategising Seminar with World Class Cities For All (WCCA) Campaign Partners. 2007. Orchidea Hotel, Braamfontein. 7–8 March.

Skinner, C. 2000. 'Getting Institutions right? Local Government and Street Traders in Four South African Cities', *Urban Forum*, 11 (1): 49–71.

———. 2008. 'The Struggle for the Streets: Processes of Exclusion and Inclusion of Street Traders in Durban, South Africa', *Development Southern Africa*, 25 (2): 227–42.

———. 2009a. 'An Open Letter to the eThekwini Municipality opposing the Proposed Mall for Warwick Junction in Durban, South Africa' *Mercury*. 03 May 2009.

———.2009b. *A socio-economic assessment of the proposal for a mall in Warwick Junction: Thousands of livelihoods under threat*. June 2009. C40 Chetty Affidavit, Case No. 11559/2009, KwaZulu-Natal High Court, Durban. Filed on 13 August 2009.

Sutcliffe, M. 2007. '20/20 Vision: The City Managers Column', *Metro Beat*, Issue 99.

Warwick Development Consortium. 2006. '*Warwick Junction Precinct Plan Status Quo Assessment*' For eThekwini Municipality. May.

8

An Anthropological Critique of Indian Diasporic Integration in South Africa: Historical Processes and the Limits of Social Justice

Ravindra K. Jain

Goolam Vahed and Ashwin Desai (2010: 10) conclude a recent paper as follows:

> There has been a (re)turn to the language of class in many communities in South Africa, if not explicitly then at least implicitly. The languages of class oppression is one powerful way in which the Indian poor can begin to forge alliances with the African poor and in this process challenge both the laager[1] of ethnic identity and poverty.
>
> The language of 'non-racialism' too ... still has a powerful resonance in South Africa for many and so does the quest to build a more equitable society. Post-apartheid South Africa remains ripe with possibilities. With increasing arguments for class to be brought into the equation this may be an important stimulus for embracing identities that cross racial boundaries.

Let me state at the outset, apropos the above conclusion, what I intend to do and not to do in this article. First, as a non-South African, whatever connotation you may attach to this statement either in terms of identity or belonging, I am reluctant to assume the role of an activist which would be necessary to pronounce a possible *solution* (as against a possible diagnosis) to the crisis of social justice in South Africa. Second, as an academic social anthropologist, I shall venture to present a largely microcosmic analysis of the problem at hand though within a macrocosmic universe of discourse, and, indeed, one informed by an 'implicit' global framework of anthropological comparisons (Jain 2010). I broadly agree with the ideological thrust of Vahed and Desai's diagnosis of the South African crisis though I do not discuss here, as they do, the play of capitalism and neoliberalism defining the political system in South Africa.

The first part of this article spells out the various concepts. In the second part, I narrate, based heavily on the recent historical work by Desai and Vahed and my own brief and provisional interpretative effort (Jain 2010: Chapter 4), three dimensions of the story of Indian diasporic integration in South Africa. I conclude the article by bringing out the implications of the historical nature of the present 'Indian diasporic integration' and the limits of social justice in contemporary South Africa.

Let me spell out the concepts of 'community', 'culture' and 'ethnicity' as used by some other scholars in their empirical work. Community is something that is constituted and reconstituted by those who belong to it. S. Dufoix points out (2008: 69–70) that there is nothing 'natural' about community, not even in the concept of 'gemeinschaft' or traditional community (sometimes translated as 'society') as contrasted with the modern 'gesellschaft' or 'association' (Tonnies 1957). He says,

> For Weber what creates community is a social relationship based on the subjective feelings of belonging to the same community ... I add that this belief is sustained by the existence of an objective community that is socially constructed and symbolised by institutions, spokespeople, emblems and myths (Dufoix 2008: 70).

It is through the exercise of individual and collective human agency that communities are constituted. Moreover, in this era of neo-functionalism we valourise the agendas or proactive purposes of conscious human agents (manifest or latent), rather than the metaphysical telos of 'systems'. The methodological and practical fallout of this realisation is that, if there is one change about human society and culture, it is the fact of purposive and planned transformation. The communities, to be sure, may not succeed in what they propose (unintended consequences and 'dysfunctions' stalk their path) but in anthropology and sociology of our times the aura of fatalism,[2] often dressed up as primordial constraints remains the overarching assumption about the mainspring of actions in communities. If in the ongoing process, the dichotomous distinction between 'gesellschaft' and 'gemeinschaft' becomes obliterated, leading to a simultaneous existence of the two (Worsley et al. 1978: 342; for an empirical example from the Indian diaspora in Malaysia see Jain 2009a: 102), so be it.

The classical anthropological concept of culture is best understood, in the context of communities, as the lens of a worldview through which fully formed or partly formulated aspirations are given shape. Values, both functional and dysfunctional, positive and negative, solidary or conflictive for communities remain in perpetual contestation (Brah 1996). They are an intrinsic component of the concept of 'culture'. I have tried to distinguish the concept of 'culture' from that of 'ethnicity':

> In sociological terms, the situational and dynamic conceptualisation of ethnicity in society is complementary to the reiterative performance of what is constructed as 'custom', 'tradition' or 'value' viz., culture. ... It makes sense to juxtapose ethnicity and culture as twin faces of dynamics of reproduction and change, respectively: both delineate process but in terms of change and continuity (Brah 1996: 234; Jain 2009a: 62).

It should be noted that the 'situational' theorisation of ethnicity right from Weber (1978) down to commentators like Barth (1969), Cohen (1974), Brubaker (2004) and Shamsul (2008) is not conceived as the cement of sustained corporate groups and is thus open to conceptualisation of change, even transformation.[3] There is, however, a reactionary catch, especially in its conceptual overlap ('family resemblances', Jain 2010b) with the concept of race. There is here an interesting historical causality. 'Ethnicity' became a sociological tool in US society, as an 'exclusive' concept, referring as it did 'initially' to the WASPs and the eastern and central *white* immigrants, as opposed to the 'inclusive' concept of 'race' in distinguishing all whites from all Blacks (Negroes). The application of ethnicity as an analytical tool elsewhere than US for example, in Malaysia or South Africa, carries with it racist connotation of its original application. Especially when race and ethnicity as antonyms of white to non-white become signifiers of identity and identification through the play of social class and power — not only does phenotype overtake whatever may remain of 'pure' genotype — they become, as masks, instruments of stereotypical, springs of social action and interaction. See in this respect M. Weber's (1978: 385–95; 933–35) failed optimism of the decline of race-and ethnicity-based status groups in the US with an increase in the population of mulattoes. The failure was socio-demographic in nature.

Indian Indenture and the Nature/Role of Cultural Factors in Resistance/Resilience

The data about Indian indenture in Desai and Vahed is amenable to be seen in terms of communities comprising mainly the various 'sub-ethnicities' of Indian workers and occupationally/functionally constituted European bosses. Mainly from the viewpoint of the workers these were 'closed communities', 'total institutions' (Beckford 1984; Goffman 1961; Jain 1970; Marimuthu 2008). In terms of their recruitment and settlement experiences, the indentured labourers were deterritorialised and reterritorialised. Reterritorialisation was hemmed in by stringent pass laws which restricted movement of labourers like in a prison. These experiences have been very fully depicted as transformative in the archives detailed by Desai and Vahed. There is one aspect of the psychological interpretation that I wish to add. The communities of indentured labourers (and the colonisers) strongly manifest features of what has been called 'the Stockholm syndrome'.[4] Colonisers, as kidnappers, soon in adaptation to life in the total institution became sympathetic co-dwellers and protectors in the estimation of the communities of both the labourers and their white masters. The mutual dependence, though sharply asymmetrical, provided the key to the adaptation process.[5] For the indenture system in South Africa the following existential circumstances for this adaptation were favourable:

(a) the emigrant indentured labourer was by and large, even in his village, impoverished and uprooted;
(b) he/she was a denizen already of a deeply stratified society; and
(c) in the social code of indenture the institutionalised relationship between the labourer, the intermediary native gang leader (Sirdar) and the European master on the plantations or on mines was highly personalised.

The racial/ethnic/sub-ethnic *identification* made by the boss was internalised as a template of *identity* by the worker?[6]

In conventional sociology and social anthropology, culture, broadly defined as 'values', is seen as the cement of social structure (Beattie 1964). Once when I made a similar point in class, one of my students said that often enough the builder weakens the cohesive power of cement by mixing sand in it. The point is well taken, that culture, though reproducing social structure, is contested, often becomes counterproductive and is usually a divisive element in society. I do not take this extreme (nihilistic) view of culture because recognising its distinctiveness retains in social science analysis an expressive dimension as against an exclusively instrumental one. However, apropos Desai and Vahed and their extensive discussion of 'resistance' among Indian indentured labourers that I wish to endorse — with sufficient justification — the ancillary concept of 'resilience' and its application in analysing cultural change in Indian society (Singh 2000). Resilience may be seen as the prerequisite of resistance. Desai and Vahed's book is replete with examples of the indentured labourers' resistance. Note, in particular, the labourers' defiance through disobedience and other 'weapons of the weak', even certain amount of violent retaliation as during the 1913 strike as a response to brutal repression and, significantly, instances of the women's sterling role in defying exploitation and contributing to 'reconstitute' a viable community in the new setting (Desai and Vahed 2010: 434–35; Jain 2010). However, those who take a rose-tinted view of this concept refuse to see any faultlines. I shall give examples where the sliding scale of its meaning reduces 'resilience' to rigidity, orthodoxy and, indeed, a resistance to adapt and change. The resistance in cultural forms like the carnivalesque reversal of roles in processually adapted traditional Indian (Hindu and Muslim) ceremonies and rituals performed in indenture community localities of South Africa may be interpreted as 'rituals of rebellion' (Jain 1970: 400–17). The sociological interpretation of these cultural protests or resistance is often a reaffirmation of the status quo. Note that M. Gluckman (1940) proposed a distinction between 'rebellion' and 'revolution'.

Desai and Vahed (2010: 310–12) write about the existence of rotating credit association (RCA) among 'Madrasi' indentured labourers on the sugar cane estates of Natal in the 1880s. The institution of RCA among the labouring classes has been extensively reported in all parts of the world (Ardener 1964). My culturalistic interpretation of this institution was in terms of an interaction between the ceremonial exchange-oriented Tamil society and plantation workers who are recipients of small but regular wages. I saw it as an adaptively cultural savings mechanism among Tamilian labourers in Malaya. However, a parallel analysis had been given by Clifford Geertz (1961) of this institution among the Javanese workers of Indonesia. Geertz generalised it as 'the middle rung in development'. Later on, I pushed my analysis of RCA further in terms of its *consequences* for the community of workers. Among other anthropological interpretations of the same institution, Sol Tax (1953) described it as 'penny capitalism' among the Guatemalan plantation workers and M. Freedman (1959) characterised its function among the Chinese immigrants in South-east Asia in the aphorism that the Chinese wage workers 'do not only work for money but they also know how to make money work for them'. In his estimation, therefore, did this institution represent a type of proto-entrepreneurship? In my follow-up studies of Indian Malaysian estate workers and ex-estate workers (Jain 2009a: Chapter 4) I highlighted the two faces of RCA: a traditional savings mechanism and a promoter and perpetrator of internal social stratification within a community of labourers working in the macro socio-economic circumstances of 'closed resources' for them.

Let me return to the depiction of RCA on the estates in Natal in the early 20th century.

> Will Gilbert of Burnesdale Estate in Ifafa ... wrote to the Protector on 28 December 1907 that the sirdar had organised a lottery. When they received their money, workers invested in jewellery. The problem for Gilbert was that some workers were selling their rations to pay the lottery, and thus going hungry (Desai and Vahed 2010: 311).

They narrate RCA as 'an astonishing story of the resourcefulness of the indentured' whereas Gilbert echoing a typical utilitarian (or a 'rational-choice theory') stance criticised the practice as being quite abnormal because his workers were 'not intelligent enough'. The resistance/resourcefulness theory and the rational choice theory both appear incomplete, if one looked at the *consequences* for the community of the 'so-called' lottery. Just to add one crucial factual detail, the RCA was both a lottery and an *auction*. In its latter incarnation, it was indeed a form of proto-entrepreneurship and hence nurtured a process of internal economic stratification in the community. There were no doubt other such processes, for example moneylending by the better-off workers to the poor ones, that led to the same result.

To generalise, the so-called egalitarian community of indentured labourers was split vertically between those who were the few proto-entrepreneurs occupying a higher stratum and those who constituted the chronically poor majority. Status discrepancy between the minority and the majority characterised the cultural nature of disputes in the 'working class' (Jayawardena 1963) on 'eye pass' or prestige-related disputes among the Guyanese plantation labourers of Indian origin), that in the life chances or social class (more accurately 'class fractions') based on market forces and relationships led to the socio-economic mobility of the few. Besides this mobility within the ranks of ex-indentured labourers there was the wider and, still wider, framework of social stratification, both internal and external to the 'Indian' community.

Historical Beginnings of Internal Social Stratification within Indian Community/ Communities and Ethnically and Demographically Disproportionate but Limited Indian Socio-economic Mobility in South Africa

That there was extreme social stratification within the plantation and mining communities and among the propertied and official stakeholders in the South African community at large[7] has been well documented. Following the sociological working out of the 'Stockholm Syndrome' in the 'total institution', both the European boss and the native *sirdar* became protectors for the majority of indentured labourers. The former was a 'benevolent' father figure and the latter his 'punitive' counterpart (Samaraweera 1981). To an extent, the benevolence of the European boss could be seen as being 'subverted' by the cruelty of the native *sirdar*. The barely concealed hostility of the labourer for the native *sirdar* was partly an outcome of envy, indeed a kind of witchcraft mentality, the logic of which ran somewhat like this, 'How could someone like us (ethnically and racially), who should 'equally' be subordinate and supplicant to the White boss, exhibit an hauteur unbecoming of his status?' If one were to sift the many complaints against management by labourers those against native *sirdars* and overseers would outnumber the ones against the 'sahibs'. The Hindi term *'mai–bap'* (mother and father) and the Tamil term, *vallaikarar*, indeed a semantic slippage between 'provider of work' and 'white man' in Tamil language, was reserved only for the White Boss and not for any Indian, of whatever high rank. The dynamic described earlier explains why the popular term of address for Gandhi became *'bapu'* (father) only in India and never in South Africa and why were none of the so-called 'popular' Indian middle-class leaders in South Africa given kinship acronyms as is only too common in India as whole.

When it comes to leadership outside the 'total institution', its common identity as 'Indian' was readily accepted by all immigrants from India because they were identified as such by the colonisers. In this respect the coloniser employers, who were the commanding bosses of the 'total institutions' were quite like anthropologists, 'in the game and out of it, watching and wondering at it'. This seems to me an explanation for the heavily European/British and now 'culturally nationalistic' (in sum, what Said would call 'Orientalist') nature of Indian *nationalism* and its disavowal as ideology and practice by an exceptional Indian visionary like Rabindranath Tagore.

If our construction of the South African narrative is to be judged by its interpretative results, I would now like to highlight the fact that in much of the post-indenture period and, particularly in the apartheid era, members of the numerically small Indian South African population, in proportion to the total population of South Africa, have occupied more positions of high office and responsibility thus constituting an 'upper stratum'. This feature was an outcome of the early formation of a proto-entrepreneurial class fraction among the Indians in solidarity with the presence in South Africa of an already entrenched affluent class of 'passenger Indians'. I have discussed the distinctive pattern of 'interstitial mobility' of an Indian component in its diasporic integration in South Africa. The point that I wish to emphasise is the *visibility* of this Indian component for the non-Indian South Africans and consequently the perceptual and sociological role of this visibility in generalising a status image for Indians as a whole, given the dominance of phenotypically-oriented perceptions in the South African plural society and the equation in perceptions and images, which have consequences for interactions, ideologies and ameliorative measures in social reality. The facts and processes of 'Indian' socio-economic mobility in South Africa despite the demographic and legal handicaps of this minority have been pointed out not only by sociologists but also by economists (Padayachee and Morrell 1991; Padayachee 1999). Padayachee in particular is seized of this paradox — the severe socio-legal disabilities of the Indians. In what follows I shall try and diagnose anthropologically the parameters of this conundrum.

Race, Ethnicity and Class: Social Stratification and Cultural Politics in Contemporary South Africa

I shall have to be very brief in the delineation of this vast subject and confine myself to the manner in which the narrative of this theme may be advanced through conceptual and empirical building blocks already provided. I begin with the crystallisation of identities through identification by the colonial masters, of Indians vis-à-vis 'natives' (Africans). In this respect too the data in Desai and Vahed is extremely rich. While in everyday life on estate and mining locations of Natal it was the diversity and differentiation among Indian identities that was paramount, the European colonisers — co-dwellers and 'direct' protectors of Indians (their common legal status as British subjects being the constant refrain in the views of professional middle class Indian leaders like Gandhi and Gokhale) — contrasted their Indian wards favourably in skills, intelligence and 'culture' vis-à-vis the African natives (Desai and Vahed 2010: 273). In saying so I wish to move a step away from a crudely constructed conspiracy and 'divide and rule' theory based on utilitarian and rational choice explanations to the practical implications of the Stockholm Syndrome. The 'racial' cast of the opposition between Indians and natives became generalised. From the point of view of the actions and ideology of middle-class Indian leaders like Gandhi, there is more than a grain of truth in the critique that they were oblivious and indifferent to participation in their emancipatory movement for the underprivileged masses, of the Blacks in South Africa. The 'racialist' perception of White guardians of law and order is well epitomised in this quote which Idris Naidoo (1982: 41) gives from his conversation with a White policeman in pre-democratic South Africa: 'What is the matter with you Indians? You've got a long history of civilisation, you wore silk before the white man, and here you are jumping from tree to tree with these barbarians, what's wrong with you man?' In contemporary South Africa even among Indians a racially inflected class distinction prevails between the so-called FBIs (Foreign Born Indians) — the well-heeled third- and fourth generation locally born youth and the recently arrived poor immigrants from India and Pakistan, the so-called 'India Papas' (Jain 2010a: 120). It has been argued with some plausibility that the Indian institution of 'caste' has been transformed over a long period of living in racialist societies like South Africa and Trinidad and Tobago, into 'race' (Niranjana 2006). The plausibility for this transformation arises also from the fact that both these institutions, caste and race, are based on a common notion of 'social heredity' (Jain 2010b). Unfortunately, the prevailing of a 'racialist' explanation for the relative affluence of Indians in the perceptions of African population has been well documented in literature.[8] The sociological critique of the Indian community as a 'model minority' in the US too uses the logic in common perceptions of a concordance between race, colour and class. In post-Obama USA the upwardly mobile young generation of NRIs has, under various existential pressures, embraced the habitus of race and class in social interaction and perceptions (Shah 2009), only partly replacing that of caste, region and language brought by their forebears as Indian 'cultural baggage'.

The perceptions by the Black South Africans of economic class and political power in racial terms — especially vis-à-vis the Indian minority — has wider consequences for diagnosing the nature of social stratification and political processes in the changing circumstances of contemporary South Africa. Vahed and Desai (2010) provide a largely macro-sociological analysis based on empirical data culled from the opinions and activities of Indians and Blacks as recorded by them and as reported in the media. These are 'apt illustrations' which in some micro-sociological and social anthropological studies have been distinguished from the analysis of 'social situations' through the 'extended case-study method' (Evens and Handelman 2010). Unfortunately we do not have many examples of such analysis for South Africa (Singh 2005). Here I give a preliminary description and analysis, by way of field notes and comments thereon, following a reformulated version of that approach to suit the context of South Africa.

Notes Dated 1 April 2010, Durban, South Africa, Captioned 'Politics as the Art of the Possible: The Macro-political Context of Multicultural South Africa and the Relationship between the (Black) Ruling Group and the (Indian) Minority'

The ethnography refers to the South African (both the ruling group and the opposition) participation in the inaugural and concluding functions of Global Organisation of the People of Indian Origin (GOPIO), South Africa, celebrating 150 years of the Indians' arrival in South Africa, specifically in the province of KwaZulu, Natal. In the inaugural function held on 28 March 2010, Buthulezi recalled his opposition, initially vis-à-vis the ANC and later in alliance with the Natal Indian Congress, firstly to White rule and apartheid and latterly to the ruling ANC. He mentioned particular Indian leaders with whom he collaborated in this struggle and opposition and ended by paying rich tributes to the late Fatima Meer. He recalled the issues common to the underprivileged Blacks and Indians and the strategies adopted to solve/overcome them. Although he referred to his own royal origins and lineage and thus, indirectly, to the traditional claims to authority in the KwaZulu Natal region (kingdom), he did not either refer explicitly to, nor asked the audience (almost entirely Indian), to participate then and there in symbolic acts of allegiance to monarchical authority. This was in contrast to the arrival of the King, the Chief Minister, Mayor et al. (all Black) who attended and spoke at length at the closing ceremony. They exhorted the audience (again almost exclusively Indian) to show allegiance and 'fealty' to the rulers (Black) by standing up and saluting the King, in the traditional Zulu manner, en masse. There were references in their speeches to the business and professional expertise of the Indians which has contributed to the wealth and wellbeing in South Africa. But there was no mistaking the (implicit) patronising tone adopted to convey how the minorities should 'of course' make contribution to the common patrimony of the (South African) nation (Williams 1989). The references to the Indian contributions as well as to Black authority were made in the language and through examples of what has been called the 'culturalisation of politics' (Jain 1994; Singh 1997) for its 'Indian' version in South Africa but the counterpoint about the 'politicisation of culture' was the hidden and instrumental transcript. It would be analytically useful to posit the copula above as a point–counterpoint strategy by the ruling group (a reformulation of Leach's [1954] 'dynamic equilibrium') to play the game of macro-politics in contemporary multicultural South Africa. The Indians in South Africa against this political backdrop are like the Chinese in Malaysia, who are an ethnic minority but economically more affluent than the Malay majority and other minorities such as the Indians. A South African Indian participant in the closing ceremony shrewdly mentioned to me (almost in a whisper), 'We have the sight of the King but very rarely. Look what a heavy price we have to pay for it.' I think he meant, of course, the very heavy economic cost made by the Indian community in the grand GOPIO ceremony especially the gala dinner, with the King as a participant. But I am sure he meant also, and importantly, the economic price of political subordination which the Indian community has to pay vs Black hegemony and authority. My informant concluded by saying that Africa is a very complex continent to understand.

In extolling GOPIO as a transnational platform for Indian solidarity, the African spokespersons in this ceremony cleverly diverted the 'national' rivalry and competition between the Blacks and the Indians on to the wider frame of global arena (thus reserving the 'national prerogative' to themselves and let the Indians explore transnational greener pastures!). This social situation conforms to my impression when the Indian Ministry of External Affairs had to make about which foreign countries with Indian diasporics should be included in the list of those where something resembling a 'dual citizenship' should be permitted. It was perceived about South Africa that though the country fares very well on the scale of affluence of its Indian diaspora (comparable to many western countries which were actually put on the list as potential investors in India) the Ministry had decided to give South Africa a go by precisely because of its newly won Black supremacy and nationalism. Giving dual citizenship or its equivalent to South African Indians would, in other words, rub the

Black ruling class the wrong way, putting the India–South Africa diplomatic relations in jeopardy. Coming back to the speeches at the concluding ceremony, the speakers made veiled references to the poverty and disempowerment of the majority (the Blacks) though unlike public pronouncements about affirmative action (for Malays or *bumiputeras*, 'sons of the soil') in Malaysia there was no mention of Black empowerment in South Africa but, interestingly enough, our speakers made far-fetched but resonant mention of parallel situations, internationally, of conflicts existing in Sri Lanka and Palestine. All this amounts to persuasion of the minorities to make a contribution to the common patrimony firmly controlled by the numerically dominant Blacks.

The semantic contexts of the above ceremonies as social situations show the rhetorical use of words about democracy, multiculturalism and multiracialism in the interaction between a ruling class and a minority. One can try to analytically penetrate this rhetoric as an instrument in the ding-dong processes of power through an overlap ('family resemblances') between the sociological concepts of race, ethnicity and class and even culture underlying almost universal notions of social heredity. In this formulation we shall have to radically modify the outmoded structural-functionalist assumptions about a metaphysical *telos* (consequences) of social solidarity and conflict in favour of the role of agency (viz. fluctuating strategies and tactics in political processes — a reformulation of Leach's 'dynamic equilibrium').

Conclusion: Indian Diasporic Integration in South Africa as Diagnosis

The nature of Indian diasporic integration in South Africa may be summed up in two points:

(a) Indians are nothing but South Africans in citizenship and legal status. They are also not vying for sovereign political power in the nation state. They are thus in one sense 'integrated' into the nation-state of South Africa.

(b) In terms of the interface between culture and politics in contemporary South Africa, their integration remains 'diasporic', first, because in the ongoing political processes they retain and deploy fragments of their Indian cultural heritage. And yet, second, their integration is characteristically 'diasporic' in that their internal cultural diversities (those of region, language, religion, caste, etc.) are being progressively subsumed in a racially defined and perceived class structure of an 'Indian' ethnic community and the multi-ethnic nation-state.

This article, in order to be complete in a certain sense, requires further research in at least two directions:

(a) It needs the socio-demographic profile of the 'poor' in South Africa, particularly their racial/ethnic break-up in the Republic and in Natal. The proportion of the poor in the Indian South African population absolutely and relative to the Black population is important. We may then be able to distinguish between the statistical picture and popular perceptions of social stratification and mobility. This could also constitute the starting point for a quantitative assessment of what we have termed the 'interstitial mobility' in the Indian South African community notwithstanding the socio-legal constraints of apartheid regime (1948–94). The marshalling of such statistical information would only supplement and not supplant the analysis based on qualitative methodology employed here.

(b) In the absence of substantial field research, my concluding statement about the progressive subsuming of internal Indian cultural diversities within a racially defined and perceived class structure remains a hypothesis. Preliminary indications of the waning salience of such factors in social action are the severely limited appeal of '*hindutva*' (fundamentalist Hindu religious thought and practice) and 'Tamilian' (regional and linguistic attachment to Tamil culture) transnational ideologies for political mobilisation among Indian South Africans. The brief ethnographic account of a social situation presented above is indicative of the direction that the field research may take to arrive at macro-sociological conclusions through the extended case study method and situational analysis.

To conclude, my narrative in this article is a story told not in terms of identity but of the ongoing social processes. The account is in the nature of a social science probe (in comparison to a theological one, for example, based on notions of sin, righteousness, expiation, etc.) as *a preliminary* to address the crisis of social justice in South Africa. I illustrate my method and results through an explication of the nature of Indian diasporic integration and I set this up as a case study of processes that may be read as either the 'price' or the 'prize' for the prospects of social justice in the Republic. A fuller discussion of that wider theme, even from the particular perspective presented above, remains a task for the future.

Notes

1. *Laager* is an Afrikaans word referring to a defensive encampment encircled by wagons (during the conflicts against the Zulus). It would refer to becoming inward looking and adopting a defensive parochial outlook.
2. This is what Amartya Sen (2006) calls 'the illusion of destiny'.
3. See in this perspective the revealing comment by Roger Sanjek (1994: 110). Speaking of intermarriage and the future of races in contemporary USA he writes: 'Both repressive processes of exclusion (race) and expressive processes of inclusion (ethnicity) must be accounted for on our analytical ledgers.'
4. In psychology, 'Stockholm Syndrome' is a term used to describe a paradoxical psychological phenomenon wherein hostages express adulation and have positive feelings towards their captors that appear irrational in light of the danger or risk endured by the victims, essentially mistaking a lack of abuse from their captors as an act of kindness. ... The syndrome is named after the Norrmalmstorg robbery of *Kreditbanken* at Norrmalmstorg in Stockholm, in which the bank robbers held bank employees hostage from 23 August to 28 August 1973. In this case, the victims became emotionally attached to their captors, and even defended them after they were freed from their six-day ordeal (Wikipedia accessed 11 September 2010).
5. It is interesting to speculate the presence of this mechanism in the unconscious bias of European interpreters, their projection of the traditional caste system in India as 'hierarchic reciprocity' (Leach 1960; Pocock 1962) sans 'power' which remains the sleeping partner.
6. For a perceptive indigenous Chinese discussion of self-identity — individual or communal — as following from identification by an 'Other' and then becoming a template for identities in general, see Wong Dehua and Li Xiaoyuan (2004). We may add that the identifier generally is someone super-ordinate in power and authority. Our Chinese authors gloss over this aspect because their argument is about Chinese ethnicities as nationalities, *ideally* equal in their diversity.
7. There is an interesting theory that the South African colonial state, contrasted with the nation-states of the usual European and North American provenance was built around three city-states, viz., Durban,

Cape Town and Johannesburg, along with their hinterlands. Further, the macro-community or nation-state of this description was based primarily on extractive (mineral) and agricultural resources rather than on manufacturing industry (personal communication from R. Thornton).
8. For a parallel example of a sophisticated and politically influential interpretation of Malay backwardness, especially vis-à-vis the Chinese, in racialist terms, see Mahathir (1970).

References

Ardener, S. 1964. 'The Comparative Study Of Rotating Credit Associations', *Journal of the Royal Anthropological Institute*, 94 (2): 201–29.

Barth, F. 1969. 'Introduction', in idem (ed.), *Ethnic Groups and Boundaries: The Social, Organization of Cultural Difference*, pp. 9–38. London: Allen and Unwin.

Beattie, J. H. M. 1964. *Other Cultures*. London: Cohen and West.

Beckford, G. L. 1984. *Persistent Poverty*. New Delhi: Selectbook Service Syndicate.

Brah, A. 1996. *Cartographies of Diaspora: Contesting Identities*. London and New York: Routledge.

Brubaker, R. 2004. *Ethnicity Without Groups*. Cambridge: Harvard University Press.

Cohen, A. 1974. 'Introduction: the Lessons of Ethnicity', in A. Cohen (ed.), *Urban Ethnicity*, pp. ix–xxiv. London: Tavistock.

Desai, A. and G. Vahed. 2010. *Inside Indian Indenture: A South African Story, 1860—1914*. Cape Town: HSRC Press.

Dufoix, S. 2008. *Diasporas*. Berkeley: University of California Press.

Evens, T. M. S. and D. Handelman (eds). 2010. *The Manchester School: Practice and Ethnographic Praxis in Anthropology*. Oxford: Berghahn Books.

Freedman, M. 1959. 'The Handling of Money: Note on the background of the economic Sophistication of Overseas Chinese', *Man*, 59: 64–65.

Geertz, C. 1961. 'The Rotating Credit Association: A "Middle Rung" in Development', *Economic Development and Cultural Change*, 10 (3): 241–63.

Gluckman, M. 1940. 'Analysis of Social Situation in Modern Zululand', *Bantu Studies*, 14 (1–30): 147–74.

———. 1958. 'Analysis of a Social Situation in Modern Zululand', Rhodes Livingstone Paper No. 28. Manchester: Manchester University Press.

Goffman, E. 1961. *Asylums*. Harmondsworth: Penguin Books.

Jain, R. K. 1970. *South Indians on the Plantation Frontier in Malaya*. New Haven and London: Yale University Press.

———.1994. 'Civilizations and Settlement Societies: Cultural Development and Identity at the End of the Twentieth Century', *The Eastern Anthropologist*, 47 (1): 1–14.

———. 2009a. *Indian Transmigrants: Malaysian and Comparative Essays*. Gurgaon: Three Essays Collective.

Jain, R. K. 2009b. 'Reflexivity and the Diaspora: Indian women in post-indenture Caribbean, Fiji, South Africa and Mauritius', *South Asian Diaspora*, 1 (2): 167–79.

———. 2010a. *Nation, Diaspora, Trans-nation: Reflections from India*. New Delhi: Routledge.

———. 2010b. 'Race and Ethnicity: A Methodological Note with Reference to the Study of Indian Diaspora', unpublished manuscript.

Jain, S. 2010. 'Transmigrant Women's Agency and Indian Diaspora', *South Asian Diaspora*, 2 (2): 185–200.

Jayawardena, C. 1963. *Conflict and Solidarity in a Guianese Plantation*. London: The Athlone Press.

Leach, E. R. 1954. *Political Systems of Highland Burma*. London: G. Bell and Sons, Ltd.

———. (ed.). 1960. *Aspects of Caste in South India, Ceylon and North-West Pakistan*. Cambridge: Cambridge University Press.

Mahathir, M. 1970. *The Malay Dilemma*. Singapore, Kuala Lumpur and Hong Kong: Federal Publications.

Marimuthu, T. 2008. 'Tamil Education: Problems and Prospects', in I. A. Bajunid (ed.), *From Tradition to Smart Schools: The Malaysian Educational Odyssey*, pp. 113–40. Kuala Lumpur: Oxford Fajar.

Naidoo, I. 1982. *Island in Chains*. Harmonsworth: Penguin Books.

Niranjana, T. 2006. *Mobilizing India: Women, Music and Migration between India and Trinidad*. Durham, NC: Duke University Press.

Padayachee, V. 1999. 'Struggle, Collaboration and Democracy: The Indian Community in South Africa, 1860–1999', *Economic & Political Weekly*, 34 (7): 393–95.

Padayachee, V. and R. Morrell. 1991. 'Indian Merchants and Dukawalahs in the Natal Economy, C. 1875–1914', *Journal of South African Studies*, 17 (1): 71–102.

Pocock, David. 1962. 'Notes on Jajmani Relationships', *Contributions to Indian Sociology*, (Old Series), 6: 78–95.

Samaraweera, V. 1981. 'Masters and Servants in Sri Lankan Plantations: Labour Laws and Labour Control in an Emergent Export Economy', *Indian Economic and Social History Review*, 18 (2): 123–58.

Sanjek, Roger. 1994. 'Intermarriage and the Future of Races in the United States', in G. Steven and R. Sanjek (eds), *Race*. New Jersey: Rutgers University Press.

Sen, Amartya. 2006. *Identity and Violence: The Illusion of Destiny*. London: Penguin Books.

Shah, S.P. 2009. 'Making Sense of the Second Generation', *Economic and Political Weekly*, 64 (30): 14–17.

Shamsul, A. B. 2008. *Many Ethnicities, Many Cultures, One Nation: The Malaysian Experience*. Bangi: UKM.

Singh, Anand. 1997. 'Cultural Entrepreneurship and the Culturalisation of Politics among Indians in South Africa', *Alternation*, 4 (1): 93–115.

Singh, Anand. 2005. *Indians in Post Apartheid South Africa*. New Delhi: Concept Publication Co.

Singh, Yogendra. 2000. *Culture Change in India*. Jaipur and New Delhi: Rawat Publications.

Tax, Sol. 1953. *Penny Capitalism: A Guatemalan Indian Economy*. Washington: Smithsonian Institute, Publications No. 16.

Tönnies, Ferdinand. 1957. *Community and Society: Gemeinschaft and Gesellschaft*. East Lansing: The Michigan State University Press.

Vahed, G. and A. Desai. 2010. 'Identity and Belonging in Post-apartheid South Africa: The Case of Indian South Africans', in A. Singh, J. Ravindra and J. Shobhita (eds), *Adversity to Advantage: The Saga of PIOs (People of Indian Origin) in South Africa,* pp. 1–12. New Delhi: KRE Publications.

Weber, M. (1968) 1978. *Economy and Society: An Outline of Interpretive Sociology*, (2 vols). Berkeley: University of California Press.

Williams, B. F. 1989. 'A Class Act: Anthropology and the Race to Nation Across Ethnic Terrain', *Annual Review of Anthropology*, 18: 401–44.

Wong Dehua and Li Xiaoyuan. 2004. 'Globalization and National Identity: Considerations based upon Chinese Experience'. International Conference on Ethnic Identity and Ethnic Conflict in Multicultural Societies. Mumbai. 3–5 March.

Worsley, Peter et al. 1978. *Introducing Sociology*. Harmondsworth: Penguin Books.

Part II

The Contemporary Contradiction of Nation-States: Democracy, Education and Environment

Part II

The Contemporary Contradiction of Nation-States: Democracy, Education and Environment

9

A Better Life for All: The Post-1994 South African Journey in the Second Decade of the New Millennium

Janis Grobbelaar

The Constitution whose adoption we celebrate constitutes an unequivocal statement that we refuse to accept that our Africanness shall be defined by our race, colour, gender, or historical origins. It is a firm assertion made by ourselves that South Africa belongs to all who live in it, black and white ... It creates a law-governed society which shall be inimical to arbitrary rule ... It rejoices in the diversity of its people and creates the space for all of us voluntarily to define ourselves as one people.

Thabo Mbeki (1996)

Not even the ANC will survive a legacy of corroded systems, political purges and politically conferred 'innocence'. But only the electorate can decide when, and if, we change course and get to where we were going back in 1994.

Njabulo S. Ndebele (2010)

South Africans are once more anguished about their futures and that of their communities and country. The journey that began with the 1994 democratic election with its culmination of a *small miracle* is in trouble and is characterised by rising social, economic and political tensions.

The country's racial and ethnic caste-like historic ordering has changed its contours somewhat but the long trend to reproduce itself survives. The latter provides the springboard in shaping a series of what can only be understood as threatening disasters. Without being reductionist or denying the complexities and historic successes of the 1994 democratic project, by 2008 statistics show that the richest 20 per cent of the population received 70 per cent of national income and the poorest 20 per cent just 1.6 per cent of it (taken from RSA 2009: 22 in Southhall 2010).[1] The white South African population has remained economically dominant whilst the majority of the black population remains trapped in poverty and segregated in apartheid fashion. This is not meant to argue that South Africa is not a *different country* since 1994 — it is.

Political stability and state legitimacy stand in sharp contrast to that of the apartheid state. The African National Congress (ANC)-led government has reduced the state debt inherited from the National Party (NP) dramatically. The currency is sound and the economy has grown in real terms. Social mobility, affirmative action, black economic empowerment and other state actions have resulted in the creation of a larger black bourgeoisie. The norm of non-racialism and non-discrimination is not officially disputed although its application has proved considerably contentious at times. But unpromising developments now worry many. The post-1994 South African state can with some justification be called a *weak* one. Roger Southall argues, for example, that the state was more dysfunctional than developmental by 2007 and is in the midst of long-term decline in 2010 (2007, 2010). In a World Economic Forum ranking in 2009 South Africa '... did exceptionally badly with regard to ... perceptions of the health of its workforce (127th out of 180) ... the business costs of crime and violence (133rd out of 180)... there being little confidence in the ability of the police to provide protection (106th out of 180)' (Southall 2010: 17). A non-racial and open political economy built on the restitution, restoration and redistribution of land, and reconciliation and social justice in a society embedded in the rule of law is proving to be more and more difficult to achieve. In the light of enormous disparities of wealth, skills and life chances still largely captured in race and ethnic dynamics and ever-growing corruption the goal of a *better life for all* in the medium term is severely threatened.

This article considers South Africa's journey from apartheid to democracy. In the first section it focuses on the settlement of a successful formal *societal transition*. In the second section the troubled and now threatened *societal transformation* that was promised to all is contemplated and, in The Third section, attention turns to the role of the South African Truth and Reconciliation Commission

(TRC) as an instrument of *societal transformation* briefly. It concludes by suggesting that should successful societal transformation play itself out by sufficiently enabling a better life for all ultimately, critical attention will need to be paid to what Dlamini (2010: 118) refers to as rescuing ' ... South African history ...' from the reification of the dominant ' ... historiography of the struggle'.

Societal Transition: South Africa's *Small Miracle*

> In the sprawling, undulating Soweto, some voting stations have(d) close to ten thousand people lining up to vote. ... In some white areas, the queues are shorter. Elsewhere they stretch over a few kilometres. These queues are a mixture of black and white, the wealthy and the destitute, domestic workers and their employers, construction staff and their bosses. ... queues all reflect the same characteristics: patience and respect (Harris 2010: 208–9).

In terms of the 1993 *Interim Constitution of South Africa*, an election based on universal franchise was held for the very first time on 27 April 1994. The ANC, having gained close to two-thirds of the votes cast over three historic days, was the outright winner.

South Africa's negotiated and revolutionary settlement had not been expected and came as a surprise. To the amazement of all, including his own party caucus and the South African military, then State President F. W. de Klerk announced the freeing of all political prisoners, including Nelson Mandela, and lifted the ban on liberation movements unconditionally on 2 February 1990. De Klerk's announcement led to four years of *talking about talks, negotiations around negotiations*, multi-party talks and legislation about the future of the country. Whilst the chief negotiating partners were in fact the ANC alliance and the incumbent still ruling NP, all political actors who wished to take part in these negotiations and discussions did and could. An exceedingly arduous and testing process was to be expected — and so it was (Friedman and Atkinson 1994). Not only were the taking up of inflexible positions of principle and ideology common but lack of trust between the parties led quite often to grave breakdowns between them. Brutal violence in Kwa-Zulu Natal and Gauteng increased over the period. The South African historian David Welsh (2009: 421–534) suggests that until the mid-1990s the scales were in favour of the NP at Kempton Park. Then they tipped. The ANC took over the moral high ground. They and their allies 'inside

134 *Janis Grobbelaar*

of the country' had by then cultivated a formidable capacity for mass action besides which they had access to an abundance of skilled negotiators drawn both from the wings of former exiles as well internals. The latter had developed well-honed negotiating skills since the re-launch of black trade unions in the early 70s and the anti-apartheid United Democratic Front (UDF) civil movement within the country in 1982 in Cape Town. Eventually an agreement was reached and the transition culminated in the 1994 democratic elections.

The broad fundamentals of the South African negotiated settlement are apparent. Colin Bundy (2000: 12), the South African social historian, captures them as follows:[2] 'the ANC first sought the political kingdom' and the NP (and corporate capital) succeeded in getting the former to turn away 'from redistribution and state regulation' of the economy — a far cry from the spirit and letter of the 1955 ANC lead Congress of the Peoples' Freedom Charter. Why and how did these indisputably momentous events occur and come about at that specific point in time and history?

A number of factors stand out. The importance of a more or less functioning societal and state infrastructure that could be and was drawn upon in 1990 should not be underestimated. It was vital to the process of the South African negotiated settlement. Key institutions had more or less survived despite apartheid and the penultimate crises for survival *white* South Africa found itself in after the second half of the 1980s. A somewhat battered judiciary and a legal facility schooled in an albeit narrow and constrained notion of the rule of law provided imperative institutional competencies and the skills and capacity required to undertake the indispensable *nuts and bolts* of a project of this nature. A working free press provided the space and capacity for public debate (surviving as it had throughout the apartheid regime despite numerous attempts to close it down). Perhaps of greatest importance, the most industrialised and commercialised economy in Africa was operating with relative health despite internal unrest and outside pressure such as the international economic boycott and United Nations (UN) sanctions. Corporate capital was moreover one of the key players in setting up the ultimate settlement. Transport infrastructure and basic utilities had moreover not yet been stripped of the ability to operate and made it reasonably easy for most basic institutions to function.

Apartheid repression had been compelled to become more coercive and costly, and in consequence the imbedded instability of the state grew ever more from the early 1970s onwards. The NP government, notwithstanding the use of the military and various promulgations of states of emergency, was unable to stop the flames of resistance and opposition that were persistently spreading and flourishing over a broad and reinvigorated front. On the other hand, elements within the ANC leadership from within as well as from exile had begun to wonder whether the overthrow of the regime by violent means and boycott was feasible in the medium term. This notwithstanding the upshot of the successes of the international boycotts and sanctions against South Africa which had led to radical cutting of its access to financial resources on the international money markets. The latter had critical consequences for the NP's political constituency and more so for white corporate elites, especially within a context in which the UDF domestic, civic movement aligned with the ANC had grown exponentially with the Cosatu-associated trade unions and the churches taking the lead by challenging the regime over a wide range of social matters, particularly those of inequality and social justice. Much of the white *modernising* bourgeoisie — above all corporate capital — no longer wanted to pay the price of apartheid. The costs of maintaining the regime were rapidly becoming too great and the benefits too small. White and black leaders and people of influence in South Africa began to visit the ANC in exile, creating fear and consternation amongst the NP leadership and its rank and file.

Although it only became fully evident after De Klerk's 1990 speech, decisive leadership was an important factor in ending the South African deadlock. Black leadership began to proliferate anew with the unbanning and growth of the black trade union movement in the 1970s. Almost 50 per cent of the black African population had moved to towns and cities by then and the benefits of urbanisation and industrialisation fed rapidly into the recruitment of informed and able leadership. Together with the emergence of the UDF in 1982 (which aligned itself with the ANC), internal organisation and mobilisation in opposition to the state reached a point of sufficient density in the 1980s. Within the ruling white elite, De Klerk had surrounded himself with small think-tanks drawn from a few party professionals, government technocrats, members of the intelligence services, white Afrikaner business and intellectual elites and other traditional institutions of Afrikaner nationalism — especially the by then infamous Afrikaner Broederbond. Whilst his inner circle remained small it should not be forgotten that De Klerk himself had never been a man of recognised leadership stature within his party. He was in fact viewed by many insiders as a useful 'committee man'.

Nelson Mandela's very special role in the making of a negotiated South African societal transition settlement can only be understood as miraculous. His special leadership qualities combining the elements of charismatic, traditional and achieved status in Max Weber's classical definition became the lynchpin upon which the negotiations often depended on. Acting more or less without an ANC mandate, he had entered into discussion with key members of the white Afrikaner establishment whilst in prison on Robben Island. Mandela's tenancy of the presidency of South Africa from 1994–98 was driven by the goals of reconciliation and national unity. Pursuing them with immense commitment and single-mindedness he sought to build sufficient societal cohesion upon which to construct a fully inclusive democratic order in the country. And so a broad leadership that had developed in South Africa over generations between people *that came from the same place* ignited and created a golden moment without which the country would have continued to stumble and break up.

The important role of ubiquitous social dynamics needs to be further and fully factored in if the South African small miracle is to be properly understood. *Social capital* amongst the warring parties *ignited* and mobilised. Whilst the notion of social capital has been so criticised and contested as to make it arguably of little value, there have been many attempts to redefine and tighten it. In so doing, scholars have countered some of the mechanistic character the concept acquired since Putman's coining of it. For example, F. Anthias presents an argument that is useful. She suggests that the concept be confined to use as a relational and/or *mobilisable* one. *Mobilisable* social capital in Anthias's terms are (2007: 788–805) '... networks and ties ...' that are relationally participatory in '... the pursuit of advantage, or the mitigation of disadvantage ...' (ibid.: 788). In other words, and in spite of the harsh South African colonial and apartheid structural status quo with its history of deep, conflicted and exploitative racial ordering, social forces and dynamics are and become by their very nature *socially cohesive* (Barolsky 2010; Chipkin and Ngqulunga 2008) at particular times. This enabled the moderation of demands in order to reach agreement during, for example, the process of South Africa's negotiated settlement. Well known South African scholar Njubula Ndebele captures Anthias's, and other, definitions of mobilisable social capital thus '... the bonding that took place among the major political negotiators seems to me too remarkable to have had no historical or social grounding ... The South Africans who sat together at the negotiating table were not total strangers to one another' (Ndebele 2000: 150).

The above domestic social dynamics need however also to be situated and understood in a broader context: international trends and seismic shifts too contributed significantly to the negotiated settlement made in South Africa. Against the background of the end of the Cold War and a worldwide realignment of power it became clear that the destruction of both a society's political economy and infrastructure were nothing to scoff at. It had a decisive impact on the thinking of the National Party elite and of De Klerk (Van Zyl Slabbert 2000: 67), as well as on the ANC leadership in exile. The exiled ANC leadership had both lived in broader Africa and in Europe for a long time and was well aware of the problems of maintaining a stable political economy. It also removed one of the major ideological justifications of the old regime that had appealed to some quarters in the West: South Africa was undoubtedly a bulwark against communism. The events in Eastern Europe in 1989 and after were significant in breaking the deadlock inside the country.

South Africa's successful societal transition — its *small miracle* — will stand in the annals of the histories of conflicted authoritarian societies as one of special note. It will also attest to definitive differences between societal transitions which consist of processes that lead to the unpacking of formal intent and the acceptance of a settlement between the parties and that of societal transformation, that is, a matter of implementation — of changing, in this instance, key values, norms and institutions of hitherto existing South African society to those of universal social justice, democracy and equal economic opportunity and the rule of law.

Societal Transformation: A Better Life for All?

... a non-racial future involves much more than simply the
enfranchisement of the 86 per cent of the population that is black.
It also involves the transformation of a sophisticated economy ...
if the next government does not make demonstrable strides in
addressing apartheid's legacy by massively expanding the delivery
of social services ... the country may experience traumatic political
destabilisation (Herbst 1994: 147).

Despite the tremendous success of its societal transition in
the early 1990s, South Africa's societal transformation has not
lived up to promises and expectations. The R800 billion annual
national economy the ANC inherited has grown to R2.2 trillion
a year — enormous growth by any standards (*Mail* and *Guardian*,
28 January 2011). However impressive this growth may be, it
masks the enduring structural problem of employment. Depending on the definition of the measure being used, unemployment
is officially at 25 per cent and broadly at 40 per cent (Makgetla
2010: 72). The global economic crisis which started in 2008 has
more-over resulted in a million jobs being lost during 2009.
The great majority of these permanent jobs were held by black
South Africans (ibid.: 68). The nature and quality of the system
of education, both past and present, determines that millions of
black South Africans remain largely unskilled. This not only results
in large-scale unemployment but also increases capital intensive
manufacture.

Under pressure and in an attempt to alleviate *jobless growth*
the ANC government has been expanding its support by a range
of grants serving unemployed people and the *working poor*. The
latest figures suggest that 14 million people are receiving government grants of some sort whilst direct taxpayers make up 6 million
people in total (*Business Report*, 22 February 2010 in Southall
2010: 10). Despite the best intentions the state has not managed
to provide economic justice for the great mass of South Africans.
Township protest against poor service delivery is growing.
Seldom does a week go by without some community or township
mobilising against local governance, and the ANC in particular.
The patterns of institutionalised poverty and inequality that
colonialism and then apartheid shaped remain in place despite
some growth in the black middle class: the poor remain trapped

within a cauldron of colour, race and a lack of the necessary skill and education 16 years into the 'new' South Africa.

Further obstructing the ideals of a societal transformation is the rise of corruption. Hardly a day goes by without the press reporting a new scandal involving the *deployment* and *redeployment* of senior ANC members to jobs in the failing parastatals or the weakening state, provincial and local government sectors — or the allocation of state tenders to, or via, party insiders. In a recent Afrobarometer report (2009) dealing with South African attitudes toward democracy compared the findings of five surveys conducted over the period 2000–2008, the respondents answered the question: *Overall, how satisfied are you with the way democracy works in South Africa?* as follows: 30 per cent were not at all satisfied or not very satisfied in 2006; by 2008 the percentage had increased to 46 per cent. The substantial drop in satisfaction over this interval is best understood as a response to seriously fractured and rupturing social cohesion inside of the ANC as well as amongst members of the alliance (Butler 2010). Arguably, so-called party 'factionalism and cronyism' around money, power and poor and corrupt(ed) governance are the key drivers of this ever-growing plague.

The abuse and misuse of the instruments of the state, including that of the South African Constitution and the criminal justice system for the personal, ideological and material pursuit of power and wealth developed during Mbeki's presidency — especially during his second term of office — continues under Zuma's presidency. Little purpose is served by repeating the sagas around the *arms deal scandal,* for example. The ignominy of *travelgate,* the actions of *the national prosecuting authority* in pursuit of Zuma in the latter's race for the presidency in opposition to Mbeki and growing *tenderpreneurship* are some examples of rapidly growing corruption in the country.

Towards the end of Mbeki's second term he lost his chairpersonship of the party at its national conference held in Polokwane in December 2007 and of the presidency in 2008. Jacob Zuma emerged as the indisputable leader of the ANC and, after the 2009 general elections, of the country. There is little doubt that the events then and those taking place currently point toward a dangerously at odds and splintered ANC within itself as well as between the members of the ruling alliance.

Despite the promises by Zuma and his supporters at Polokwane of a return to alliance, party and parliamentary accountability and participation, wealth and political power accumulation as a consequence of the membership of various competing centres of support and influence has been replaced — or been added to those existing under Mbeki. The momentum of abuse of the state apparatus as well as dishonesty and fraud in the pursuit of the spoils is mounting as a perusal of the press will illustrate. The trickle-down effect of this kind of behaviour has become institutionalised at increasing levels of both government and society, weakening the state and its apparatuses and hence, inevitably, societal order and social cohesion (Ramphele 2008; Southhall 2007; Terreblanche 2002). Unless these practices can be remediated, *a better life for all* will remain a *dream deferred* and South Africa's societal successful democratic transformation an illusion.

The South African Truth and Reconciliation Commission (TRC)

In 1995 the National Unity and Reconciliation Act was passed. It was the second piece of substantive societal 'transformation' legislation enacted by the South African democratic government[3] of national unity and was to be implemented forthwith. The first was the Restitution of Land Rights Act of 1994. Both were provided for in the 1993 negotiated Interim Constitution of South Africa and both were viewed as foundational to the new democratic country. Both these acts are essential and reflective of what Cherryl Walker has referred to as the theme of the struggle *master narrative* underpinning South African society. They were to deal with the all-embracing trauma and suffering of the loss of land and human dignity (Walker 2008: 34–35). *Master narratives* tend to undermine and distort or limit possible solutions by homogenising and reifying both the circumstances and the people involved. Without recognising this, Walker suggests that solutions are difficult to find and more so to implement and that the failures of the policy should be readdressed in the light thereof (ibid.: 11–33).

The TRC's key task was to promote and establish social cohesion and the necessary national unity across the deeply institutionalised divisions and inequalities between hitherto disenfranchised and enfranchised groups of black and white South Africans through reconciliation and restorative justice facilitated by truth-telling. Whilst the concerns of the commission were primarily those of the restoration of the loss of human rights to the dispossessed majority of South Africans who were stripped of their dignity by colonialism and its more modern form of apartheid given the colour of their skins, it was also meant to open up so-called second generation human rights which include economic rights to all.

Embedded and contextualised as it was within the Mandela presidency, the TRC was an instrument of the *master narrative* although it was not understood as that by the majority of the former ruling elite. Mandela's mandate and task was to put into place the infrastructure required to build a South African democracy. A presidency concerned to build a *better life for all* via the institutionalisation of the restoration of all social and human rights. The theme *of* Mandela's *reconciliation presidency* as well as the life chances via economic redistribution linked to it was central to the ANC-led government's vision of reconstructing South Africa. Even those who saw and see the TRC as a symbol in service of the interests of the *little people* and not in itself an instrument of societal transformation — it was in fact an intrinsic part of the first presidency and of primary instrumental importance. Its *master narrative* was and is concerned with the losses and suffering of the past and with restoration. Two of the three committees of the commission, the Human Rights Violation Committee (particularly its public hearings) and the work of the Reparations and Rehabilitation Committee were designed to promote national unity and reconciliation.

As a form of transitional justice truth commissioning lies at the core of an ongoing and much contested debate (Elster 2004; Hayner 2002; Minow 2002), internationally amongst all those concerned with rebuilding and reconstructing conflict-ridden societies. The central divide is concerned with retributive justice, that is, applying the rule of law without compromise of principle versus that of restorative justice aimed at achieving restitution, tolerance and reconciliation. In the South African case the latter was organically aligned with the socio-political and economic processes and dynamics of negotiation that had led to South Africa's *small miracle* of societal transition viz., the formal Kempton Park agreement driven by a minimum consensus-based set of values towards democracy.

There is no doubt that truth commissioning allowed thousands of ordinary people the opportunity to express their pain and some to tell their stories in the public domain, bringing catharsis for many. They were accorded the dignity of being lis-tened to in an official state sponsored hearing. The commission was a formal government body and its very creation was an acknow-ledgement of South Africa's *crime against humanity*.[4] Its legacy is closely tied up with the fact that it is no longer easy for any South African to plead ignorance of the horror and evil of apartheid.

However it also failed in many ways. Perhaps most importantly, having omitted to point out that the expectations and under-standing captured in the *master narrative* by the victims were not going to be, nor could they be, acted on by the TRC outside of its life which was meant to be a maximum of two years. That when victims were asked by commissioners and statement takers what could be done to help them to look after the children of their dead sons and daughters, for example, they did not know that the com-mission had no *chequebook* — nor that it did not have the capacity to bring back the bodies of their children from the countries in which they had died and which were buried in the exile[5] of foreign soil. Restorative justice has proved to be illusive and partial for most.

Conclusion

The article's concern was to analytically and substantively divide South Africa's early societal transition success — *the small miracle* — from the many difficulties of attempts to transform and restore the country. To achieve a *better life for all* a serious rethink-ing of socio-economic policy with regard to employment is the most pressing need so that the restitution and restoration of eco-nomic opportunity is not tied to the *master narrative*.

Exacerbated by widespread state corruption and the persisting coincidence between poverty and race, the economy nonethe-less remains relatively attractive to international investment. Perhaps increased pressure needs to be placed on international investment by the state to help create more jobs according to Southall (2010: 18). On the other hand, the state must clearly act a lot more decisively against dishonesty and fraud. A massive amount of money is lost each year in the drive towards the accu-mulation of wealth by the abuse of ever-growing corrupted systems of governance.

Second, the article has sought, in the light of Walker's and to some extent that of Dlamini's recent work (2008; 2010), a way towards a better understanding of South Africa's problems and solutions around the role of the TRC by suggesting a shift away from the rigid ideologically-driven notion of a not always real and objective past towards one which challenges this *master narrative* in the hope that a rewriting of struggle historiography of inter alia the TRC that will help facilitate *a better life for all* in South Africa.

Notes

1. The South Africa Statistical services estimate the 2010 population at 50,725 million people of which 9 per cent are white and 91 per cent black (i.e., 2.4 per cent Asian, 9.1 per cent coloured and 79.5 per cent African).
2. This survey is conducted biennially.
3. The first was the Restitution of Land Rights Act of 1994.
4. Resolution 3068 adopted by the United Nations General Assembly in 1973, the International Convention on the Suppression and Punishment of the Crimes of Apartheid.
5. Personal experience: I acted as the information manager of the Johannesburg office of the TRC over a period of two years on sabbatical from my university.

References

Act Number 200 of 1993. 'The Interim Constitution of South Africa'.

Act Number 34 of 1995. 'The National Unity and Reconciliation Act'.

Afrobarometer. 2009. 'Popular Attitudes toward Democracy in South Africa: A Summary of Afrobarometer Indicators, 2000–2008'.

Anthias, F. 2007. 'Ethnic Ties: Social Capital and the Question of Mobilisability', *The Sociological Review*, 55 (4) 788–805.

Barolsky, V. 2010. 'A Better Life for All: Social Cohesion and Social Conflict', Human Sciences Research Council, Seminar Draft Paper, Sociology Seminar Series. University of Pretoria.

Bundy, C. 2000. 'The Beast of the Past: History and the TRC', in W. James and L. van de Vijver (eds), *After the TRC: Reflections on Truth and Reconciliation in South Africa*. Cape Town and Athens: David Philip Publishers and Ohio University Press.

Butler, A. 2009. *Contemporary South Africa* (2nd edn). New York: Palgrave Macmillan.

———. 2010. 'The Africa National Congress under Jacob Zuma', in John Daniel, Prishani Naidoo, Devan Pillay and Roger Southhall (eds.), *New South African Review 1. 2010: Development or Decline?* Johannesburg: Wits University Press.

Chipkin, I. and B. Ngqulunga. 2008. 'Friends and Family: Social Cohesion in South Africa', *Journal of Southern African Studies*, 34 (1) 61–76.

Coleman, M. 1998. *A Crime against Humanity: Analysing the Repression of the Apartheid State*. Johannesburg: David Philip Publishers.

Dlamini, J. 2010. *Native Nostalgia*. Auckland Park: Jacana Media.

Du Toit, F. and E. Doxtader (eds). 2010. *In the Balance. South Africans debate re-conciliation*. Auckland Park: Jacana Media.

Elster, J. 2004. *Closing the Books: Transitional Justice in Historical Perspective*. Cambridge: Cambridge University Press.

Friedman, S. and D. Atkinson (eds). 1994. *South African Review 7: The Small Miracle. South Africa's Negotiated Settlement*. Johannesburg: Ravan Press.

Grobbelaar, J. and M. Ghalib. 2007. 'Security and Reconciliation in Post-Conflict Society: The Matter of Closing the Books in South Africa and Somalia', *Bildaan, an International Journal of Somali Studies*, 7: 1–38.

Harris, P. 2010. *Birth. The Conspiracy to Stop the '94 Election*. Cape Town: Umuzi.

Hayner, P. B. 2002. *Unspeakable Truths: Facing the Challenge of Truth Commissions*. New York: Routledge.

Herbst, J. 1994. 'Populist Demands and Government Resources in the New South Africa', *Journal of Commonwealth Comparative Politics*, 32 (2): 147–65.

Kaminski, M. M. and M. Nalepa. 2006. 'Judging Transitional Justice', *Journal of Conflict Resolution*, 50 (3): 383–404.

Makgetla, N. S. 2010. 'The International Economic Crisis and Employment in South Africa', in John Daniel Prishani Naidoo, Devan Pillay and Roger Southhall (eds), *New South African Review 1. 2010: Development or Decline?* Johannesburg: Wits University Press.

Mamdani, M. 1998. 'When Does Reconciliation Turn into A Denial Of Justice?' *Sam Nolutshungu Memorial Lecture*. Human Science Research Council: Pretoria.

Mbeki, Thabo. 1996. 'Statement of Deputy President Thabo Mbeki on behalf of the ANC, on the Occasion of the Adoption by the Constitutional Assembly of the Republic of South Africa Constitutional Bill'. *Cape Town. 8 May.* http://www.newsimbabwe.com. Accessed 10 January 2011.

Ramphele, M. 2008. *Laying Ghosts to Rest*. Cape Town: Tafelberg.

Minow, M. 2002. *Breaking the Cycles of Hatred*. Princeton: Princeton University Press.

Ndebele, N. 2000. 'Of Lions and Rabbits: Thoughts on Democracy and Reconciliation', in W. James and L. van de Vijver (eds), *After the TRC: Reflections on Truth and Reconciliation in South Africa*. Cape Town and Athens: David Philip Publishers and Ohio University Press.

———. 2010. 'Toxic Politics: Diary of a Bad Year', *Mail & Guardian*. 23 December.

SA Reconciliation Barometer. (2009) 2010. 'Institute for Justice and Reconciliation'. http://www.ijr.org.za. Accessed 28 January 2010.

Southhall, R. 2007. 'The ANC State more Dysfunctional than Developmental?' in Sakhela Buhlungu, John Daniel, Roger Southhall and Jessica Lutchman (eds), *State of the Nation. South Africa 2007*. Cape Town: HSRC Press.

Southhall, R. 2010. 'South Africa 2010: From Short-term Success to Long-term Decline?' in John Daniel Prishani Naidoo, Devan Pillay and Roger Southhall (eds), *New South African Review 1. 2010: Development or Decline?* Johannesburg: Wits University Press.

Terreblanche, S. 2002. *A History of Inequality in South Africa 1652–2002.* Pietermaritzburg: University of Natal Press.

'Truth and Reconciliation Commission of South Africa Report'. 1998. Vols 1–5. Cape Town: Juta.

———. 2003. Vols 6 and 7. Cape Town: Juta.

Van Zyl Slabbert, F. 2000. 'Truth without Reconciliation, Reconciliation without Truth', in W. James and L. van de Vijver (eds), *After the TRC: Reflections on Truth and Reconciliation in South Africa.* Cape Town and Athens: David Philip Publishers and Ohio University Press.

Walker, C. 2008. *Landmarked: Land Claims and Land Restitution in South Africa.* Johannesburg: Jacana.

Welsh, D. 2009. *The Rise and Fall of Apartheid.* Johannesburg: Jonathon Ball Publishers.

10

South Africa: Conceptualising a Politics of Human-oriented Development

Adam Habib

The first year of South Africa's second decade of democracy witnessed the unfolding of a political drama: the outcome will define the future character of the society. Who was to succeed President Mbeki in the African National Congress (ANC) involved a formidable political cast, comprising not only the then President of the Republic and Jacob Zuma, now President of the ruling party, but also almost every significant figure in South Africa's ruling political hierarchy. Moreover, the script was organised around the political contest between different sets of heroes and villains, themselves personified in the individual personalities of Thabo Mbeki and Jacob Zuma. The distinguishing feature of this theatre was that its heroes and villains changed depending on who was doing the narrative.

In one version, South Africa's transition is presented in a positive light. It is a story of macro-economic stability, sustainable growth, low inflation, high productivity and demographic and racial transformation. South Africa is presented as the example of the modern African state. The benefits of the democratic transition are to be broadly shared across society (PCAS 2003). Where it has not been, it is suggested that it has less to do with the policies pursued, and far more to do with the structural dynamics of South African society (Mbeki 2003, 2004a, 2004b). The heroes in this story are Thabo Mbeki, Trevor Manuel, Tito Mboweni and the cadre of officials and technocrats surrounding them. The villains are the populists located mainly in the Congress of South African Trade Unions (COSATU), the South African Communist Party (SACP) and the ANC Youth League who support Jacob Zuma and mislead what is in effect the rabble of largely young, uninformed, lumpen elements.

The second version presents South Africa's transition as having been derailed. Of course there is an acknowledgement of the positive features of this transition. Its peaceful character, the establishment of new democratic institutions and the racial transformation of the state are recognised as advances on South Africa's apartheid past. But the story is also seen as one of missed opportunities, the enrichment of a few and the capture of the ANC by a new breed of politically connected businessmen and the marginalisation of the urban and rural communities (COSATU 2006; SACP 2006a, 2006b). The heroes in this version are Jacob Zuma, Zwelinzima Vavi, Blade Nzimande and the groups of activists who are perceived to have stood up to the then imperial presidency and the comprador bourgeoisie that surround it. The villains are President Mbeki, his cabinet and the technocrats who operated in the unfeeling world of statistics and who are alienated from the lived realities of South Africa's poor and the marginalised.

Both versions of the story have one common feature. They are organised around agency. The stories are about personalities and political advance is only possible if one's band of heroes success-fully ascend to high political office in the ANC and the state. These stories have very little to say about institutional constraints and structural conditions. Where there is a discussion of structural conditions, it is presented often by the mainstream political and economic elites, as a 'no-alternative' scenario, with the intention of intellectually disarming critics.

Yet a structural analysis of the transition, one that emphasises configurations of power and how individual leaders' choices are constrained by the institutions they inhabit, need not strategically disarm political agencies interested in a more inclusive human-oriented development. Such agencies do not have to conceive development as a product of individuals who occupy high office. For them South Africa's transition is conditioned by the structural configurations of power, and as a result a human-oriented development agenda is dependent on a political programme that prioritises engaging these structural conditions to make a different set of socio-economic policies viable. How this can be theoretically conceptualised, and the elements comprising this political programme, is the focus of this article.

Structural Reforms for Human-oriented Development

The argument here is for an engagement with structural conditions so that power is dispersed and reconfigured in the social setting; a substantive uncertainty is thereby achieved where political and economic elites become uncertain, and their accountability is as a result re-established between the latter and citizens and policy becomes responsive to the interests of the poor and the marginalised. Even if the need for a substantive uncertainty is recognised, how is it to be generated in South Africa at this historical juncture? Of course the character of the contemporary international system is unlikely to assist in this regard. Not only are the impulses to substantive uncertainty severely weakened as a result of the erosion of the bipolar world, but the economic and technological transformation of the last two decades hitherto captured under the term 'globalisation', have also strengthened predictability through a concentration of power in favour of trans-national capital and international financial agencies and to the disadvantage of national political elites and marginalised groups (Held and McGrew 2003; Marglin and Schor 1992). Neither is a revolution or a national revolt on the scale of that which occurred in South Africa in the 1980s or in Malaysia in 1969 on the cards for the foreseeable future. The frequent revolts that do spontaneously occur are sporadic, localised, largely oriented to accessing rights and do not constitute an immediate political challenge to national elites (Ballard et al. 2006b).

Substantive uncertainty has to be created within the framework of the democratic political system which is not only an advance on apartheid, but also the product of the endeavours of poor and working people. There is also a long tradition of thought in progressive and socialist circles on how to advance the interests of workers and the poor within democratic non-socialist contexts. The most recent scholarly conceptual exercise on South Africa in this regard was undertaken by John Saul who, following Boris Kagarlitsky (1990), made the case for what he termed structural reform, that is, reforms that have a snowball effect and facilitate the emergence of other reforms, all of which collectively constitute a project of self-transformation.

In addition, such reforms are, in Saul's words:

> Rooted in popular initiatives in such a way as to leave a residue of further empowerment — in terms of growing enlightenment/class consciousness, in terms of organizational capacity — for the vast mass of the population, whom thus strengthen themselves for further struggles, further victories (Saul 1991: 6).

But Saul floundered when it came to specifying the reforms that had to be defined as structural. Caught up in the euphoria of the transition and the rhetoric of intellectuals, progressive academics and union leaders, he proceeded to give credence to a slew of policies that would by no stretch of the imagination be described as transformative (Desai and Habib 1994). Nevertheless, Saul's conceptual departure point, structural reform, can be usefully harnessed to understand how to advance a human-oriented development. For reforms to warrant the title 'structural' they must enhance the leverage of working and marginalised communities, diffuse power in favour of these social groups and promote the substantive uncertainty of political elites.[1] What policy reforms and strategies can advance this agenda? Of course these have to be determined in a contextually specific manner. They must emanate from a concrete analysis of a spatial context in a specific time. And for South Africa, in this historical period, five decisions, developments and/or reforms, can be identified as useful for increasing the leverage of poor and marginalised citizens, and thereby enhancing the substantive uncertainty of both national and global elites.

First, electoral reform would go a long way to enhance citizens' leverage over political elites. Currently, the proportional electoral system enables the representation of a maximum number of political parties. This positive feature, however, is counterbalanced by a negative, the empowerment of the party leadership over rank-and-file legislative representatives. Given that electoral votes are cast for the party rather than individual candidates and that the parliamentary list is largely determined by the party leadership, the accountability dynamic of legislative representatives to their constituencies is severely weakened. Indeed, accountability is structured hierarchically to party leaders, which consequently

ensures that individual legislative representatives are conditioned to act not with their conscience, but in line with party diktat
(COSATU 2006).

These consequences have prompted a number of civic actors
and political parties to call for an overhaul of the electoral system. Indeed, the Slabbert Commission, appointed in May 2002
to investigate the issue recommended that the electoral system,
be changed to a Mix Member Proportional (MMP) System with
75 per cent of legislative representatives elected from 69 multi-
member constituencies, while the remainder would come from
the party list to ensure overall proportionality as per the mandate
of the constitution.[2] This recommendation reflected, according
to the majority on the Slabbert Commission, a popular view that
while the national list PR system was fair and representative, it did
not enable individual legislators to be accountable to the voters
(Mattes and Southall 2004). The express purpose of the majority
recommendation of the Slabbert Commission was to enhance
the leverage of citizens over their representatives and contribute
to a political system that generates a substantive uncertainty for
its political elites. It should be noted that this majority view was
contested by a minority report which found, in favour of the status
quo, a recommendation that was ultimately accepted by the ANC
government.

The second related but distinct development that can greatly
contribute to this end is the establishment of a viable, competitive political system. At present, South Africa has all institutional
characteristics of a robust democratic political order. Yet its
political system cannot be interpreted as being competitive. This is
because not only does the ANC overwhelmingly dominate in terms
of electoral support, but the largest opposition parties are also
unable to seriously serve as competitors to the ruling party because
their support base is largely among minority racial groups. As a
result, no viable political system exists, and a viable parliamentary
opposition has no prospect of emerging from the collection of
parties currently represented in the national legislature (Habib
and Taylor 2001).

The only way this competitive political system will be established is if the Tripartite Alliance was to fracture and COSATU
and the SACP were to go it on their own.[3] This is of course to ask
quite a lot from individuals who have fought together throughout

the dark years of apartheid. But this is essential if the dispersal of power and substantive uncertainty of political elites is to be achieved. COSATU and the SACP, were they to go separate ways, would compete in the same electoral pool as the ANC. This means that they need not come into power to succeed in shifting the policy agenda to the left. Their mere presence and a respectable showing in the elections would force the ruling party to address the immediate concerns of the working and unemployed poor in order to compensate for the greater electoral competition on its left flank.

Two objections are often made when this idea of a break in the alliance is broached. First, it is feared that leaving the alliance would enable the upper classes, both black and white, to have free rein in determining the policy agenda of the ruling party (Marais 2001). This, however, is to make the assumption that policy influence only occurs through participation in internal forums. Yet as many studies would demonstrate, they can as easily be influenced by extra-institutional action and/or the external deployment of other forms of leverage by social actors within society (Ballard et al. 2006b; Zuern 2006). With regard to the latter, it is worthwhile noting that capital was able to influence the ANC's policy since 1996 without much substantive presence within the party itself (Habib and Padayachee 2000). Finally, as COSATU (2006) and the SACP (2006a, 2006b) themselves would recognise, the alliance with the ruling party has not prevented the slide to what they perceive as neoliberalism.

Second, a break in the Tripartite Alliance is often objected to on the grounds that the overwhelming majority of workers and shop stewards would prefer the alliance to continue. This fact is not only articulated by the leadership of COSATU and the SACP, but by a group of scholars loosely associated with the Sociology of Work Programme (SWOP) in the University of Witwatersrand, who have demonstrated over three surveys in the last decade that more than two-thirds of COSATU's rank and file are supportive of the alliance (Buhlungu 2006). A survey data, however, cannot replace analysis. Demonstrating that a majority of workers support the alliance does not address the issue of whether a break could strategically advance the agenda of the working and unemployed poor.[4] All it demonstrates is that the subjective will for the alliance does not as yet exist. After all, it is worthwhile noting that majorities have been known to support inappropriate or even incorrect strategic perspectives.[5]

Third, the erosion of the corporatist institutions and processes that have tended to proliferate in South Africa since the early 1990s would not automatically advance a human-oriented development. This is probably treasonous to argue given the ideological ortho--doxy that has developed in favour of corporatism in both the academy and the public sector (Adler and Webster 1995; COSATU 2006; Maree 1993; Seekings and Nattrass 2006; Webster and Adler 1999). But it would be worthwhile to bear in mind that corporatism facilitated social democracy in Western Europe in particular because of the Keynesian macroeconomic environment, itself a product of a particular configuration of power in the global order (Maier 1984: 49; Panitch 1986). Its use in a more neoliberal economic climate is, therefore, unlikely to lead to the same outcome. Indeed, as Przeworski (1991) maintained, corporatist institutions can become mechanisms of co-optation in the present era, enforcing a predictability that detracts political elites from their accountability to their citizens.

The alternative, of course, need not involve a pristine non-engagement or a wish for revolutionary rupture as corporatist advocates often caricature it. Indeed, one option may simply be to constitute the establishment of a pluralist labour system, similar to that existing in the USA, where participation and negotiations are not institutionalised and governed by formal political rules or by a broader public discourse that stressed the necessity of partnerships among conflicting social forces (Schmitter 1974). Rather, the negotiations that do occur are simply the outcome of the everyday interplay and contested engagements of social actors in the economic and market arena. It would be useful to note, of course, that this pluralist labour system has precedence in South Africa; it existed in the 1980s and its reintroduction can only but compel the organised expressions of workers and the poor to focus on a politics of power in which collective organisation comprises its essential component.[6]

But it is also possible to have a social pact that is facilitative of human-oriented development. The social pact attempted in the 1990s failed because structural conditions did not result in equitable outcomes for all social partners. In essence it became a co-optive mechanism to emasculate labour's demands. Now, however, structural conditions seem to be shifting — COSATU's leverage within the state has been enhanced, political and economic elites are more uncertain as a result of Polokwane, the global and national macro-economic environment is moving in a Keynesian direction — creating the potential for a social pact to succeed. Yet for this to happen, bold political leadership is required. Such leadership needs to manage the expectations of both citizens and workers and the business community. The ANC and government leaders have tried the former, but not the latter. Paralysed by a fear of markets and their reaction, political elites are reluctant to rein in the expectations of business executives and the upper middle classes. But as long as they fail to do so, or are perceived to be doing so, they will fail to rein in popular expectations. Popular and privileged expectations are tied by an umbilical cord, and neither can be reined in without the other. The irony is that whereas the social pact of the 1990s failed because of structural conditions, the one of the post-April 2009 era may be stillborn because of a failure of political courage and imagination.

Related, but distinct from this is a fourth development which involves the emergence of an independent, robust plural civil society. Already there has been much progress made in this regard. In two separate reflections on the issue, I have argued that civil society has not only been fundamentally transformed in the post-1994 era, but that sections of it are also having a dramatic systemic impact by contributing to a substantive uncertainty that is making elites more responsive to the poor and marginalised citizens. The first of these reflections entitled *State-Civil Society Relations in Post-Apartheid South Africa* (2005), attempts to demonstrate that political democratisation and economic liberalisation have essentially transformed an ostensibly homogenous, black progressive anti-apartheid civil society into one composed of at least three distinct blocs — non-governmental organisations (NGOs), survivalist agencies and social movements — all with very distinct relationships with the state. It concluded that: 'Diverse roles and functions undertaken by (these) different elements of civil society, then collectively create the adversarial and collaborative relationships, the push and pull effects, which sometimes assist and other times compels the state to meet its obligations and responsibilities to its citizenry' (ibid.: 688–89).

The second, more specific contribution, co-edited with Richard Ballard and Imraan Valodia, focused on post-apartheid social movements, maintaining that they 'contribute to the restoration

of political plurality in the political system', facilitate 'the accountability of state elites to our citizenry' and 'contributed to the emergence of a political climate that prompted government's recent
shift to a more state interventionist and expansive economic policy
with a more welfare orientation' (Ballard et al. 2006a). These
developments then effect what Jeremy Cronin recently termed
enabling a popular agency, which is necessary for the dispersal of
power that at least makes possible the emergence of a more human-
oriented development trajectory.[7]

Finally, a strategic foreign policy can be instrumental in
establishing the political space and enhancing the capacities of
national stakeholders, including its political elites, to pursue a
human-oriented development. The literature review undertaken
above of the political conditions under which elites become
responsive to their citizens clearly indicates that a contested
international environment defined by rivalry among global elites
and great powers is positive for human-oriented development
(Johnson 1999). Moreover, it suggests that resource endowments,
such as mineral wealth, strategic location and even population
size, can become a useful leverage for national political elites in
their engagements with their foreign and global counterparts.[8]
The application of these lessons to the South African case involves
two elements. First, it requires South Africa to undertake the role
of leadership in the continent, or in the words of some of the
international relations literature, to play the role of benevolent
hegemony that not only prioritises stability, democracy and
economic development, but also the development of regional and
continental common markets. These increases in market size can
greatly enhance the leverage of national and continental politicians
in their relations with other actors in the global economy, and
can be particularly favourable for attracting foreign investment.
Second, it would require prioritising multilateral institutions
and endeavours and strategic alliances both among the South
and between Northern and Southern countries in order to con-
tain not only the unilateralism of the USA, but also that of big
economic powers when they act in concert as often happens in
global trade negotiations.[9]

Some of these roles are already being taken by South Africa.
It has increasingly begun to play the role of regional and continental hegemon, even if this is done unevenly and sometimes

reluctantly (Habib and Nthakeng 2006).[10] South Africa has also played an active role in multilateral institution building both at the continental and international levels (le Pere 1998; Schoeman 2003). Moreover, it has also begun to prioritise strategic alliances as in the case of India, Brazil, South Africa (IBSA) and the Brazil, Russia, India, China and South Africa (BRICS) partnerships and in the Group of 20 (Flemes 2006), some of which were crucial in preventing, particularly in the trade negotiations in Cancun, an unfair trade deal being imposed on the countries of the South.[11]

Despite these successes, there are some significant weaknesses in some of South Africa's foreign policy engagements. First, it has to prioritise South–North strategic alliances less in addition to the South–South ones, if power is to be significantly dispersed in the global setting and development opportunities for the South are to be maximised. Second, some of South Africa's politicians have to learn to transcend their market fundamentalism so apparent in some of the documentation of NEPAD (Bond 2004), their refusal to regulate South African investment on the continent (Habib and Nthakeng 2006), and in the almost timid reforms undertaken at the level of the IMF and World Bank. It would be useful to note that the current success story of China is not one of simply its resort to the market, but also its pragmatism in manipulating the latter through a fixed currency for instance, to suit its own ends (Breslin 2006). Third, South Africa's foreign policy practitioners and trade negotiators need to become bolder in their engagements. This would involve a greater willingness to involve itself in the politics of brinkmanship, as occurred in Cancun, and in engaging global civil society who could be far better engaged than at present to advance a human-oriented development agenda. Finally, none of this would be possible without more significant capacity being built both at the level of technical skills within state institutions, and the internalisation of these strategic perspectives among state personnel far beyond the narrow band that currently occupies the presidential and foreign policy apparatus (Alden and le Pere 2004). In any case, the five developments and/or reforms suggested above are not meant to be an exhaustive list. Many more may be conceived to be relevant. To earn the title of 'structural', however, all must be directed to dispersing power so as to make elites substantively uncertain of their futures, a necessary political precondition for establishing the shift to a more human-oriented development trajectory.

Conclusion

It would be worthwhile to note that the strategies and policies recommended suggest that not only human-oriented development is a product of a political process, but also that it requires an intricate mix of representative and participatory democratic elements. The first two strategic and policy reforms are intended to strengthen the representative character of the political system so as to promote a contestation between political elites. The next two speak to strengthening the participatory character of the political system, to facilitate what Steven Friedman (2005) has so often termed 'providing voice to the poor'. This mix of representative and participatory democratic elements is meant to create the substantive uncertainty, which is the political foundation that generates the accountability between elites and their citizens so necessary for realising a human-oriented development agenda. The political programme then challenges the perspectives of those who view participatory and representative democracy as distinct political systems. The perspective advanced here suggests that it is the intricate mix of participatory and representative elements that enhances the accountability of political elites to their citizens.

There is a precedent for this in South Africa's recent political history. Elsewhere, I have argued that South Africa's economic and social policies have undergone a significant change since 2001. Senior government figures are no longer so enamoured with the market as they once were. Privatisation has been put on the backburner and is no longer mentioned with any regularity. There has been a steep rise in social expenditure as welfare grants have now been extended to cover almost 10 million people. State intervention is back in vogue and is reflected in both the driving of infrastructure spending through state owned enterprises and the establishment of equity and transformation targets in the industry charters. Finally, senior government's rhetoric has dramatically changed in recent years — now there is emphasis on the need to correct market failures, and poverty alleviation and even inequality reduction is now given as much emphasis as is growth (Habib 2004).

There are two explanations why this happened. The first advanced mainly by government ministers, policy technocrats and researchers associated with government suggests that the shift in policy was either part of an original long-term vision, or is at least a product of an incremental learning process where officials correct for earlier policy failures (Hirsch 2005). But it is hard to give much weight to this explanation. Not only is it founded on the earlier critiqued assumption that policy is merely an outcome of a rational process involving policy technocrats and state officials, but it also does not recognise that much of the rationale advanced in, and outcomes expected of the Growth, Employment and Redistribution Strategy (GEAR) did not materialise (Habib and Padayachee 2000).

The second explanation is far more persuasive. It explains the shift in policy as an outcome of the partial reconfiguration of power that occurred in the late 1990s. This reconfiguration resulted from three related but distinct factors. First, was the failure of GEAR both in terms of attracting foreign investment and increasing employment and thereby alleviating poverty? Second, was the concomitant rise of social movements and community organisations and/or their more adversarial stance vis-à-vis state policies? This more independently aggressive posture affected organisations and collectives both within and outside the Tripartite Alliance (Ballard et al. 2006b). Finally, there was the partial shift in the ideological consensus at the global level most dramatically reflected in the critiques of previous insiders Joseph Stiglitz (2002) and Jeffrey Sachs (2005), both of whom began to criticise the structure of the international financial institutions and their policy prescriptions. These developments facilitated the emergence of at least a partial substantive uncertainty of political elites at the national level, regularly reflected in the President's annual state of the nation addresses, and which prompted the shift in economic and social policies in the new millennium.

The role of substantive uncertainty in facilitating a more ideologically diverse public discourse and a reconsideration of policy is also evident in the succession crisis within the ANC. A number of public commentators have indicated that one of the positive consequences of the contestation between President Mbeki and his previous deputy and now President of the ANC, Jacob Zuma, has been the opening up of the policy discourse in particular on AIDS, the macro-economy, and Zimbabwe (Friedman 2006). Yet, as I argued in a panel debate with Aubrey Matshiqi and Steven Friedman at the Institute for Security Studies (ISS), this openness is vulnerable and unlikely to be sustainable so long as it is premised on a contest between two leaders in the ruling party. For it to be truly sustainable, the uncertainty must be institutionalised within the political system as a whole.

This is worth noting for even today the general policy shift, while significant, is by no means absolute or uncontested. Indeed, South Africa's existing policy architecture is currently very contradictory. There are significant sections of it that have a developmental, Keynesian and social democratic flavour, especially when it comes to welfare and infrastructure spending. Yet, it also has strong continuities with the GEAR framework, particularly reflected in the Reserve Bank and Treasury's rigid commitments to deficit and inflation targeting (Habib 2004). As argued earlier, this contradiction will never be resolved by clever technocrats in rational conversation. It will be fundamentally determined by the configuration of power and how it evolves over the next few years.

This, then, is one of the principal lessons to be learnt from some of the comparative development experiences across the world. South Africa has had some policy shifts in recent years that have benefited poor and marginalised communities. But for these stakeholders' interests to be addressed fully, and for the country's problems of poverty and inequality to be tackled comprehensively, not only must the policy shift be sustainable, but the current contradictions in the policy architecture need also to be resolved. And this is not going to be merely done through rational conversation between policy technocrats. It will be ultimately resolved when power is dispersed and reconfigured in the social setting; political and economic elites are made substantively uncertain of their futures; accountability is thereby re-established between the latter and citizens; and policy as a result becomes responsive to the interests of the poor and marginalised. The vision of social citizenship enunciated by Marshall (1950) in his classic text and which now underlies the scholarly works of most progressive academics will only truly be realised when activists, public intellectuals and scholars transcend their ideological and political orthodoxies and begin to truly interrogate the politics of development in this historical era.

Notes

1. This perspective is similar to that articulated by the SACP. In part two of its controversial discussion document released by its Central Committee in May (2006), entitled *Class Struggles and the Post-1994 state in South Africa*, the SACP argues that 'if it is to have any prospect of addressing the dire legacy of colonial dispossession and apartheid oppression, a national democratic strategy has to be revolutionary, that is to say, it must systemically transform, class, racial and gendered power …' This is not new. For instance, the slogan adopted by the SACP at its 1995 strategy conference, 'Socialism is the future — build it now' reflects similar sentiments.

2. COSATU is in favour of the general recommendation, although it suggests that the proportion between constituency and party list be 65 per cent and 35 per cent, respectively (COSATU 2003: 7). Its support is just shy of 70 per cent, up between 66.36 per cent and 62.65 per cent in 1999 and 1964, respectively. Although critics sometimes qualify this point by noting that voter turnout in national elections has declined to 76 per cent, down from 88 per cent in 1999, this should not detract from the fact that the party has increasingly consolidated its electoral support in the country (HSRC 2006: 9).

3. This is the peculiar logic that has become common in this debate. See Southall and Wood (2003), COSATU (2003) and a number of the chapters in Buhlungu (2006). Ultimately, Jeremy Cronin, Deputy General-Secretary of the SACP and Chairperson of the Transport portfolio in the national legislature, is probably correct to recognise that were the alliance to break, it would not do so neatly, but will probably fracture almost all of the constituent units (Butler 2007: 35–52; Cronin 2002; Southall 2003; Suttner 2006). But then political and social advance is often a messy affair, and it is precisely the acrimony and broken relationships that give rise to the substantive uncertainty of elites, which is so necessary for a policy agenda that is responsive to the interests of working and poor communities. Is this likely to happen? Almost certainly not in the short term. As indicated earlier, the political will among both the leadership and its supporters just does not currently exist for such a radical course of action. It may, however, in the future. The problem is whether COSATU and the SACP will at that point be sufficiently viable so as to constitute an alternative political pole of attraction.

4. COSATU has begun to reflect on the organisational lessons of its practice of the 1980s, although it is careful to acknowledge that this experience must not be romanticised (see COSATU 2006).

5. He suggested this at a seminar, hosted by the Centre for Conflict Resolution (CCR) of the University of Cape Town on 18 October 2006, where he served as a discussant to a presentation I made on our co-edited book on social movements, *Voices of Protest*.

6. Note, for instance, how China has used population and therefore market size as a leverage to attract foreign investment.

7. Note, for instance, the coincidence of interests on agricultural subsidies that prevailed for so long between the USA and Europe in the World Trade negotiations.
8. There are of course scholars who dislike the term 'hegemon', preferring instead to describe South Africa as a pivotal state (see Adebajo and Landsberg 2003; le Pere 1998).
9. The negotiations ended in stalemate and generated enormous criticism of both the USA and Europe and increased pressure on them from domestic stakeholders to reconsider their positions.
10. Panel discussion on the theme, 'The Presidential Succession and the Tripartite Alliance', hosted by the Institute for Security Studies (ISS), Pretoria, 14 September 2006.
11. This contradiction has most recently reflected itself in a debate between Treasury and the Department of Trade and Industry (DTI) officials on the recommendations advanced by scholars and in particular Dani Roderik, associated with Harvard University's Center for International Development, which was commissioned to investigate the constraints on South Africa's growth prospects. Roderik's focus is on employment which he recommends be addressed through an expansion of the export-oriented tradable sector which often employs low skilled workers. This is to be done in part through the creation of a competitive exchange rate, which means that the Reserve Bank needs to go beyond its narrow inflation-targeting regime to incorporate tradable output and employment as criteria for its decision-making. This recommendation, it is reported, is heavily supported by DTI officials, and is simultaneously strongly opposed by the National Treasury, which insists on addressing the problems through a continued reliance on market measures such as a competitions policy (Roderik 2006).

References

Adebajo, A. and C. Landsberg. 2003. 'South Africa and Nigeria as Regional Hegemons' in M. Baregu and C. Landsberg (eds), *From Cape to Congo: Southern Africa's Evolving Security Challenges*, pp. 171–203. Boulder, CO: Lynne Rienner.

Adler, G. and E. Webster. 1995. 'The Labor Movement, Radical Reform, and Transition to Democracy in South Africa, *Politics & Society*, 23 (1): 75–106.

Alden, C. and G. le Pere. 2004. 'South Africa's Post-apartheid Foreign Policy: From Reconciliation to Ambiguity', *Review of African Political Economy*, 31 (100), 283–97.

Alexander, N. 2002. *An Ordinary Country: Issues in the Transition from Apartheid to Democracy in South Africa*. Pietermaritzburg: University of Natal Press.

Ballard, R., A. Habib and I. Valodia (eds). 2006a. *Voices of Protest: Social Movements in Post-apartheid South Africa*. Pietermaritzburg: UKZN Press.

Ballard, R., A. Habib and I. Valodia. 2006b. 'Conclusion: Making Sense of Post-apartheid South Africa's Voices of Protest', in idem (eds), *Voices of Protest: Social Movements in Post-apartheid South Africa*. Pietermaritzburg: UKZN Press, pp. 397–418.

Barker, R. (ed.). 1971. *Studies in opposition*. London: Macmillan.

Bhorat, H. and R. Kanbur. 2006. *Poverty and Policy in Post-apartheid South Africa*. Cape Town: HSRC Press.

Blondel, J. 1997. 'Political Opposition in the Contemporary World', *Government and Opposition*, 32 (4), 462–87.

Bond, P. 2000. *Elite Transition: From Apartheid to Neoliberalism in South Africa*. Pietermaritzburg: University of Natal Press.

———. 2004. *Talk Left, Walk Right: South Africa's Frustrated Global Reforms*. Pietermaritzburg: UKZN Press.

Bratton, M. and N. van de Walle. 1997. *Democratic Experiments in Africa: Regime Transitions in Comparative Perspective*. Cambridge: Cambridge University Press.

Breslin, S. 2006. 'Interpreting Chinese Power in the Global Political Economy', presented at the Conference on Regional Powers in Asia, Africa, Latin America and the Middle East. German Institute of Global and Area Studies (GIGA). 11–12 December.

Buhlungu, S. 2006. *Trade Unions and Politics: COSATU Workers after 10 Years of Democracy*. Cape Town: HSRC Press.

Butler, A. 2007. 'The State of the African National Congress', in Sakhela Buhlungu, John Daniel, Roger Southhall and Jessica Lutchman (eds), *State of the Nation: South Africa 2007*. Cape Town: HSRC Press, pp. 35–52.

Chin, K. F. and K. S. Jomo. 2000. 'Financial Sector Rents in Malaysia', in M. Khan and K. S. Jomo (eds), *Rents, Rent Seeking and Economic Development: Theory and Evidence in Asia*, pp. 304–26. Cambridge: Cambridge University Press.

COSATU. 2003. 'Resolutions of the COSATU 8th National Congress, Electoral System, Part 5'.

———. 2006. 'COSATU Political Discussion Document: Possibilities for Fundamental Change'. Prepared for the 9th National Congress. 18–21 September.

Cronin, J. 2002. 'An Interview with Helena Sheehan'. http//www.comms.deu. ie/sheehanh/ za/cronin02.htm. Accessed 17 November 2005.

Dahl, R. A. 1966. *Political Oppositions in Western Democracies*. New Haven, CT: Yale University Press.

Desai, A. 2002. *The Poors of South Africa*. New York: Monthly Review Press.

Desai, A. and A. Habib. 1994. 'Social Movements in Transitional Societies: A Case Study of the Congress of South African Trade Unions', *South African Sociological Review*, 6 (2): 68–88.

Doner, R., B. Ritchie and D. Slater. 2005. 'Systemic Vulnerability and the Origins of Development States: Northeast and Southeast Asia in Comparative Perspective', *International Organization*, 59 (2): 327–61.

Epstein, L. 1967. *Political Parties in Western Democracies*. New York: Praeger.

Evans, P. 1995. *Embedded Autonomy: States and Industrial Transformation*. Princeton, NJ: Princeton University Press.

Flemes, D. 2006. 'Can Emerging Middle Powers Challenge the International System? State and Perspectives of the IBSA Dialogue forum, presented at the Conference on Regional Powers in Asia, Africa, Latin America and the Middle East. German Institute of Global and Area Studies (GIGA). 11–12 December.

Freund, B. 2006. 'State, Capital and the Emergence of a New Power Elite in South Africa: 'Black Economic Empowerment' at National and Local Levels', paper presented at the Harold Wolpe Memorial Trust 10th Anniversary Colloquium. Cape Town. 22–23 September.

Friedman, S. 2005. 'South Africa: Globalization and the Politics of Redistribution', in J. S. Tulchin and G. Bland (eds), *Getting Globalization Right: The Dilemmas of Inequality*, pp. 14–73. London: Lynne Rienner.

———. 2006. 'Spring of Hope, Winter of Worry for South African Democracy', *Business Day*. 6 September.

Habib, A. 2004. 'The Politics of Economic Policy-making: Substantive Uncertainty, Political Leverage, and Human Development', *Transformation*, 56: 90–103.

———. 2005. 'State-civil Society Relations in Post-apartheid South Africa', *Social Research*, 72 (3), 671–692.

Habib, A., J. Daniel and R. Southall. 2003. 'Introduction', in J. Daniel, A. Habib and R. Southall (eds), *State of the Nation: South Africa 2003–2004*, pp. 1–24. Cape Town: HSRC Press.

Habib, A. and S. Nthakeng. 2006. 'Constraining the unconstrained: Civil Society and South Africa's Hegemonic Obligations in Africa', in W. Carlsnaes and P. Nel (eds), *In Full flight: South African Foreign policy after Apartheid*, pp. 175–94. Midrand: Institute for Global Dialogue.

Habib, A. and U. Padayachee. 2000. 'Economic Policy and Power Relations in South Africa's Transition to Democracy', *World Development*, 28 (2): 245–63.

Habib, A. and R. Taylor. 2001. 'Political Alliances and Parliamentary Opposition in South Africa', *Democratization*, 8 (1) 207–26.

Held, D. and A. McGrew. 2003. *The Global Transformations Reader*. Cambridge: Polity Press.

Hirsch, A. 2005. *Season of Hope: Economic Reform under Mandela and Mbeki*. Pietermaritzburg: University of KwaZulu-Natal Press.

HSRC. 2006. 'Survey on South African Voter Participation in Elections'. Prepared for the Independent Electoral Commission (IEC), South Africa.

Huntington, S. 1991. *The Third Wave: Democratization in the Late Twentieth Century*. Norman, OK: University of Oklahoma Press.

Johnson, C. 1999. 'The Development State: Odyssey of a Concept', in M. Woo-Cumings (ed.), *The Developmental State*, pp. 32–61. Ithaca, NY: Cornell University Press.

Jung, J. and I. Shapiro. 1995. 'South Africa's Negotiated Transition: Democracy, Opposition and the New Constitutional Order', *Politics & Society*, 23 (3): 269–306.

Kagarlitsky, B. 1990. *The Dialectic of Change*. London: Verso.

le Pere, G. 1998. 'South Africa: An Emerging Power', *Global Dialogue*, 3 (1): 1–2.

Maier, C. 1984. 'Preconditions for Corporatism', In J. Goldthorpe (ed.), *Order and Conflict in Contemporary Capitalism*, pp. 39–60. Oxford: Clarendon Press.

Mamdani, M. 1996. *Citizen and Subject: Contemporary Africa and the Legacy of Late Colonialism*. Princeton, NJ: Princeton University Press.

Marais, H. 2001. *South Africa: Limits to Change: The Political Economy of Transition*. London: Zed Books.

Maree, J. 1993. 'Trade Unions and Corporatism in South Africa', *Transformation*, no. 21: 24–54.

Marglin, S. and J. Schor. 1992. *Golden Age of Capitalism: Reinterpreting the Post-war Experience*. Oxford: Oxford University Press.

Marshall, T. H. 1950. *Citizenship and Social Class*. Cambridge: Cambridge University Press.

Mattes, R. and B. Southall. 2004. 'Popular Attitudes towards the South African Electoral System', *Democratisation*, 11 (1): 51–76.

May, J. 2000. *Poverty and Inequality in South Africa: Meeting the Challenge*. Cape Town: David Philip.

Mbeki, T. 2003. 'Address of the President of South Africa, Thabo Mbeki, to the National Council of Provinces'. 11 November.

———. 2004a. 'Address of the President of South Africa, Thabo Mbeki, to the First Joint Sitting of the Third Democratic Parliament'. Cape Town, 21 May.

———. 2004b. 'State of the Nation Address of the President of South Africa, Thabo Mbeki: Houses of Parliament'. Cape Town, 6 February.

Moore, Jr B. 1989. *Liberal Prospects under Soviet Socialism: A Comparative Historical Perspective*. New York: Averell Harriman Institute.

Nabudere, D. W. 2006. 'The Development State, Democracy and the Global Society in Africa', presented at the Conference on Investment Choices for Education in Africa. Faculty of Education, University of Witwatersrand. 20 September.

O'Donnell, G. 1993. 'On the state, Democratization and some Conceptual Problems: A Latin American View with Glances at some Post-communist Countries', *World Development*, 21', (8): 1355–1369.

———. 1994. 'Delegative Democracy', *Journal of Democracy*, 5 (1): 55–69.

O'Donnell, G. and P. Schmitter. 1986. *Transitions from Authoritarian Rule: Tentative Conclusions about Uncertain Democracies* (vol. 4). Baltimore, MD: John Hopkins University Press.

Panitch, L. 1986. *Working Class Politics in Crisis: Essays on Labor and the State*. London: Verso.

PCAS (Policy Coordination and Advisory Services). 2003. 'Towards a Ten Year Review — Synthesis Report on Implementation of Government Programmes'. PCAS, The Presidency. October.

Przeworski, A. 1991. *Democracy and the market*. Cambridge: Cambridge University Press.

Roderik, D. 2006. 'Understanding South Africa's Economic Puzzles', Working Paper No. 130. Centre for International Development, Harvard University.

Sachs, J. 2005. *'The End of Poverty: How We can make it Happen in our Lifetime'*. New York: Penguin Books.

SACP, 2006a. 'Class, National and Gender Struggle in South Africa: The Historical Relationship between the ANC and the SACP, Part 1', *Bua Komanisi*, Special Edition pp. 3–16. May.

———. 2006b. 'Class Struggles and the Post-1994 State in South Africa, Part 2', *Bua Komanisi*, Special Edition, pp. 16–31. May.

Saul, J. 1991. South Africa: Between 'Barbarism' and 'Structural Reform', *New Left Review*, 188.

Schedler, A. 2001. 'Taking Uncertainty Seriously: The Blurred Boundaries of Democratic Transition and Consolidation', *Democratisation*, 8 (4): 1–22.

Schmitter, P. 1974. 'Still the Century of Corporatism', *Review of Politics*, 36 (1): 85–131.

Schoeman, M. 2003. 'South Africa as an Emerging Middle Power 1994–2003', in J. Daniel, H. Adam and R. Southall (eds), State of the nation: South Africa 2003–2004. Cape Town: HSRC Press, pp. 349–67.

Seekings, J. and N. Nattrass. 2006. *Class Race and Inequality in South Africa*. Pietermaritzburg: UKZN Press.

Sen, A. 1999. 'Democracy as a universal value', *Journal of Democracy*, 10 (3), 3–17.

Shapiro, I. 1994. 'Three Ways to be a Democrat', *Political Theory*, 22: 124–51.

Southall, R. 2003. 'State of the Political Parties', in J. Daniel, A. Habib and R. Southall (eds), State of the nation: South Africa 2003–2004, pp.53–77. Cape Town: HSRC Press.

———. 2006. 'Introduction: Can South Africa be a Developmental State', in Sakhela Buhlungu John Daniel, Roger Southhall and Jessica Lutchman (eds), *State of the Nation: South Africa 2005–2006*, pp. xvii–xlv. Cape Town: HSRC Press.

Southall, R. and G. Wood. 2003. 'COSATU, the ANC and the Election: Wither the Alliance?' *Transformation*, no. 38: 68–83.

Stepan, A. 1978. *The State and Society: Peru In Comparative Perspective*. Princeton, NJ: Princeton University Press.

Stiglitz, J. 2002. *Globalization and its Discontents*. New York: Norton.

Suttner, R. 2004. Democratic Transition and Consolidation in South Africa: The Advice of 'the Experts', *Current Sociology*, 52 (5): 755–73.

———. 2006. 'African National Congress as Dominant Organisation: Impact of the Attainment of Power and Phases of Post Liberation Development and Crisis', presented at the Wits Interdisciplinary Research Seminar. Johannesburg. 2 October.

Terreblanche, S. 2002. *A History of Inequality in South Africa 1652–2002.* Pietermaritzburg: University of Natal Press.

UNDP. 2003. *South African Human Development Report.* Cape Town: Oxford University Press.

Wade, R. 1999. *Governing the Market: Economic Theory and the Role of Government in East Asian Industrialization.* Princeton, NJ: Princeton University Press.

Webster, E. and G. Adler. 1999. 'Towards a Class Compromise in South Africa's 'Double transition': Bargained Liberalization and the Consolidation of Democracy', *Politics & Society*, 27 (3): 347–85.

Wiarda, H. 1981. *Corporatism and National Development in Latin America.* Boulder, CO: Westview Press.

Zuern, E. 2006. 'Elusive boundaries: SANCO, the ANC and the post-apartheid South African State', in R. Ballard, A. Habib and I. Valodia (eds), *Voices of Protest: Social Movements in Post-apartheid South Africa.* Pietermaritzburg: UKZN Press, pp. 179–202.

11

Indian Democracy in Search of a Democratic State: Socio-political Challenges and State Responses in Contemporary India

Ujjwal Kumar Singh

Comprehending democracy and the state, and indeed the relationship between state and democracy, has remained a conundrum. There is an impressive range of writings on Indian democracy and politics, focusing on the vicissitudes of electoral democracy, the democratic upsurge, changing party system, democratisation through the enhanced capacity of the state to represent diversity and overcome group discrimination and deprivation, the increase in participatory networks through institutional changes at the local level, public policy, and the role of civil society towards their effective implementation.

Most of these writings, however, do not offer any physical or conceptual space — symbolic or substantial — to the 'un-democratic' aspects of democracy in India, occluding what should have been an indispensable component of any study of democracy. The neglect of the 'un-democratic' makes studies of democracy vacuous, for not only is this aspect crucial to understanding the distinctively graded experiences of democracy, but the un-democratic is not just an undesirable residue of the functioning of modern democracies, but indeed an inextricable aspect of its duality. Moreover, there have been few attempts to explore the manner in which democracy works in tandem with the 'reason of state' (Friedrich 1957: 4–5),[1] in particular the relationship between procedural democracy and the aggregate of societal relations which are embodied in the state (Mohanty 1982),[2] and the ideological role that the former may play in sustaining political regimes and specific forms of the state.

In this article, I will map the broad contours of the debates on state and democracy in India, identifying the faultlines discernable in this vast and erudite scholarship. Through an examination of illustrative cases, I propose that the historically specific form of the modern state in India has unfolded along processes which exhibit an expanding register of electoral democracy, redistribution and entrenchment of constitutionalism. At the same time, however, the governance register of the state has unfolded simultaneously, to consolidate the power of the state, and give effect to modes of legitimation, which erode constitutionalism and the rule of law, and make for a 'weak' democratic state. The 'power' and 'rule' registers of the state manifest themselves in its institutional ensemble, and its responses to specific challenges of democratic churnings. These responses are often, and paradoxically so, effected through the institutional mechanisms of electoral democracy, so much so that elections become surrogate for democracy. These are accompanied with extraordinary measures of legal coercion, presented as 'dilemmas' generated by 'unbridled' democracy, necessitating the recourse to hard choices.

This article will explore this ambivalence of the democratic state in India by arguing that electoral democracy has become a substitute for political resolution of challenges in Kashmir and Chhattisgarh, and the pursuit of order through the coercive apparatus of the state continues simultaneously. In states like Chhattisgarh with large *adivasi* populations and prolonged armed struggles, development concerns are addressed through 'special' laws protective of the rights of the adivasis, such as the Scheduled Tribes and Other Traditional Forest Dwellers (Recognition of Forest Rights) Act (FRA 2006) and the Panchayat Extension into Scheduled Areas Act (PESA 1996). Yet, these laws, based on notions of substantive participation of the adivasis in decision making, are often subjected to procedural subversions, even as extraordinary laws like the Unlawful Activities Prevention Act (UAPA 1967, 2004, 2008) and the Chhattisgarh State Public Security Act (CSPSA 2005) are used indiscriminately.

The Indian State and Democracy: The Logic of Constitutive Contradiction

Early authoritative writings on the post-colonial state in India placed themselves within the modernisation framework. The institutions of the state were seen as primarily concerned with the task of political development, and judged for their ability to discard the vestiges of their pre-modern pasts and achieve the 'modular forms' of western liberal democracies (Morris-Jones 1964). Later scholarship on the Indian state, however, distanced itself from prescriptive frameworks of 'progressive' development, arguing that the experience of building the modern state in India, as has been the case in all societies, has revealed a process of differentiation rather than singularity of form (e.g., Kaviraj 2000, 2003; Kothari 1970; Rudolph and Rudolph 1967).

Most of these writings characterise the post-colonial state in India, as possessing dual and mutually contradictory registers, logics, tendencies and processes. Democracy is seen as *one* element of this duality, the other element being that of 'governance' and 'rule'. While the governance and rule registers are seen as carrying forward the structures put in place by the colonial state, the demo-cratic register is construed as marking the creative and inaugural moment of the modern state in India (Baxi 2005, 2000). Yet, while writing about the specificity of the trajectory of democracy in India, most scholars focus on electoral democracy, or adhere almost exclusively to an examination of the characteristic elements of a 'functioning' democracy, to the total occlusion of its undemocratic obverse, which is integral to the experience of democracy in all societies. Thus, while mapping the 'relative success' of Indian democracy, they rely on the evidence of 'regular and reasonably fair elections, institutionalised multiparty system and adversarial politics' and 'the other trappings of a democratic society, such as free speech and free media' (Jayal 2007), or the changing character of the politics of representation in the electoral arena (Kaviraj 2003; Jayal 2006) and the democratic upsurge as a manifestation of the possibilities of participation that the electoral process offers (Yadav 2000).

While it was in these registers of deviation from the mimetic mode that democratic churnings are witnessed in post-colonial India, the paradox of the national-state, as was the case with the colonial state, is precisely that it has not been able to address the continuing churnings, through an expansion of its demo-cratic register. While the processes of eliciting 'consent', through the mechanisms of franchise and representative government is a necessary condition for democracy, it does not exhaust the democratic possibilities of the state. On the other hand, by institutionalising the 'separateness' of the state from society, elections often serve as modes of legitimation, in conditions of democratic and political deficit. While writing about the success of India's democracy, most frameworks appear to lose sight of the state and the manner in which it interacts with society, regulating, ordering and organising it, through a vast panoply of governance power/resources.

Indeed, these two elements/tendencies/processes of the state, which seem to run *parallel* to each other in the writings on the Indian state, I suggest, *interlock* and interweave in actual practice. As an embodiment of aggregate power relations in society, the state allows the governance register to overwhelm democracy, through a range of vocabularies of rule, including that of development. The logic of governance, which under colonial rule focused on efficiency and production of power-effects necessary to keep the subject population in a state of habitual obedience, came also to include the rhetoric of development in independent India (Mohanty 1989).[3] The state in independent India took upon itself massive industrialisation programmes, entailing production of essential goods and creation of infrastructure, and also the generation of and redistribution of wealth (Kaviraj 2003).

The developmental role of the state forms an inextricable part of its legitimation practice, made possible by the specific composition of the ruling classes in post-colonial India. This aspect of the state has been discussed extensively by scholars from both non-Marxist and Marxist perspectives. The framework of 'passive revolution' has been used in some quarters to argue that institutional structures in independent India through much of 1970s and part of the 1980s functioned through 'compromise and alliance' between the bourgeoisie and other dominant classes (Kaviraj 1984, 1988; Chatterjee 2010). The structures of domination could work through this alliance mediated by a power bloc, which got ossified in the bureaucracy and the ruling structures of the state. It perpetuated itself through the containment of the lower orders of society, and the assertion of 'brahmanical values' under the veil of 'bourgeois virtues of governance' (Alam 2004: 116). With globalisation and neoliberal restructuring of the state, however, the bureaucratic apparatus is constrained by a relative loss of autonomy and salience in matters of economic policy (ibid.: 116–17). On the other hand, there is an exponential augmentation of the law and order and security functions of the neoliberal state, to address democratic churnings in society.

In the following sections, through illustrations from Kashmir and Chhattisgarh, I will attempt to show how the interlocking between registers of democracy and rule becomes pronounced, with attempts to secure stability through electoral democracy, alongside an accumulation of laws which repress movements, and those which seek to provide protective rights. This ultimately shows how the logic of bureaucracy (or the governance register) may cohabit with the logic of democracy, appropriating it into the logic of rule. It may be argued that movements for autonomy/liberation in the case of Kashmir and movements against land acquisition and dispossession by *adivasis* and by armed Maoist groups have been addressed by the state through the dominant logic of governance. The logic of democracy, while being relegated to a subordinate and subsidiary position, is made to appear, however, as the primary concern of the state.

The Democratic Paradox: The National Security State and the Substitution of the Political

Kashmir and Chhattisgarh perhaps most appropriately manifest what has been called the democratic paradox (Mouffe 2000: 3–4), i.e., the paradox of putting together in 'liberal democracies' the 'divergent and irreconcilable logics' of the liberal tradition and the democratic tradition. The tension between these two incompatible logics and their corresponding 'grammars' are visible in both states. The struggles over democracy in both the states have been addressed by the state through elections, while other constitutional measures for democratic participation have been subverted. Simultaneously, the developmental state, which had previously secured legitimacy for the state through redistribution, has entrenched itself more firmly into the logic of the national security state.

The national-security state is associated with specific state practices which have emerged in the context of the 'war on terror', involving both the exponential rise in laws for dealing with terror, and also ways by which these legal regimes, elicit the consent of the people. The security state, which presents itself as a means for collective security, is in practice embedded in the raison d'etat or 'reasons of the state' (Friedrich 1957; Gross 2001). The considerations of reasons of state are generally understood as emerging in exceptional or extraordinary conditions, which imperil the existence of the state. Theoretically, therefore, notions of state sovereignty, the identification and delineation of an exceptional and imperiling condition, and its correlate — the definition of normalcy — are necessary derivatives of raison d'état.

Democratic regimes see restrictions and limitations on governmental powers as fundamental, with rights, liberties and the rule of law being so integral that they may not be diluted even in times of acute danger, limiting thereby the range of activities that the state may pursue to protect itself. Yet, the reason of state is often perpetuated behind a veil of democracy. In the context of anti-terror or security laws, for example, the state justifies the use of these laws as 'calibrated and just response' to a dilemma, which the state claims is thrown up by a surfeit of democracy, necessitating resolution through exceptional measures. Thus extraordinary laws, understood within the framework of the 'dilemma of democracy', come across as responses to the 'extraordinary situations' that emerge primarily because of the openness and freedom which democracy allows. These laws, moreover, going by this logic, are not only necessitated by conditions of unbridled democracy; they are also not inimical to democracy, but rather integral to its functioning, as necessary correctives serving important restorative and curative purposes.

In both Kashmir and Chhattisgarh, the 'security state' is buttressed by legal regimes of exception, and extraordinary reinforcement of the 'security apparatus' of the state, made operational by 'democratically' elected regimes. While addressing the armed struggles in tribal areas of Chhattisgarh, Orissa, West Bengal, Jharkhand, etc., the Indian state has converted developmental issues almost exclusively into a security issue, with an 'effective police response' overriding all other solutions (Sundar 2007). The annual report of the Ministry of Home Affairs (2008–2009) proposes 'a holistic approach' to dealing with 'naxalite activities', which prioritises 'security', suggesting a timeframe whereby 'law and order' issues pertaining to the Maoists are to be sorted out first for any effective development to take place.[4]

The 'securitisation' of development has resulted in the creation of 'borderlands' in the heart of India.[5] In these areas within the territorial boundaries of India, which are 'borderlands' precisely because of warlike conditions that exist there, a web of securitisation networks exist. While the presence of armed forces in Jammu and Kashmir (as in much of the north-east) is facilitated by extraordinary laws like the Armed Forces Special Powers Act (AFSPA 1958), in the 'Maoist-affected' states like Chhattisgarh, the paramilitary and the state police are buttressed by special security laws like the Chhattisgarh Special Public Security Act, 2005. The state law works in tandem with the Unlawful Activities Prevention Act, 2004, 2008 which has become the foremost law in the country to curb political dissent, and to continue with the electronic surveillance methods put in place under POTA (Singh 2007).[6]

Simultaneously, the state governments have sought to raise civilian militias drawn from within the community, leading to the setting up of village defence councils in Jammu and Kashmir and the Salwa Judum in Chhattisgarh.[7] In seeking a solution to the 'law and order' problem, the state government in Chhattisgarh claims to have evolved a 'governance' paradigm for policing. Taking recourse to the practice of policing in colonial times, respective state governments have invoked provisions of the Police Act (1861), to set up a force of Special Police Officers (SPOs), leading to new faultlines within the community, and escalation of social conflicts around the forms of domination that emerge from the militarisation of the community by the state. Moreover, while colonial forms of community policing elicited an obligation from the subject population to participate in a disciplinary regime of total subjection, in its new avatar of armed community policing in conflict situation, the invocation of special policing provision produces new forms and loci of power, which both legitimate state practices of rule, and also reconstitute the community in significant ways.

Amidst this, in states ridden by people's struggles, elections are made a surrogate for substantive democracy. Indeed, in a manifestation of a strategy of pragmatic modus vivendi, the state is able to present the stability of elections as the substitute for any 'unsettling' political solution. Indeed, the question whether in conflict situations the 'freedom' and 'fairness' of elections can at all be assured is pertinent, given that significant political actors choose to abstain from the political process, and those that remain are often those who wield coercive power in the region. In situations of long-drawn conflict, the credibility of elections and electoral mechanisms are put to test, so much so that in such a context, rather than a mechanism 'enabling' the people to exercise fair, free and informed political choice, elections may come to be seen as representing and furthering the hegemonic interests of the State, as opposed to the democratic aspirations of the people (Lyngdoh 2004; Singh 2004).

In Jammu and Kashmir, for example, since 1995, the elections in the state for both the Lok Sabha and the State Assembly were held by the Election Commission under the full sway of 'counter-insurgency' forces, including the army, paramilitary and armed police of the state. In a comparable situation in Mizoram, it was only when a political process was set in motion with the Mizoram Accord of 30 June 1986, conferring statehood and a special status to Mizoram, that 'conditions were seen as conducive for holding free and fair elections', and the process of elections to the Assembly was subsequently initiated.[8]

In Chhattisgarh, the state assembly and parliamentary elections were held in 2003, 2004 and 2009, amidst the Maoist enforced election boycott. The electoral outcomes were widely projected as a victory of democracy (of votes over the gun). In actual practice, however, there was only 50 per cent electoral turnout in the state, and a large part of the state did not go to the polls. Indeed, as testimonies by democratic rights activists and independent poll observers bear out, elections in the state, under the circumstances, were not the medium by which the *adivasis* of the Bastar region in Chhattisgarh expressed their consent to or discontent with the existing regime.[9] In both Kashmir and Chhattisgarh, despite successfully conducted elections, and installation of governments on the basis of majority votes, the political crisis continues.

Development for Whom: Procedural Subversions

If elections remain an inadequate and insufficient measure of democracy, what about the protective laws which affirm *adivasi* ownership and control over their resources? In states like Chhattisgarh where special constitutional provisions pertaining to Scheduled Areas apply, laws like Panchayat Extension into Scheduled Areas (PESA, 1996) and Forest Rights Act (FRA, 2006) provide the frameworks for participation in matters relating to ownership, transfer and use of community resources. The PESA was expected to protect the control of the *adivasi* population over their land and prevent indiscriminate acquisition of land by the state by providing for a system of participation whereby tribal land could be acquired only through a process eliciting their consent. Under PESA, state laws have to be in consonance with 'customary law, social and religious practices and traditional management practices of community resources'. The approval of the Gram Sabha is imperative for plans, programmes and projects of social and economic development.

Interestingly, under the contemporary development discourse, Chhattisgarh is being projected as being on the course of rapid industrialisation, as the largest producer of thermal power, cement and sponge iron in the country. Industrialisation involves largescale acquisition of agricultural and forest land and dispossession of the *adivasi* population in the state. Ironically, the acquisition of land is done following procedures under the PESA, giving it a façade of democratic decision making, and the *adivasis* are made complicit in their dispossession. Among the most indicting testimonies to this process has come significantly from the government itself. Chapter 4 ('Alienation of Tribal and Dalits Lands') in the voluminous draft report of the Committee on State Agrarian Relations and Unfinished Task of Land Reforms (vol. I) submitted to the Ministry of Rural Development, while identifying the trends toward land alienation in tribal areas of Jharkhand, Orissa and Chhattisgarh, terms it the 'biggest land grab since Columbus'.[10] The two cases discussed below show how, in the context of the securitised development regime in Chhattisgarh, the PESA is subverted to facilitate land acquisition by the state.

In Darrawada village in Raigarh district of Chhattisgarh, the villagers were put through a mandatory public hearing on 17 May 2010 under the PESA for the acquisition of land for a power plant. Held amidst tight security of about 1,500 policemen, the apparent outcome of the hearing was that the villagers had consented to part with their land. The villagers revealed, however, to a fact-finding investigation, that they were coerced into selling their land, in exchange for freedom for imprisoned villagers.[11]

In another incident, a robust Gram Sabha in Premnagar village, located in the vicinity of reserved forest area in the Scheduled Area district of Sarguja, was smothered through its elevation in March 2010 into a Nagar Panchayat. The Gram Sabha had been actively exercising its powers under the PESA by raising objections to the setting up of a coal-based power plant and mines, which would have destroyed around 1,70,04,900 trees and livelihoods of villagers, since 90 per cent of the village depended upon minor forest produce and agriculture. The villagers petitioned the High Court, stating that their constitution into a Nagar Panchayat was done through subterfuge, 'whereby the wide, special and significant powers of the Gram Sabha', as spelt out under the PESA, were taken away 'unconstitutionally and illegally'.[12] Indeed, the documents obtained by the petitioners under the Right to Information (RTI) and placed before the court revealed that the Secretary of Urban Administration and Development had submitted a fabricated resolution of the Gram Sabha and inflated the population figures of the village to allow for its conversion into a Nagar Panchayat, confirming that the decision was taken by 'the political party in power' and was 'connected with the establishment of the Coal based Power Plant, which the Gram Sabha had consistently resisted'.[13]

The November 2010 announcement of the Integrated Action Plan (IAP) by the Cabinet Committee on Economic Affairs for 'quick resolution' of problems concerning healthcare, drinking water, education and roads in selected 'Naxal-hit' districts focuses on 'improvement in governance' and compliance with specific preconditions. These preconditions include 'effective implementation' of the provisions of the PESA 1996 and FRA 2006. It may be recalled that the PESA allowed *adivasi* populations dependent on forests, control over minor forest produce (MFP), and the FRA gave communities the right to manage and conserve these resources. The discussion in the preceding paragraphs shows how a facade of participatory democracy and effective implementation of the PESA can easily be created. Another survey has shown that in some of the 'Naxal-hit' districts, for which the IAP was devised, which have so far been the target of the central government's ₹ 13,000 crore Integrated Development Package, the states have continued to retain control over MFPs through their respective forest departments.[14]

Conclusion

This article argues that more often than not, studies exploring the register of democracy as a constituent element of the modern state in India remain confined to electoral democracy. Debates and discussions about the success or limits of democracy then become restricted to achievements of Indian democracy in terms of holding periodic elections and the institutional ensemble that enables peaceful transitions of political regimes. The transitions themselves are unpacked and measured in terms of voter turnouts, vote shares and seats won. The effects of the governance register on democracy is explored with less confidence and zeal. More often than not, it is seen as lying in the domain of activism, devoid and divested of academic rigour. This article has shown that the power and rule aspects of the state erode the democratic structures in ways which may not be captured by the stability/success of electoral democracy models. Electoral democracy may in practice occlude concerns of substantive democracy and studies of electoral democracy may not identify substantive concerns in their preoccupation with numbers.

Specific examples of Kashmir and Chhattisgarh have shown that in order for electoral democracy to not become a substitute for a democratic state, it is important not to conceptualise the registers of democracy/rights/justice and governance/power/rule as two contradictory registers which run parallel to each other, but as registers which in practice interlock and often produce effects which are undemocratic. A search for the democratic state in India is precisely a quest towards the unraveling of its rule register and looking for possibilities of making it correlate and correspond with the democratic register.

Notes

1. The 'reason of state' advocates the exercise of unrestricted panoply of measures by the state when faced with existential challenges. Carl J. Friedrich suggests that 'reasons of state' are *considerations*, which exist 'whenever it is required to insure [that] the survival of the state must be done by the individuals responsible for it, no matter how repugnant such an act may be to them in their private capacity as decent and moral men' (1957).
2. The state, according to Manoranjan Mohanty, is the political organisation of society, the organisation of power at the societal level (1982).
3. The ruling practices of the post-colonial state made themselves manifest through a duality of processes, involving overt coercion and repression, as well as through the state's developmental role (Mohanty 1989).
4. See Annual Report 2008–2009, departments of Internal Security, States, Home, Jammu and Kashmir Affairs and Border Management, Ministry of Home Affairs, Government of India, Delhi, 2009, pp. 16–17. The Chhattisgarh government increased the police budget for the fiscal year

2010–2011 by 17 per cent to 'strengthen law and order' and 'combat red terror in the country's worst Naxal-infested state', proposing a new police district at the diamond rich Gariaband, where 'the administration spotted the movement of naxalites' (*Business Standard* 2010). The security forces in the region include the paramilitary police such as the IRBs and the CRPF. According to a December 2007 report of the Ministry of Home Affairs, 13 battalions of central paramilitary forces were deployed in Chhattisgarh, a substantial bulk of which is stationed in Dantewada and Bijapur districts. The numbers have increased substantially since then. In November 2010, the Cabinet Committee on Economic Affairs approved an Integrated Action Plan (IAP) in 60 selected 'Naxal-hit' districts, involving a grant of ₹ 25 crore each, for 'quick resolution of problems concerning healthcare, drinking water, education and roads' (*The Hindu* 2010).

5. The Border Roads Organisation traditionally deployed in frontier areas has been deployed to build roads in this region, alongside the proliferation of highly specialised and special police units (which go by threatening names like Greyhound in Andhra Pradesh, Alpha Hawks in Maharashtra and Cobra in other states) and the paramilitary/state police/armed constabulary (as in the Operation Greenhunt in Chhattisgarh).

6. Indicating a process of normalisation of extraordinary laws, the UAPA has become a receptacle for laws which have been forced into disuse due to political/democratic pressure (e.g., POTA). The UAPA has elaborate procedures for declaring political organisations 'unlawful' and 'terrorist', and electronic surveillance, without the procedural safeguards that existed in the repealed POTA (Singh 2007).

7. Translated from the Gondi language, *salwa judum* means 'purification hunt'. The Salwa Judum had its precursors in sporadic *jan jagaran abhiyans*, which were then enforced as a compulsory campaign by the government. See Sundar (2007: 277). The Salwa Judum, which emerged in the state in 2005, was presented as 'a real Gandhian movement' by K. P. S. Gill, Security Advisor to the Chhattisgarh government, and by the state government as a 'spontaneous peace movement' of the people against the Maoists. The Salwa Judum unfolded as a government-supported and by some accounts enforced (through local leaders and police) civilian organisation which accompanied the security forces in arson and forcible evacuation of villages. Fact-finding investigations and academic works on Chhattisgarh have shown that the Salwa Judum used violent intimidation methods, resulting in massive forced internal displacement. Two petitions, *Nandini Sundar and Others v. State of Chhattisgarh*, 2007 and *Kartma Joga and Others vs. State of Chhattisgarh and Union of India*, 2007, have been filed in the Supreme Court seeking its intervention against the Salwa Judum operation and a rehabilitation plan for the region. An order was delivered by Justices B. Sudershan Reddy and Surinder Singh Nijjar, on 5 July 2011, in *Nandini Sundar and Others vs. the State of Chhattisgarh* directing the Chhattisgarh government to disarm SPOs, and confine their use only to functions specified under

section 23 of the Chhattisgarh Police Act 2007, which did not include armed combat. About a month later the central government moved the Supreme Court for a review/recall of its order on the ground that the order was against the spirit of the constitution, violated the principle of separate powers, and would have an adverse impact upon the government's anti-naxal operations in various states as well as the fight against militants in Jammu and Kashmir and the northeastern states of India.

8. Noorani (2002).
9. A PUCL Chhattisgarh team along with Nandini Sundar visited Dantewada district where a poll boycott had been called by the CPI(ML) People's War, on 20 April 2004, which was the polling day. The team visited seven villages on a randomly selected basis in Konta, and three notified polling stations Kolaiguda (118), Gachanpalli (119) and Pentapad (67). In none of these polling stations did the team find any evidence of polling booths or agents.
10. Draft Report 2009.
11. Chhattisgarh's industrial jungle, *Down to Earth*, 15 September 2010, http://www.downtoearth.org.in/node/1862, accessed 20 September 2010.
12. Writ Petition no. 6872/2010 against the 30 July 2009 notification consti- tuting village Premnagar into a Nagar Panchayat under the Chhattisgarh Municipalities Act, 1961, by members of the erstwhile Gram Sabha of village Premnagar in the Scheduled Area district of Sarguja. I am grateful to Sudha Bhardwaj from Chhattisgarh for drawing my attention to this petititon, and making a copy available to me.
13. Ibid.
14. A survey by *Down to Earth* of the 33 worst-affected districts in eight states (Chhattisgarh, Jharkhand, Madhya Pradesh, Bihar, Orissa, Uttar Pradesh, Bihar, Maharashtra), which have some of the poorest areas in the country, and are the richest in forest and MFP, shows that none of these states have implemented the provisions pertaining to MFPs under PESA. The data which is till September–October 2010 for all states except Chhattisgarh, for which the data is till December 2009, shows that the state governments have sought to retain control over MFPs through the Van Suraksha Samitis under the forest departments (as in Andhra Pradesh), dragged their feet over transfer of ownership to Gram Sabhas (as in Jharkhand), have not implemented the PESA (as in Maharashtra) or denied the panchayats, control over MFPs by making the PESA subject to state laws (as in Orissa). Incidentally, while the MFPs are a much sought after resource with over 10 million *adivasis* dependent on them for survival, the Forest Department's revenue from MFPs is steadily increasing. See 'Red Flag', *Down to Earth*, 1–15 November 2010, http://www.downtoearth.org.in, accessed 20 November 2010.

References

Alam, Javeed. 2004. *Who Wants Democracy?* Delhi and Hyderabad: Orient Longman.

Baxi, Upendra. 2005. 'The (Im)possibility of Constitutional Justice', in Zoya Hasan, E. Sridharan and R. Sudarsan (eds) *India's Living Constitution*. Delhi: Permanent Black.

———. 2000. 'Postcolonial Legality', in Henry Schwarz and Sangeeta Ray (eds), *A Companion to Postcolonial Studies*. Malden, MA: Blackwell.

Chatterjee, Partha. 2010. 'The State', in Niraja Gopal Jayal and Pratap Bhanu Mehta (eds), *Companion Volume to Politics in India*. New Delhi: Oxford University Press.

Friedrich, Carl J. 1957. 'Constitutional Reason of State — The Survival of the Constitutional Order', 4–5.

Gross, Oren. 2001. 'Cutting Down Trees: Law Making Under the Shadow of Great Calamities', in Ronald D. Daniels, Patrick Macklem and Kent Roach (eds), *The Security of Freedom*. Toronto: University of Toronto Press.

Hindu, The. 2010. 'Action Plan for 60 Naxal Hit Districts'. 27 November.

Jayal, Niraja Gopal. 2006. *Representing India: Ethnic Diversity and the Governance of Public Institutions*. New York: Palgrave Macmillian.

———. 2007. 'The Role of Civil Society', in Sumit Ganguly, Larry Diamond and Marc F. Plattner (eds), *The State of India's Democracy*. Baltimore: Johns Hopkins University Press.

Jayal, Niraja Gopal and Pratap Bhanu Mehta (eds). 2010. *The Companion Volume to Politics in India*. New Delhi: Oxford University Press.

Kaviraj, Sudipta. 1984. 'On the Crisis of Political Institutions in India', *Contributions to Indian Sociology*, 18 (2). July–December.

———. 1998. 'A Critique of Passive Revolution', *Economic and Political Weekly*, 23 (45/47), Special Number, pp. 2429–44. November.

———. 2000. 'Democracy and Social Inequality', in Francine Frankel et.al. (eds), *Transforming India: Social and Political Dynamics of Democracy*. New Delhi: Oxford University Press.

———. 2003. 'A State of Contradictions: The Post-colonial State in India', in Quentin Skinner and Bo Strath (eds), *State and Citizens: History, Theory, Prospects*. Cambridge: Cambridge University Press.

Kothari, Rajni. 1970. *Caste in Indian Politics*. Delhi: Orient Longman.

Lyngdoh, James Michael. 2004. *Chronicle of an Impossible Election*. Delhi.

Mohanty, Manoranjan. 1982. 'The Contemporary State, An Outline', *Teaching Politics*, VIII Nos. (1 & 2).

———. 1989. 'Duality of the State Process in India: A Hypothesis', *Bharatiya Samajik Chintan*, XII (1–2). March–June.

Morris-Jones, W. H. 1964. *The Government and Politics of India*. London: Hutchinson.

Mouffe, Chantal. 2000. *The Democratic Paradox*. London and New York: Verso.

Noorani, A. G. 2002. 'One-horse Race', *Hindustan Times*. 28 May.

Rudolph, Lloyd and Susanne Rudolph. 1967. *The Modernity of Tradition: Political Development in India*. Chicago: University of Chicago Press.

Singh, Ujjwal Kumar. 2004. *Institutions and Democratic Governance: A Study of the Election Commission and Electoral Governance in India*, Monograph no. 9. New Delhi: Nehru Memorial Museum & Library.

———. 2007. *The State, Democracy and Anti-Terror Laws in India*. New Delhi: Sage Publications.

Sundar, Nandini. 2007. *Subalterns and Sovereigns: An Anthropological History of Bastar (1854–2006)* 2nd edn. New Delhi: Oxford University Press.

Yadav, Yogendra. 2000. 'Which Reforms? Whose Democracy? A Plea for a Democratic Agenda of Electoral Reforms', in Subhash Kashyap, D. D. Khanna and Gert W. Kueck (eds), *Reviewing the Constitution?* Delhi: Shipra Publications.

Government Reports

'Annual Report 2008–09'. 2009. Departments of Internal Security, States, Home, Jammu and Kashmir Affairs and Border Management, Ministry of Home Affairs. New Delhi: Government of India.

'Unfinished Task of Land Reforms' (vol. I). 2009. Draft report of the Committee on State Agrarian Relations and Unfinished Task of Land Reforms submitted to the Ministry of Rural Development.

12

Reproduction, Contestation and the Struggle for a Just Education in India

Padma Velaskar

Education was perceived as a key player by the liberal, democratic Indian state in pursuance of its modernist project. Of the multiple roles assigned to it in terms of economic, political and cultural modernisation, it is education's role as a vehicle of equality and justice that proved most contentious in the nation's colonial and post-colonial educational history. This was understandable given the historical relationship between educational exclusion and caste-feudal patriarchy and the elitist, segmented character of indigenous education. The colonial system, unequal and unevenly spread, was skewed in favour of elite society. It made sense in terms of a colonial logic of cultural imperialism and distorted capitalist penetration. While inheriting this system, the post-colonial, sovereign Indian state claimed commitment to an opposing ideology — using education as the chief instrument of ending invidious caste, gender, tribe and ethnic inequalities and injustice. What has unfolded over the 60 years of post-colonial experience of pursuing the political agenda of educational equality and justice, is a complex social history of educational expansion and an equally complex social impact. As is obvious, egalitarian goals have only been partially fulfilled. Spectacular educational achievements coexist with glaring under-achievements and failures, the most persistent being that of fulfilling even the minimalist constitutional goal of universalising elementary education.

Currently, the educational scenario is further complicated by the entry of global capitalism in the Indian political economy and the rise of cultural majoritarian forces that render the social fabric more fragile. In the new liberalised context, education has come to hold greater importance as an economic resource for the state, economy and the individual. A new dynamism and soaring educational aspirations are matched by unprecedented levels of demand and supply and of intense competitiveness. In a rapidly changing economic and political scenario, there is a greater consciousness about the benefits of education among the poorest. At the same time, the older state discourse of equality and justice is muted by competing discourses of market choices and new claims about quicker attainment of the goal of growth with equity under a liberalised economy. As multiple players representing diverse interests have entered into the educational field, there is explosion of activities and conflicting assessments of progress. This has obscured the actual picture.

Patterns of educational distribution and attainment reflect rampant gender, caste, class, tribe and ethnic inequalities. To understand the educational situation it is important to undertake structural analyses that links state, society and the education system. Political economists and critical theorists from a range of disciplinary and multi-disciplinary perspectives have analysed the education systems in western and other societies. Drawing basically from political economy and critical sociological perspectives that view education as part of economic and ideological configuration (Apple 1982), this is a preliminary exploration of the Indian schooling system as a social and cultural enterprise. While the article underlines education as a significant avenue of justice in India, it also explores its impact from the point of view of those most affected by state failure: India's subordinated classes, with a focus on Dalits and Dalit girls. Overall the scenario is marked by reproduction, change, conflict and contradiction. The dominant reality is that of reproduction of structures of caste, class and gender inequality which reveals the limits of education as an instrument of social justice.

Reproduction is a major organising idea informing socialist theories that were developed in advanced capitalist societies. To avoid mechanistic determinisms, ideas of resistance and opposition have entered the critique of schools. I have drawn upon these ideas and adapted them to analyse the Indian educational situation (Giroux 1983). The key issue underlying the theories is that of power, its different but overlapping dimensions of economic, cultural and state power and how education mediates the three. Close links exist between state, capitalist economy and schooling which reproduce socio-cultural orders, divisions of labour, dominant forms of knowledge and ideologies and capitalist relations of production. As the main funder and provider of education, centrality is accorded to the role of the State. Education contributes to cultural reproduction and to the reproduction of the structure of power relations and symbolic relations between the dominated and subordinated. Feminist critique has enlarged the scope of these theories to take account of women and sexual divisions of labour that are embedded in capitalist relations and has emphasised the stultifying role of patriarchal ideology in excluding women and denying them equal opportunities (Althusser 1971; Apple 1982, 1985, 2000; Bourdieu and Passeron 1977; Giroux 1983; Sharp 1980; Wolpe 1978).

Education does all this in India in distinct structurally and culturally specific ways. There is a need to examine the relevance of this powerful set of ideas and develop our own perspectives. State and societal stratification operating through two dominant arms of the economic and the political are key agents of reproduction of educational advantage and disadvantage and the social relations of domination and subordination. The article explores the roles of state and private capital in Indian education. It examines the implications of state educational policy and provision from an egalitarian perspective, locating both in the wider political economy and socio historic context. Little attention has been given to the role of the private schooling system in shaping the ethos and structuring of the schooling system. The inegalitarianism and domination inherent in it, its implications and consequences, outlining the systemic aspects that militate against the subordinated are issues that are rarely analysed. Together, both state and the private sector legitimise the reproduction of educational and social inequality.

Education has been both a contested site and an instrument of struggle against caste and gender domination in Indian society. The paper explores resistance and struggle posed by the Dalits of India to contest their exclusion, discrimination and hegemony. In the light of a brief discussion of systemic changes brought about under the impact of economic liberalisation, it concludes that nothwithstanding the attainment of education based mobility by Dalits, their continued struggles for mobility and their widespread political consciousness, the role of education is likely to be largely reproductive of old and new structures of inequality.

Role of the State in Education and the Development of Educational Structures

A theory of the Indian state would be critical to understanding the role of the state and political processes with respect to state control of education, and the development of educational structures. The Indian State has been variously characterised as capitalist, dualist or elitist (Kaviraj 1997; Mohanty 1990). The bureaucracy of the Nehruvian state by virtue of class and caste background was unresponsive to welfare tasks. Powerful societal groups of business, rich peasantry, managerial and bureaucratic classes and organised working class turned redistributive ideas into mere rhetoric (Kaviraj 1997). In post-Nehruvian times, a new political class of bureaucrats and political professionals had even less interest in social reform and traded electoral support for the private use of state resources.

The formation of state policy and action in education can be located in the phenomenon of the duality of state in which forces of capitalism, state authority and coercion, techno-managerial system pursuing non-secular policies coexisted with welfare and democratisation (Mohanty 1990). In this context education policy reflected dualism — it was a response to dominant as well as newly emergent groups in society. I wish here to develop the idea that reproduction takes place through state intervention, primarily through the politics of exclusion, weak inclusion and vertical segregation of the subordinated at the bottom of a hierarchical system. Three distinct processes are at work:

(a) elitist policy that overemphasises educational needs of a modernised urban industrial economy at the expense of rural or social goals;
(b) state sponsored exclusion through non-provision, under-provision and non-implementation of programmes and schemes in favour of the subordinated; and
(c) ignoring caste, gender and other forms of discrimination in state schools.

Recognising that there is a reciprocally determining relation between structure of state apparatus and nature of policies is useful (Kaviraj 1997). As an aspiring democratic capitalist–developmental state, the new nation defined development in terms of capitalist transformation of rural economy and rise of urban-industrial society. Educational expansion was geared to scientific and technological knowledge development, political and cultural modernisation and development of a skilled labour force. The egalitarian agenda was circumscribed to only mean a constitutional 'promise' to educate all children up to 14 years, with an obligation to promote with 'special care' the educational interests of the weaker sections. The compensatory principle which is underscored by notions of justice, fairness, restitution and reparation was applied rather frugally to elementary education, amounting to meagre state allocations of finances and facilities in order to compensate for centuries of oppression and educational exclusion.

The first educational policy (1968) incorporated a strong egalitarian perspective in the policy imperative of a common school system. However, in the absence of any financial, curricular or pedagogic commitments it remained merely on paper. It evoked overt political endorsement but stiff resistance in practice. It was both politically inexpedient and socially repugnant to a caste- and status-conscious society (Naik 1982). Clearly, state policy embodied the exclusive and exclusionary interests of dominant elites. Both policy and patterns of implementation revealed themselves as prime expression of the dominant cultural world-view and provided firm ground for the advance of education's role as a social reproducer in the evolving capitalist social formation that also accommodated pre-capitalist formations.

Educational policy in contemporary times is shaped world-wide by neoliberal ideologies and economic agendas of global capitalism. In India, the 'New Education Policy' of 1986 was the harbinger of neoliberalism in education — a fact that went relatively unnoticed at the time was the ideological shift from the commitment to equal opportunity to the new principle of equity. In an antithesis to notions of socialist collectivism of Nehruvian times and varied populisms of post-Nehruvian era, neoliberalism spelt a celebration of self-interested individualism and a conscious turn against the ideal of social justice. Synchronising with the opening up of markets, the decade of the 1990s saw a major redefinition of relations between state, market and schools (Velaskar 2010).

As we shall see below, state policy continues to keep the education system connected to structures of caste, class and gender.

Exclusion through Non-provision and Under-provision

The state holds a pre-eminent position as the main provider, financer, regulator and controller of education and monitors its growth and development (Dale 1989). In India, patterns of state provision and social cultural factors associated with historical patterns of educational diffusion have not been matters of serious study. The basic significance of equitable provision was highlighted in the context of less developed societies having multiple bases of social inequality (Foster 1977). The first task for the Indian state was to extend elementary schooling and overturning colonial under provision and create an expansive public education system. Given the massive regional, caste, class, gender and tribe inequalities, it had to be a gigantic effort. The state was also confronted with providing for neglected regions and populations — subordinate classes, rural areas, Dalit, interior and tribal-dominated areas. These were huge collectivities that were outside the fold of formal education. However, in the context of a capitalist political economy of state funding, the pace of expansion of schools for the poor remained slow and stilted. The state itself paved the way for a politics of exclusion.

Today, the reality of under-provision continues to be serious. Patterns of expansion have reproduced imbalances and unevenness (interstate and regional) in the diffusion of schooling. The shortfalls that exist are found particularly in but are not confined to Bihar, Madhya Pradesh, Rajasthan and Uttar Pradesh (BIMARU) states that have experienced pathetically slow and unsatisfactory educational expansion.[1] Under largely feudal set-ups and conditions of economic backwardness underscored by slow transition to industrialisation, rural masses were largely engaged in peasantry, artisan production and farm and non-farm labour. Patterns of utilisation were characterised for long stretches in the post-colonial period by poor enrolment and high dropout rates. Low-caste and class households were resigned to family-taught labour and production skills useful in caste and gender-based divisions of labour in rural and urban economies. In the BIMARU states, given the magnitude of economic developmental and political neglect, the state obligation to educate all children receded to the background. Consequently, a strong association between caste, economic deprivation, gender practices and school dropout persists. A new state policy in the mid-1980s underscored a commitment to equity and adopted a targeted approach to Dalits, tribals and girls but continued to provide quantitatively inadequate and qualitatively inferior education to them and and ignored the specific needs of girls belonging to these communities. Thus while expansion of government schooling led to a shift from mass exclusion to mass inclusion, it has been an incredibly delayed, weak and highly discriminatory inclusion (Velaskar 2005). Pressures and demands by the subordinated groups and their political representatives have impelled only meagre and grudging state action.

The dynamics of educational provision is a phenomenon that needs explanation both structurally and politically. A theory of the workings of the federal structure of the Indian state and its relation to education decision making and governance is critical to understanding political dynamics of state control and the development of local educational systems. It has been argued that the Nehruvian state was overruled in post-Nehruvian times by a new political class of bureaucrats and political professionals with little interest in social reform. Politicians and politically ambitious and socio-economically dominant groups gained local control of public resources and used them for private gain (Kaviraj 1997). The history of educational expansion has been marked by politicians capturing educational resources to advance personal, party and partisan politics and also advance the fortunes of ethno classes based on caste status and other cultural identities and economic wealth (Rudolph and Rudolph 1972). The state of Uttar Pradesh is a revealing case in point. In the course of their analysis of Uttar Pradesh 'burden of inertia', J. Dréze and H. Gazdar attribute the failure of public service delivery of education to lack of public accountability and low commitment and value to education. However, they also touch upon a range of factors — poverty, distorted spending, women's low status, poor teaching management, caste politics and factionalism that reflect the complex of structural forces at work (Dréze and Gazdar 1997).

Today, under the imperatives of structural adjustment, there is global pressure for withdrawal of public funds from the social sector. The new dispensation has given rise to a new expansionism which is driven by parallel pressures to achieve globally defined targets. The state-school system continues to expand but it now comprises 'alternate' learning centres, under-resourced and under-equipped. Moreover, the state now invokes NGO outreach partnerships with the private sector and an amorphous 'community' support to fulfil functions which its own massive educational machinery has hitherto failed to perform. A number of studies have testified to abysmal teaching–learning conditions prevailing in the worsening state system.[2]

The 'Power and Ideology'[3] of Private Schooling

A crucial part of state policy is the facilitation of a private sector which, under state control, not only enjoys considerable autonomy but exercises considerable power and ideological influence over the entire system. Charged with provision of elementary and higher education, the state left secondary education almost completely to private initiative — an established provider during colonial times. Unable to fulfil the demand for western education, the middle and upper classes, encouraged by colonial grants-in-aid policy, set up their own schools. The trend began in big cities and towns and was emulated in smaller towns (Kamat 1985). In the post-independence period, the 'private' sector both aided and unaided grew steadily under a benevolent state and perhaps contributed to the decline of the state system. The processes of expansion and provision accommodated significant elitist economic class as well as ethno-class interests based on religion, language, regional and caste identities, the latter encouraged by the policy of minority rights in education. Class interests converge more often than not with ethnic ones. Private enterprise in education thus comprises well-defined sectional and sectarian ideological interests and the private sphere displays a remarkable inter-institutional cultural diversity. The systemic outcome is the institutionalisation of horizontally and vertically stratified schooling systems of multiple tiers that mirror local systems of class, status and caste/ethnic privilege and hereditary social honour (Velaskar 1990).

Though there has historically existed and continues to exist a socially conscious educational entrepreneurship, private schooling is predominantly driven by sectarian interests rather than by public purpose or public obligation to egalitarianism. It is the

economically and politically powerful who can operate successfully as education entrepreneurs or managers.[4] The private sector,
especially its most elite segments, exercise tremendous political
clout and social influence and impact on shaping the ethos of the
national education system.

Schooling systems are important avenues for the promotion
of dominant status cultures (Collins 1971). The cultural ethos of
private schools selects, reflects and teaches carefully developed
caste, class, religious values, aesthetic tastes, language, cultural
symbols and practices, etiquette and manner. Official curricula are
contextualised in and imparted through informal and hidden
curriculum shaped by these ethnic cultures. Knowledge, values,
norms, thought and beliefs are largely in consonance with home/
community/caste cultural/ethnic backgrounds and expectations of
children and their parents and draw upon their cultural resources
and repertoires.[5] Since cultural preservation and protection of cultural identity is the important driving force behind a social group's
desire to establish schools, cultural transmission and perpetua-
tion are important aims. State-prescribed/sanctioned curricula
are defined and redefined to accommodate secular discourses of
citizenship and economic lifestyles within a religio-cultural school
ethos.

Despite the diversity which camouflages the cultural cleavages
produced by an ethnically marked school system, there is also an
underlying homogeneity and unity brought about by common
class interests which the private schools hold in the capitalist job
market. There is tremendous competition between and within
the schools to secure and consolidate highest and best market
credentials as well as secure access for their wards to prestigious
branches of higher and professional education. Private schools,
bolstered by the parallel institution of the coaching class, share
values, assumptions and beliefs that sustain inequality and capitalist logic and do little to challenge social stereotypes and preju-
dices that act as very real, if invisible, unifying forces against the
subordinated sections.

The entire system works as a force of social segregation,
cultural boundary maintenance and ethno-centric ideas, providing
spaces for the ideologies of caste hierarchy and cultural difference
if not communal antagonism, and for the construct of culturally
specific masculinities and femininities that continue to restrain

the girls. Even as it waves the flag of universalism and meritoc-racy, the power and ideology of private schooling provides the space to avoid unwanted groups and/or enforce 'consent' of 'outsiders'. Schools, both state and private, are not the democratic equal arenas that it was hoped they would be. The elite private sector is openly exclusionary and adopts stringent selection processes to make it totally exclusive. However, even in the middle rungs of state and state-aided schools that draw a diverse class and socio-cultural representation, several mechanisms of exclusion, discrimination and domination operate in social relations, organisational and classroom practice and curricular forms. Caste, class, religion, language and gender powerfully shape everyday life of schools, through cultural rituals and common-sense meanings. The pro-cesses can have visceral emotional, cognitive and pedagogic effects on children of subordinated and minority communities (NCERT 2005).[6]

Stratified Education and its Implications for Justice

Evidently, the combined effect of state neglect of education and a vibrant private sector with different ideological persuasions and educational motivations stratifies schools, children, curriculum, pedagogy, the teaching–learning process and teachers. The hierarchical system with the 'best' schools at the top and 'worst' at the bottom corresponds roughly but definitively to societal caste-class and ethnic formations. It is a key mechanism of reproduc-tion of educational advantage and disadvantage (Velaskar 1990). Largely based on age-old principles of ascription, particularism, exclusion and closure, it permits privileged access to the most economically and socially rewarded education to elite minorities of economically and culturally powerful and ensures safe and exclusive passage of their cultural capitals which are the ones that count in elite higher and professional education and elite job markets. The real underlying ideology is of non-meritocratic ascription which is acceptable in a political culture that is marked by hierarchy, patronage and corruption.

In contemporary times the combined impact of political con-sciousness, economic liberalisation, class differentiation and new state educational policies has accentuated caste, class, caste and gender divisions and fuelled mobility aspirations of all, including hitherto excluded groups. As the stratification system gets more complex, each new emergent stratum is fitted into an educational subsystem which gets increasingly differentiated to accommodate them. The undercutting of the state system has entailed a new commercial private sector catering to the needs of the growing middle classes as well as of less well-off sections who can muster up the purchasing power. Its scale of operation and patterns of geographic spread are linked to demand. The impact of new privatisation initiated under state liberalisation can be felt across the system. The middle class has bloated with greater affordability among newly better-off and mobility-seeking sections of the middle and lower middle classes which also includes those from subordinated groups. For the poorest and most marginalised is reserved the expanded but impoverished and dysfunctional system of state schooling. They are the prime victims of state withdrawal.[7] The overall outcome is the further differentiation of the school system and greater polarisation of the systemic hierarchy. It also needs emphasis that unfettered privatisation facilitates easy entry of neo-right elements into the system. Increasingly, Hindutva forces are succeeding in establishing upper-caste cultural and religious hegemony in schools.[8] However, contestations from below attempt to pose challenges to this hegemony.

Contestations from Below

Education emerged as an instrument of resistance and contestation in the context of emancipatory struggles which broke out of the contradictions generated by colonial rule. Subaltern ideologies of low-caste and Dalit protest saw in education a powerful weapon that could fulfil social transformation goals. Though the movements encompassed varied ideological strands, goals and strategies, they shared a common faith in education and it emerged as a powerful force in Dalit liberation.[9] Thus was forged a symbiotic relation between education struggles and liberation ones, both energising each other. Significantly, education was redefined as a critical material and cultural resource that would help challenge the hierarchical structure of the caste Hindu social order and Brahminical hegemony and enable a shift from hereditary, stigmatised, caste-ascribed social positions to new positions, identities and selves based on self-respect and dignity. In the context of Dalit movements, not only was there demand

and struggle for education but also an attempt to infuse education with a new radical political purpose and meanings that contested dominant meanings and carved out alternate ideologies. In general, education was to serve as a mode of self-recovery.

Defined thus, the pursuit of education turned the field into an arena of conflict. At first, missionaries and Hindu reformers vied for Dalit patronage and initiated them into modern formal education as a means of 'social uplift'. Later the Dalits themselves, including Dalit women, engaged in various types of educational struggles that revolved around the issue of access to the existing system, and combated caste prejudice and hostility. Segregation was a key feature of the colonial system and separate schools were set up by the state for the depressed classes as a result of intensified demand.[10] Soon Dalits made valiant efforts to start their own schools and succeeded in doing so to a limited extent, with the help of funding by the state as well as their own caste people who had achieved some economic affluence (Yagati 2002; Zelliot 2002).[11] Education provided a much needed focus for autonomous and meaningful activity for the common people in pursuit of an agenda of liberation and equality. Educational awareness and struggle became an integral part of the processes of political conscientisation and struggle.

With the arrival of Dr Babasaheb Ambedkar, the movement for Dalit liberation acquired a radical edge. In this context, the liberating purpose of education was further clarified and sharpened. Ambedkar emphasised the importance of education in creating a moral and social conscience and saw it as a means of rejecting and overcoming inferior ascribed status and equipping Dalits intellectually and morally to wrest power. Thus, for Ambedkar, higher education was of critical significance in the battle to end social slavery and to create, among Dalits, to quote his words, 'the consciousness of the significance of their lives for themselves and their country'.

In the post-independence period, education continues to command powerful counter-symbolic and substantive value as a liberating tool. Ambedkar's slogan — 'Educate, Agitate, Organise' — continues to exert a huge inspirational and motivational impact on people's consciousness. The symbolic and substantive value of education is embodied in the very persona of Ambedkar who serves as the ultimate role model (Velaskar 1998). While the pursuit of political power is the main strategy for Dalit liberation, for common Dalits education is structurally the main source of change in social location and status. The post-independence era has seen resilient efforts and caste conflicts over the issue of the implementation of positive discrimination policy in education. While the multiple effects of educational advance registered by the Dalits may remain largely intangible, it is apparent that education has brought about changes in social class and status as well as carved out new politico-cultural spaces and new positive identities and forms of consciousness. This has happened among both Dalit men and women. However, barring a few regions and caste groups there exists marked gender disparity in Dalit educational attainment as a majority of Dalit girls are subject to a secondary familial and community status.

The Ambedkar legacy is evident in continuing expressions of protests and cultural politics, efforts towards cultural emancipation, self-conscious rejections of hegemonic discourse and practice and the rise of organic intellectuals who search for alternative paradigms of justice and emancipation. It is difficult to imagine that this would have happened on a scale and intensity that it did without the spread of education (Velaskar 1998). Educated Dalit leadership plays important role in processes of cultural challenge, setting new parameters and engaging in new politics of liberation that constructs varied emboldened collective agendas and self-image. Dalit literary work has revolutionised regional and national literary scenes. As they gave critical expressions to subordinations and humiliations of the past, they now provide wide-ranging cultural critiques, conceptions of alternate modernities with sophisticated dimensions that include self-criticism and self-protest. Economically, educational advance has paid off as evident in significant levels of horizontal and vertical occupational and social mobility.

In Conclusion: Reproduction and Contestation in Neoliberal Times

The article has attempted an exploration of how power relations operating within the domains of economy, polity and society/community have shaped and interacted with the schooling system to create and reinforce educational inequality and injustice and the responses the situation has evoked from Dalit subalterns for a just education. Education has played an integral part in furthering the state's programme of redistributive justice. More dominantly, however, its role as a means of social division and control has enlarged multifold. The dominant story is one of persistent inequality and structural reproduction. While education has fetched material and social benefits and is well established as a value among them, the educational battle, fought long and hard by subordinated people, is as yet unfinished.

As the neoliberal state shifts to a new paradigm of economic growth based on free market principles, contemporary patterns of provision seem to hark back to the old order of exclusion and colonial theories of downward filtration. However, the forms of exclusion are new: they exclude through inclusion in expanding but, diminished subsystems of state and private schooling.[12] State-institutionalised practices of education delivery reveal the state's key role in aggravating the dynamics of educational disadvantage based on caste, class and gender. The state is now more openly complicit with the private sector in consolidating the power of economic and cultural capital, of privilege and hegemony. The political philosophy underlying educational expansion has undergone basic shifts; most importantly, education is viewed as a private rather than public good. In the changed milieu, state and private expansionism give the subordinated greater access to the system, but lower the possibility of obtaining an education that would serve the goals of relevance and equitable opportunity. The consequence is a complex pattern of attenuating and widening educational inequalities that needs to be carefully deconstructed.

Thus, we are confronted today not with an unchanging scenario of gross educational deprivation but a new complex intersectional educational social hierarchy of inclusions and exclusions. At its very bottom end, children confront situations of low-grade inclusions, selective exclusions and ejections and self-defined rejections. Their poor educational attainments are not enough to lead the subordinated people out of conditions of economic want and political disadvantage but serve merely to legitimise caste/gendered labour allocation patterns where they are likely to occupy pre-assigned places in poorly paid, exploitative sectors of the informal economy. At best, they gain a foothold in low-security, low knowledge–skills–status segments of the formal. Educational and social destinies of girls within these groups are predominantly determined by patriarchal subordination and exploitation in the institutions of family and economy.

To conclude, this broad sketch of past and present trends suggests that education's role as social and cultural reproducer is being strengthened and its limited capacity to help overcome societal barriers of stratification is being considerably eroded, seriously affecting the life chances of those stuck at the bottom. Indeed, both policy and system serve to freeze educational inequalities and positions of relative advantage and disadvantage at present levels. The neoliberal educational agenda seems designed to accord greater power to the privileged. However, it remains effectively unchallenged and uncontested by ideological agendas and politics from below. On the politico-economic front, capitalist processes have breached economic and cultural divides among the subordinated. And the democratic politics of the day, while bringing political empowerment has not revived the spirit and essence of the Ambedkarian ideology of social democratic transformation. It would need much more than cultural critique to confront and alter the conditions of intersectional inequality and rise of new conservative hegemonies propagated by the market and civil society. There is a need to push for equitable economic and educational agendas and not the panaceas which the state periodically doles out.

Clearly, the education system is being geared to instrumentalist needs of the market and not to meet goals of educational justice or impart empowering knowledge for the majority. 'Democratisation', defined within such confining parameters and assuming the narrow forms that it has, cannot lead to the emergence of truly democratic and egalitarian schools.

Notes

1. BIMARU states, including Bihar, Madhya Pradesh, Rajasthan and Uttar Pradesh, are the bunch of Indian states most backward in terms of human development indicators and suffer from high rates of mortality, fertility, morbidity, undernutrition, illiteracy, slow pace of poverty decline and low levels of non-agricultural employment.
2. See, for example, NCERT (2005); PROBE (1999); Bhatty (1998); Leclercq (2003).

3. The title of this section is adapted from the seminal volume edited by J. Karabel and A. Halsey (1977).
4. For some regional accounts of sectarian and segregated expansion of education in the post-independence period see Rudolph and Rudolph (1972); Kamat (1985); Tharakan (1984); Nagaraju (1998); Jeffery et al. (2005). See also Vaidyanathan and Nair (2001).
5. For accounts of schools as institutions of cultural ideology, identity and power, see Waldrop (2004); Kumar (2000); Talib (1998); Scrase (1993).
6. See note 2.
7. This discussion is based on Velaskar (2010). It draws upon evidence from recent studies: for example NCERT (2005); Vaidyanathan and Nair (2001); Jha and Jhingran (2002); Velaskar (2006).
8. Several studies are now available of RSS schools: see Bakaya (2004); Chaturvedi and Chaturvedi (2004); see also Sundar (2004); Sarkar (1996).
9. Studies include: Gooptu (1996); Jaffrelot (2003); Jeffrey et al. (2008); Khare (1984); Lynch (1969); Pai (2002); Dube (2001: 308); Geetha and Rajadurai (1998).
10. For historical accounts of educational struggles of the Dalits see in particular studies by Eleanor Zelliot, K. Satyanarayana and Chinna Rao Yagati in Bhattacharya (2002); see also Constable (2000); and Velaskar (2007).
11. For specific illustrations of efforts made by Dalits to set up schools see Zelliot (2002) and Yagati (2002); see also Velaskar (1998) and Constable (2002).
12. Recent studies which have established sizeable differentials in educational access and attainment in terms of region, caste, class, religion, gender and tribe include Govinda (2002); Vaidyanathan and Nair (2001); Jha and Jhingran (2002).

References

Althusser, L. 1971. 'Ideological State Apparatuses, Notes towards an Investigation', *Lenin and Philosophy and Other Essays*, pp. 242–73. New Left Books.

Apple, M.W. (ed.). 1982. *Cultural And Economic Reproduction In Education*, pp. 1–31. London: Routledge & Kegan Paul.

———. 1995. *Education and Power*. New York and London: Routledge.

———. 2000. *Official Knowledge Democratic Education in a Conservative Age*. London: Routledge.

Bakaya, A. 2004. 'Lessons from Kurukshetra: The RSS Education Project', in Anne Vaugier-Chatterjee (ed.), *Education and Democracy in India*. New Delhi: Manohar.

Bhatty, K. 1998. 'Education Deprivation in India: A Survey of Field Investigations', *Economic and Political Weekly*, 33 (28): 1858–1869. 11 July.

Bhattacharya, S. 2002. *Education and the Disprivileged: Nineteenth and Twentieth Century India*. Hyderabad: Orient Longman.

Bourdieu, P. and J. Passeron. 1977. *Reproduction in Education, Society and Culture.* London: Sage Publications.

Bowles, S. and H. Gintis. 1976. *Schooling in Capitalist America.* London: Routledge and Kegan Paul.

Carnoy, M. 1974. *Education as Cultural Imperialism.* New York: Longman.

―――. 1982. 'Education, Economy and the State', in Michael Apple (ed.), *Cultural and Economic Reproduction in Education*, pp. 79–126. London: Routledge and Kegan-Paul.

Chaturvedi, J. and G. Chaturvedi (2004). 'Construction of Saraswati: Formation and Transformation of Saffron Identity in Contemporary Uttar Pradesh', in Anne Vaugier-Chatterjee (ed.), *Education and Democracy in India.* New Delhi: Manohar.

Collins, R. 1971. 'Functional and Conflict Theories of Educational Stratification', *American Sociological Review*, 36: 1002–19. December.

Constable, Philip. 2000. 'Sitting on the School Verandah: The Ideology and Practice of Untouchable Educational Protes in Late Nineteenth Century Western India', *The Indian Economic and Social History Review*, 37(4): 383–419.

Dale, R. 1989. *The State and Educational Policy.* Milton Keynes: Open University Press.

Dreze, J. and H. Gazdar. 1997. 'UP: The Burden of Inertia', in J. Dreze and A. Sen (eds), *Indian Development: Selected Regional Perspectives* pp. 33–138. New Delhi: Oxford University Press.

Dube, Saurabh. 2001. *Untouchable Pasts: Religion, Identity, and Power among a Central Indian Community, 1780–1950.* New Delhi: Vistaar.

Foster, P. 1977. 'Education and Social Differentiation in Less-Developed Countries', *Comparative Education Review, Special Issue: The State of the Art*, 21 (2 & 3): 211–29. June–October.

Geetha, V. and S. V. Rajadurai. 1998. *Towards a Non-Brahmin Millennium: From Iyothee Thass to Periyar.* Calcutta: SAMYA.

Giroux, H. 1983. 'Theories of Reproduction and Resistance in the New Sociology of Education: A Critical Analysis', *Harvard Educational Review*, 53 (3): 257–93. August.

Gooptu, N. 1996. 'Caste, Deprivation and Politics: The Untouchables in UP Town in the Early Twentieth Century', in Peter Robb (ed.), *Dalit Movements and the Meaning of Labour.* New Delhi: Oxford University Press.

Govinda, R. (ed.). 2002. *India Education Report: A Profile of Basic Education.* New Delhi: Oxford University Press.

Jaffrelot, C. 2003. *India's Silent Revolution: The Rise of Low Castes in North Indian Politics.* New Delhi: Permanent Black.

Jeffery, R. et al. 2005. 'Social Inequalities and Privatisation of Secondary Schooling in North India', in R. Chopra and P. Jeffery (eds), *Educational Regimes in Contemporary India*, pp. 41–61. New Delhi: Sage.

Jeffrey, Craig, Patricia Jeffery and Roger Jeffery. 2008. *Degrees without Freedom? Education, Masculinities and Unemployment in North India.* Stanford: Stanford University Press.

Jha, J. and D. Jhingran. 2002. *Elementary Education for the Poorest and Other Deprived Groups: The Real Challenge of Universalisation*. New Delhi: Centre for Policy Research.

Kamat, A. R. 1985. *Education and Social Change in India*. Bombay: Somaiya Publications.

Karabel, J. and A. Halsey. 1977. *Power and Ideology in Education*. Oxford: Oxford University Press.

Kaviraj S. 1997. 'The Modern State in India', in Martin R. Doornbos and S. Kaviraj (eds), *Dynamics of State Formation*, pp. 225–50. New Delhi: Sage Publications.

Khare, R. S. 1984. *The Untouchable as Himself: Ideology, Identity and Pragmatism among the Lucknow Chamar*. Cambridge: Cambridge University Press.

Kumar, N. 2000. *Lessons from Schools: The History of Education in Banaras*. New Delhi: Sage.

Leclercq, F. 2003. 'Education Guarantee Scheme and Primary Schooling in Madhya Pradesh', *Economic and Political Weekly*, XXXVIII (19): 1855–1869.

Lynch, O. M. 1969. *The Politics of Untouchability: Social Mobility and Social Change in Cities of India*. New York: Columbia University Press.

Mohanty, Manoranjan. 1990. 'Duality of the State Process in India', in Ghanshyam Shah (ed.), *Capitalist Development Critical Essays*, pp. 149–61. Bombay: Popular Prakashan.

Nagaraju, C. S. 1998. 'Political Economy of Education Development: Karnataka in Historical and Contemporary Perspectives', *Journal of Social and Economic Development*, 1(1): 128–52.

Naik, J. P. 1982. *The Education Commission and After*. New Delhi: A. P. H. Publishing Corporation.

NCERT. 2005. 'Position Paper of National Focus Group on Problems of Scheduled Caste and Scheduled Tribe Children'. New Delhi: NCERT.

Pai, S. 2002. *Dalit Assertion and Unfinished Democratic Revolution: The Bahujan Samaj Party in Uttar Pradesh*. New Delhi: Sage.

PROBE. 1999. *Public Report on Basic Education in India*. New Delhi: Oxford University Press.

Rizvi, F. 1993. 'Critical Introduction: Researching Racism and Education', in B. Troyna (ed.), *Racism and Education: Research Perspectives*, pp. 1–17. Buckingham: Open University Press.

Rudolph, S. and L. Rudolph (eds). 1972. *Education and Politics in India: Studies in Organization, Society, and Policy*. New Delhi: Oxford University Press.

Sarkar, T. 1996. 'Educating the Children of the Hindu Rashtra: Notes on RSS Schools', in P. Bidwai, H. Mukhia and A. Vanaik (eds), *Religion, Religiosity and Communalism*. New Delhi: Manohar.

Scrase, T. J. 1993. *Image, Ideology and Inequality: Cultural Domination, Hegemony and Schooling in India*. New Delhi: Sage.

Sharp, Rachael. 1980. *Knowledge, Ideology and Politics of Schooling: Towards A Marxist Analysis of Education*. London: Routledge and Kegan Paul.

Sundar, N. 2004. 'Teaching to Hate: RSS's Pedagogical Programme', *Economic and Political Weekly*, 39(16): 1605–12.

Tharakan, P. K. M. 1984. 'Socio-economic Factors in Educational Development', *Economic and Political Weekly*, 19(45): 1913–28.

Talib, M. 1998. 'Educating the Oppressed: Observations from a School in a Working Class Settlement in Delhi', in S. Shukla and R. Kaul (eds), *Education, Development and Underdevelopment*, pp. 199–209. New Delhi: Sage.

Troyna, Barry. 1993. 'Racism and Education: Research and Perspectives', *Modern Educational Thought*. Buckingham: Open University Press.

Vaidyanathan, A. and P. R. Gopinathan Nair (eds). 2001. *Elementary Education in Rural India: A Grassroots View*. New Delhi: Sage.

Velaskar, Padma. 1990. 'Unequal Schooling as a Factor in the Reproduction of Social Inequality in India', *Sociological Bulletin*, 39 (1 and 2): 131–146.

———. 1998. 'Ideology, Education and the Political Struggle for Liberation: Change and Challenge Among Maharashtra Dalits', in S. Shukla and R. Kaul (eds), *Education, Development and Underdevelopment*, pp. 210–40. New Delhi: Sage Publications.

———. 2005. 'Educational Stratification, Dominant Ideology and the Reproduction of Disadvantage in India', in S. M. Dahiwale (ed.), *Understanding Indian Society: The Non-Brahmanic Perspective*, pp. 194–220. Jaipur and New Delhi: Rawat Publications.

———. 2006. *Inequality, Opportunity, Emancipation: The Education of Dalit Men and Women in India*, pp. 223–40. New Delhi: IHD Publications.

———. 2007. 'Caste, Gender and Education: Dalit Girls' Access to Schooling in Maharashtra', in J B.G. Tilak (ed.), *Women's Education and Development*. New Delhi: Gyan Publishing House.

———. 2010. 'Quality and Inequality in Indian Education: Some critical Policy Concerns in Contemporary Education Dialogue, 7 (1): 58–93.

Waldrop, A. 2004. 'The Meaning of the Old School-Tie: Private Schools, Admission Procedures and Class Segmentation in New Delhi', in A. Vaugier-Chatterjee (ed.), *Education and Democracy in India*, pp. 203–27. New Delhi: Manohar.

Walters, P. B. 2000. 'The Limits of Growth: School Expansion and School Reform in Historical Perspective', in M. Hallinan (ed.), *Handbook of the Sociology of Education*, pp. 241–61. New York: Kluwer Press.

Wolpe, A. 1978. 'Education and the Sexual Division of Labour', in A. Kuhn and A. Wolpe (eds), *Feminism and Materialism*. London: Routledge and Kegan Paul.

Yagati, Chinna Rao. 2002. 'Education and Identity Formation Among Dalits in Colonial Andhra', in S. Bhattacharya (ed.), *Education and the Disprivileged: Nineteenth and Twentieth Century India*, pp. 84–118. Hyderabad: Orient Longman.

Zelliot, Eleanor. 2002. 'Experiments in Dalit Education: Maharashtra, 1850–1947', in S. Bhattacharya (ed.), *Education and the Disprivileged: Nineteenth and Twentieth Century India*, pp. 35–49. Hyderabad: Orient Longman.

13

Reflexive Education to Re-envision Modernity

Anita Rampal

Ten years after Independence, the Rural Schools Project in South Africa (Nelson Mandela Foundation 2005) had called for a review of how the vision of a new democratic nation had shaped its schooling. In planning the meeting I had inadvertently stirred a hornet's nest. I had wondered why plastic tables and chairs were held in such priority in primary schools, often even at the cost of other pressing needs to ensure better learning. Amidst loud indignation some black educators declared that things they had earlier been deprived of in schools should now be 'rightfully' theirs. How can children write otherwise? It was demeaning and inhuman 'to sit on the floor and write', they proclaimed. Well-meaning emotion, but perhaps somewhat overstated. An interesting debate ensued, and at one point I physically demonstrated how most people in India still sat on the floor cross-legged, even in prestigious political meetings or musical soirees in a posture many westerners paid substantial sums to emulate in their yoga classes! However, the question remained. Why was Africa, the Cradle of Writing, held in deference for its ingenious and imaginative use of papyrus and quill, now finding it demeaning to write without tables and chairs?

Ironically, the words 'culture' or 'identity' in South Africa still carry connotations of the colonial past and apartheid, when 'culture' was used as a marker of colour and 'race'. However, the present seemed defined through markers of another culture — western dress, furniture, architecture, and teaching in the English language (often without comprehension, and mostly through rote) — now translated as 'basic rights' at schools. In India too popular perceptions of the 'quality' of education are tied to similar markers of class and cultural capital. Moreover, the hegemony of globalising aspirations of upwardly mobile urban communities now make it even more difficult for a contemporary 'indigenous' discourse on education to sustain.

The 'indigenous tradition' of schooling had emerged out of alternative educational ideas rooted in the anti-colonial struggles of India and some African countries that challenged 'imported' knowledge, images, values and beliefs. For instance, Mahatma Gandhi and Julius Nyerere both stressed education for self-reliance, equity and rural employment. In the contemporary discourse on education, the indigenous tradition is seen as one that:

(a) reasserts the importance of education's relevance to the socio-cultural circumstances of the nation and the learner;
(b) assures that relevance implies local design of curriculum content, pedagogies and assessment, using learners' rich sources of prior knowledge; and
(c) moves beyond the boundaries of the classroom/school through non-formal and lifelong learning activities (UNESCO 2005: 34).

The Gandhian model of Basic Education (Hindustani Talimi Sangh 1938) called for 'education for life, through life' and used a productive craft — weaving, carpentry, agriculture or pottery — as the *medium* of interdisciplinary hands-on learning in the primary curriculum, with the mother tongue as the medium of instruction. At the upper primary stage the distinction between traditional 'academic' and 'vocational' streams was sought to be reduced through flexible tracks, where science, home science or agricultural science could be placed at par. This matched the anti-colonial agenda for inclusive schools independent of government funding. It also attempted an interrogation of the traditional caste system that stigmatised the 'low castes' and their vocations. Basic Education schools continued to run till after India became independent, but did not receive sustained support from the government and the elites aspired for white-collar employment through 'modern' education.

The decolonising discourse on education saw a historic debate (Bhattacharya 1997) between two major Indian thinkers — Gandhi and Tagore — whose respect for each other refined their differences and enriched the dialogue on development, modernity, nationalism, education, language, science and its domination. Gandhi led the movement of 'non-cooperation' and supported the *swadeshi* (the indigenous) with the boycott of British goods, including British-run schools. Tagore ran his own school but did not support the boycott, and wrote to Gandhi in 1921, that the 'struggle to alienate our heart and mind from those of the West is an attempt at spiritual suicide ... [as indeed] for a long time we have been out of touch with our own culture' (ibid.: 62). However, Gandhi asserted: 'I want the cultures of all the lands to be blown about my house as freely as possible. But I refuse to be blown off my feet by any' (ibid.: 64). Both developed distinct models of indigenous education. Tagore was critical of the centrality of manual work in Gandhi's Basic Education, at the cost of art and aesthetics, and wondered if it amounted to a differentiated education 'doled out in insufficient rations to the poor' (ibid.: 34), who thus gets assigned to a limited place and vocation.

Education and the Modernisation–Indigenisation Dilemma

The historic Gandhi–Tagore engagement reconnects with several contemporary educational debates. Indeed, the curriculum continues to manifest as an ongoing 'complicated conversation' and a 'social and subjective reconstruction', that allows an analysis of 'one's experience of the past and fantasies of the future in order to understand more fully, with more complexity and subtlety, one's submergence in the present' (Pinar 2004: 4). The modernisation–indigenisation dilemma for education continues to reconfigure now in several countries, around differently nuanced curricular dimensions, ranging from the 'developmental–ecological' crisis, 'rational–moral' values, 'academic–everyday' knowledge, 'intellectual–manual' work, English or mother tongue as the medium, to the material–cultural politics of identity (Rampal 2010).

The last Indian Education Commission (GOI 1966) was steered by a majority of male scientists influenced by the spirit of science and education for national development. Educational reconstruction for modernisation was seen as a way to deal with the rapid pace of 'explosion of knowledge', where knowledge itself was to be reconceptualised as not 'passively received' but 'actively discovered'. Traditional learning, 'where the assimilative faculties tend to be emphasised to the neglect of the critical and creative ones' (GOI 1996: Section 1.70), was to be abandoned for modern education, aimed to create a new social order, by awakening curiosity, developing attitudes, values and essential skills for independent study and thinking, befitting responsible democratic citizenship.

The Commission was also influenced by Orientalist thought, which viewed the culture of the West in terms of its science, technology and rationality, as distinct from the culture of spirituality of the East. Nationalist scientists had negotiated 'spirituality' as a means to indigenise the modernisation project, and also to preserve the 'insider' domain of national identity, free from the material 'outsider' domain of colonial sovereignty (Chatterjee 1994). Some had even perceived Indians as children learning to 'suckle the virtues of western science' from the British, who needed to be 'weaned' through qualities of self-reliance instilled by the 'cultivation' of science on their own (Chakravarty 2004). The instrumental Baconian spirit of mastery over nature was sought to be tempered with more humanising forms of knowledge. The Commission cautioned that though modern science had helped man gain mastery over outer space, having neglected knowledge of his own inner self, he faced 'the choice of rolling down a nuclear abyss to ruin and annihilation or of raising himself to new heights of glory and fulfilment yet unimagined' (GOI 1996: Section 1.86). The Commission thus sought an ambivalent synthesis of belief and action, of *ahimsa* (non-violence) and science. It hoped that India could engage in 'reinterpretations and re-evaluations' of its deep fissures of inequality and social injustice, using 'its own cultural resources of compassion, tolerance and spirituality', while it drew upon the new liberalising forces that had emerged in the West with the 'French revolution, the concept of the welfare state, the philosophy of Marx and the rise of socialism'(ibid.: Section 1.77).

The dominant 'western' influence of modernisation theory had called for a 'modern man' as an ideal subject, who could shrug off the burden of 'tradition' and underdevelopment through rational relationships limited to the public sphere, while his affiliations with women, children or the community were relegated to the private and often non-modern sphere (Unterhalter 2010: 782). However, a slightly different version of modernity was associated with the struggles for decolonisation, and was less critical of certain forms of 'tradition', but called upon citizens of the new nation states to subordinate their local cultural identities to the larger national project defined by a Constitution. Indeed, both perspectives on modernity failed to acknowledge large majorities of those citizens who had ambiguous relationships with their nation-states, either because they lived in regions inaccessible to modern institutions or because they had been dispossessed by the politics of development or exclusion (Unterhalter 2010).

Education for All: Questions of Quality and Equity

Despite the call for democratising education, curricula have circumvented policy commitments in most nation-states, since 'modern education, despite its egalitarian rhetoric, was never designed to provide equal or even appropriate education for all', having been created by and for the centre to consolidate its power through peripheralism of the majority (Cummings 2003: 277). The egalitarian vision of Basic Education, *Hindustani Talimi* (Hindustani Talimi Sangh 1938), was similarly marginalised by the hegemony of 'modern' education, which after independence dismissed 'work education' to the margins of irrelevance, to the 'low ability' and low desirability 'vocational' tracks.

The Education Commission (GOI 1966) recommended 'common schools' and was concerned that the

> children of the masses are compelled to receive sub-standard education ... while the economically privileged parents are able to 'buy' good education for their children. This is bad not only for the children of the poor but also for children from the rich and privileged groups. ... By segregating their children, they prevent them from sharing the life and experiences of the children of the poor and coming into contact with the realities of life. In addition to weakening social cohesion, they also render the education of their own children anaemic and incomplete (Section 1.36, 1.37).

However, the challenge of translating strong policy visions into consonant conceptions of what must form a democratic and 'equalising' curriculum proved to be daunting. A series of National Curriculum Framework (NCF) documents (GOI 1975, 1988, 2000) continued to project the 'diversity' of children only in terms of 'the special needs of the talented, the backward, and those coming from non-formal channels' (GOI 1975: Section 2.15). These reinforced deeply discriminatory constructions of the 'slow learner' in need of 'remedial' programmes, and the 'bright' deserving 'enrichment', through problematic 'deficit' theories of learning.

Mass-schooling systems and transmission pedagogies employed to further the aims of modernity for nation building, through 'scientific' principles of curriculum design in 'official' languages, have now been called into question. The thrust on uniformity of curricula and 'equal opportunities of access' to schooling is seen to be linked to 'the assumptions about the person in relation to the institutions of modernity' (Unterhalter 2009: 783). The 'civilising' agenda of school is righteously imposed on poor children, who supposedly need to be 'rescued' through discipline from the chaos and squalor in their homes. The textbook usually maintains an inert distance, refusing to acknowledge the lives of the dispossessed, and deals with survival issues in a cold, sterile manner. Assuming that everyone lives in a brick-and-mortar bungalow provided with tapped water, it preaches 'water conservation' so that taps are not kept running while brushing one's teeth. It diligently evades issues of conflict, seen as 'uncomfortable' by the dominant middle class, with an implicit understanding that while it must inform 'those backward' children on how to conduct their lives 'properly', it should project only 'positive' situations to protect the 'innocence' of the privileged (Rampal 2007).

In contrast, the National Curriculum Framework 2005 acknowledges that despite several radical policies, the system continues to reproduce social conformity and inequality, through learning regimes and values that valourise authority, competition and mindless memorisation of meaningless information (Rampal 2005). It calls for 'critical pedagogy' that underscores issues of inequality and power relations along with social constructivist approaches to learning, where the focus is on active meaning making by learners who develop their understanding through lived experiences in multicultural contexts (GOI 2005).

There have been concerns about growing influences of neo-conservatism in education across the world as well as in India, which attempt to restructure schooling in conformity with 'traditional' values and 'national culture'. Ironically, these educational reforms that claim to invoke standardised educational regimes for better quality, actually rebel against diversity and criticality and strive to manufacture consent in an ambience more suited for a globalised market economy. With few commitments towards 'quality' and even fewer about 'equality', the transformative agency of education is easily forgotten. Egged by neo-liberal policies and demands for a global workforce equipped with 'basic skills', there is pressure on the Indian state to roll back through investments not on schools but in giving children 'vouchers' to exercise 'choice' so that schools compete in the market despite experiences of other countries that show how such measures have increased inequalities. Standardised and managerial modes of assessing school quality through a culture of testing have led to the 'deskilling' of teachers who find their motivation and creativity undermined while 'teaching' is reduced to the model of the industrial workplace (Apple 1993).

The human development approach to Education For All (EFA) with an 'expanded vision' — for the empowerment of children, youth and adults — views the person as an active and reflective agent. However, national curricular aims across countries are seen to be shifting to facilitate rather than interrogate the global neoliberal agenda. An EFA review (Amadio et al. 2005) of the trends in national aims between the 1980s and 2000s, shows that though there are calls for 'expanding human capabilities' with a shift towards student-centred approaches, yet the role of education in helping individuals to transform society — a notion expressed in several country statements of the 1980s — now lies abandoned in favour of 'facilitating successful adaptation to an ever-changing world' (ibid.).

Reflexive Schools as Indigenous Sites of Knowledge Production

The systems approach to mass modern schooling, encapsulated by 'delivery' metaphors, fails to allow for a meaningful participation of learners and teachers, owing to its non-negotiable and 'given' character arising out of what J. Eggleston calls the 'received' perspective (Eggleston 1977). On the contrary, 'reflexive' education deals with knowledge which is actively constructed, negotiated, criticised and suitably transformed by the participants. In the former model, knowledge is considered to exist independent of the learner arranged into deliverable bits, encapsulated within rigid articulations or definitions, and severely constrained by 'subject' and 'discipline' boundaries. However, the reflexive curriculum views knowledge not as a fixed product but as a holistic process, strongly influenced by the personal meanings of learners (Rampal 1991).

Language for meaning making plays a central role in the indigenous discourse on education as a medium of thought, reflection and identity. After India gained independence, religious chauvinism combined with the political hegemony of the Hindi heartland demanded a highly chaste Hindi as the 'national' language. The country refrained from declaring a 'national' language, but instead termed Hindi the 'official' language with English as an 'associate additional official language' to serve as a link between the pluralities of regional or state languages. The Official Language Commission (GOI 1956) recommended that new terminologies should not be 'concocted in a literary workshop' but 'mined from the quarries' of artisanal 'dialects' and vocational knowledge of craftspersons, artisans, technicians and semi-skilled workers who manage to devise their own hybrid forms of technical and scientific terminologies. However, the course of events that followed unfortunately went contrary to the wise counsel of the Commission. The official Sanskritised Hindi was not carved from the dynamic heteroglot and extensively used Hindustani, which grew out of the composite culture of diverse communities, forging strong emotional bonds of shared memories and continuing to shape the classrooms of today, silencing popular expression and knowledge (Rai 2001).

Indeed, similar concerns have been voiced in South Africa where unlike the context of Indian schools, English remains the dominant language, and efforts are on to ensure the development and 'intellectualisation' of local languages (Dlodo 1999; Odora-Hoppers 2002). Moreover, attempts to incorporate cultural or civilisational resources in education have been part of major political contestations, especially in multicultural countries with complex colonial histories. An indigenous discourse on schooling calls for new metaphors for the notion of a 'national' or 'multicultural identity'. One metaphor for the dynamic and diverse society sought in post-apartheid South Africa is that of the 'Garieb' (*The Great River*), proposed by N. Alexander (Alexander 2002: 107). In this the mainstream is composed of a confluence of all the tributaries, which in their ever-changing forms continue to constitute and reconstitute the river, such that no single current dominates, and there is no 'main stream'.

The violent history of Partition had challenged the process of carving a national identity through the education system. The Committee for Emotional Integration (GOI 1962: 3) asserted that

> '[u]nity is not uniformity. No one is asked to give up his faith in the religion of his fathers, his love for the language which the poets — who have inspired his life and the life of thousands like him — chose as the medium of expression, for their sense of truth and beauty. ... Such loyalties do not detract from the loyalty to the nation: rather they add depth to it and, in turn, derive meaning and significance from that over-all loyalty which is the nation's due'.

However, the nationalist-chauvinist agenda continues to assert the cultural hegemony of the dominant Indian 'main stream'. Education thus remains a politically contested site for the schooling of dominance — of caste, class, language, religion and gender — despite radical committees and secular policies that have challenged these divisive designs. Moreover, there is often a fine line between interpretations of what constitutes 'local' or 'indigenous' knowledge, and the reflexive perspective with a thrust on critical pedagogy must be invoked to deal with complex issues of re-appropriation.

Africa, South America as well as South Asia have seen moves for a critical re-appropriation of indigenous knowledge (Goonatilake 1998; Ogunniyi 1989) with an end to 'extroversion' of all forms, including economic, scientific and technological. For instance, school history curricula in Central and South America, reviewed from the subaltern perspective, have declared 12 October, the day Columbus reached the 'New World', as the 'Indigenous Resistance Day'. Similarly, social movements represented at the World Social Forum have called for an audit of the 'ecological debt' of the colonising countries which, through centuries of exploitation of mineral and other natural resources of the South, have caused its deep economic debt. Cognitive heritage too needs to be critically re-examined, not through a patenting regime, but to enrich the indigenous 'commons' for economic and knowledge production.

Schools can serve as indigenous sites of production of new knowledge, through reflexive curricula and, equally, of relegitimisation and appraisal of some of the lost traditions (Rampal 2009). In fact, received models of formal education often lead to the de-legitimisation and loss of knowledge traditions. The tribal or rural child is knowledgeable about the natural world, and does not need to look at 'pictures' to count the legs of a spider, identify the eggs of a frog or the leaves of a neem tree. She may learn from her community about metal casting, identification of medicinal herbs through the rich biodiversity of her forests, which foreign companies may aggressively vie to patent and commercially exploit, but ironically, schools do not value (Rampal 2002).

The National Curriculum Framework (2005) and the new textbooks developed by the National Council of Educational Research and Training (NCERT) have attempted to creatively address the lives and knowledge systems of the underprivileged majority. These focus on the processes by which learners actively construct knowledge, and attempt to remove rigid disciplinary boundaries while departing from the traditional approach of 'imparting information'. Many textbooks incorporate oral narratives, representations of different genres of folk and contemporary art, true-life experiences and examples of indigenous knowledge, humour, satire and also complex questions that promote criticality even on controversial issues. For instance, the chapter 'Whose Forests?' from the Environmental Studies textbook for Class V, uses the real-life narrative of an indigenous woman to interrogate the issue of forest rights. It presents the perspective of forest dwellers who believe that 'the forest is our collective bank — not yours or mine alone. We take from it only as much as we need' (NCERT 2008a: 183). The book asks learners to respond to not 'What is a forest?', but to the constructivist query 'What do you think is a forest?' The woman describes her struggle for an education that would enable her to fight for her community's rights, and continues to take young children into the forests to help them know their cultural roots, with an almost Frierian declaration that 'To learn to read the forest is as important as reading books' (NCERT 2008a: 182).

Situated Learning: Challenges of Integrating Education and Work

Research in 'everyday cognition' has moved psychology beyond the individual, to look at human thinking through cultural, anthropological, social and historical perspectives. The most frequently examined area of everyday cognition is mathematics

Gerdes 1985; Lave 1988; Nunes et al. 1993; Zaslavsky 1973, and studies between processes of mathematical performance in the two settings — the school and the street — have indicated that the striking difference lies in the processes of teaching and learning. While school learning focuses on individual cognition, abstract thought and general principles, out-of-school learning depends on shared cognition, contextualised reasoning and situation-specific competence. Rigid rule-bound solutions, taught in formal schools, do not carry meaning or help learners solve problems in practical contexts. In contrast, the strategies they develop while 'doing mathematics' in everyday contexts are flexible and help them to stay close to the meaning of the situation and the quantities involved (Rampal et al. 1998, 2000). These folk and street math strategies have been consciously used for the new NCERT primary mathematics textbooks, often through living examples of people engaged in everyday contexts. Moreover, chapters such as 'Building with Bricks', 'The Fish Tale' or 'Kiran the Junk Seller' (NCERT 2007, 2008b for classes IV and V) are meant to focus on the knowledge systems of 'real-life' masons, fish-workers or the enterprising young woman who was intimidated by school math but now effectively manages her junk business.

A persistently challenging terrain has been education for out-of-school children and youth, especially girls, as well as the increasingly popular option of open schooling. This demands more concerted effort through academic–activist partnerships to bring insights from theory and praxis, to address the situated knowledge and often fragile literacies of adolescent learners. Such effort was evident in the National Literacy Campaigns which, inspired by the Frierian approach to 'read the word and the world', in some districts, went beyond reading and writing, to encompass issues of social justice and transformative action (Rampal 2003, 2005).

The school curriculum still continues to be largely located within an 'academic' domain, not having engaged enough with the more difficult issues of work and vocation. It is somewhat ironical that in a low-income country such as India, vocational education curricula are perceived as having 'low quality', meant only for the 'non-academic' or 'low-ability' learners, even as working-class families despair that schools continue to alienate their children from their own vocations and livelihoods. Institutes or polytechnics that offer these 'low-track' courses are not creatively or academically engaged with curriculum development, while some are even placed under the Department of Labour, not Education. In a new globalised manifestation of the 'brain versus body' skills dichotomy, higher-order '21st century skills' of creativity and interpersonal communication are being competitively nurtured by school education in industrialised countries to somehow justify the outsourcing of 'low-skill' jobs to low-income countries. This offers a challenge for both India and South Africa to break fresh ground and design indigenous vocational curricula which have an innovative, creative and academic 'high skill' technological edge for the majority of our learners.

A study of rural schools of South Africa (Nelson Mandela Foundation 2005) had noted that vocational education was resisted by teachers and learners, because it was associated with 'impoverished curricula' and visions of colonialism and apartheid. Bantu education was meant to limit African aspirations through minimum literacy skills, sewing and housecraft for girls and woodwork and gardening for boys. In the absence of serious academic re-envisioning of education in a reflexive mode, parents continue to be ambivalent about the aims of schooling.

> Whereas parents seek a solution through skills and education for agricultural and community development, learners want a modern and meaningful education, equal to the best in the country and in which they enjoy rights *within* and *through* education that will enhance their capabilities as human beings (Nelson Mandela Foundation 2005: 102).

However, despite a high level of disillusionment about the state of rural education, and faced with the challenges of poverty, hunger and sometimes despair, most people still felt that education offered tangible hope and possibilities to improve capabilities.

A dialectical relationship between education and society lends itself to a dual dynamic of change so that while, on the one hand, education is invoked to transform social values, there remains the need for simultaneous social action to transform the values of education itself. Instead of drifting with the often instrumental rhetoric of the 'knowledge economy' and focusing narrowly on the glamour of modern information and communication technologies, we need to restructure education to address the diverse spectrum of knowledge systems that relate to work and production patterns of the majority (Rampal 2010). The Right to Education Act in India was implemented in 2010, six decades after the Constitution promised all its children free and compulsory education. This shift from a highly stratified and selective system premised on limited notions of achievements to a rights framework that nurtures and develops the capabilities of all children, will be possible through reflexive education that also re-envisions modernity.

References

Alexander, N. 2002. *An Ordinary Country*. Scottsville, South Africa: University of Natal Press.

Apple, M. W. 1993. *Official Knowledge: Democratic Education in a Conservative Age*. New York: Routledge.

Amadio, M., S. Gross , P. Ressler and N. Truong. 2005. 'Quality Education for All: World Trends in Educational Aims and Goals between the 1980s and the 2000s' thematic paper for the 'UNESCO Global Monitoring Report'. Paris: UNESCO.

Bhattacharya, S. (ed.). 1997. *The Mahatma and the Poet: Letters and Debates between Gandhi and Tagore 1915–1949*. New Delhi: National Book Trust.

Chatterjee, P. 1994. *Nation and its Fragments: Colonial and Post-Colonial Histories*. New Delhi: Oxford University Press.

Chakravarty, P. 2004. *Western Science in Modern India*. Delhi: Permanent Black.

Cummings, W. K. 2003. 'The Limits of Modern Education', in E. R. Beauchamp (ed.), *Comparative Education Reader*. London: Routledge Falmer.

Dlodlo, T. S. 1999. 'Science Nomenclature in Africa: Physics in Nguni', *Journal of Research in Science Teaching*, 36 (3): 321–31.

Eggleston, J. 1977. *The Sociology of the School Curriculum*. London: Routledge and Kegan Paul.

Gerdes, P. 1985. 'Conditions and Strategies for Emancipatory Mathematics Education in Underdeveloped Countries', *For the Learning of Mathematics*, 5 (1): 15–20.

Goonatilake, S. 1998. *Toward a Global Science*. Bloomington: Indiana University Press.

Government of India. 1956. *Report of the Official Language Commission*. New Delhi: Government of India Press.

———. 1962. *Report of the Committee for National and Emotional Integration*. New Delhi: Ministry of Education.

———. 1966. *Report of the Education Commission: Education and National Development*. New Delhi: Ministry of Education.

———. 1975, 1988, 2000, 2005. *National Curriculum Framework*. New Delhi: National Council for Educational Research and Training.

Hindustani Talimi Sangh (All-India Education Board). 1938. *Report of the Zakir Hussain Committee on Basic Education*. Wardha, Maharashtra.

Lave, J. 1988. *Cognition in Practice*. Cambridge: Cambridge University Press.

NCERT. 2008a. *Looking Around: Textbook for Class V Environmental Studies*. New Delhi: National Council for Educational Research and Training. www.ncert.nic.in.

———. 2007 and 2008b. *Math-Magic: Textbook for Mathematics* (for Classes IV and V). New Delhi: National Council for Educational Research and Training. Also available at www.ncert.nic.in

Nelson Mandela Foundation. 2005. *Emerging Voices: A Report on Education in South African Rural Communities*. Cape Town: HSRC Press.

Nunes, T., A. D. Schliemann and D. W. Carraher. 1993. *Street Mathematics and School Mathematics*. Cambridge: Cambridge University Press.

Odora-Hoppers, C. (ed.). 2002. *Indigenous Knowledge and the Integration of Knowledge Systems*. Claremont, South Africa: New Africa Education.

Ogunniyi, M. B. 1989. 'Traditional African Culture and Modern Science', in E. Ekeh and A. Ashiwaju (eds), *Nigeria Since Independence: Volume on Culture*. Nigeria: Heinemann Educational Books.

Pinar, W. F. 2004. *What is Curriculum Theory?* Mahwah, NJ: Lawrence Erlbau Associates.

Rai, A. 2001. *Hindi Nationalism: Tracts of the Times, 13*. New Delhi: Orient Longman.

Rampal, A., R. Ramanujam and L. S. Saraswati. 1998. *Numeracy Counts!* National Literacy Resource Centre, Mussoorie: LBS National Academy of Administration.

———. 2000. *Zindagi Ka Hisaab*. National Literacy Resource Centre, Mussoorie: LBS National Academy of Administration.

Rampal, A. 1991. 'Deliverance from the 'Delivery' Metaphor: Curriculum Innovation in India. *Journal of Education for Teaching*, 17 (3): 237–44.

———. 2002. 'Texts in Context: An EFA 2000 Review', in R. Govinda (ed.), *India Education Report*. New Delhi: Oxford University Press.

———. 2003. 'Counting on Everyday Mathematics', in T. S. Saraswathi, (ed.), *Cross cultural Perspectives in Human Development: Theory, Research and Applications*. Thousand Oakes, CA: Sage Publications.

———. 2005. 'Revaluing Education', in R. Chopra and P. Jeffery (eds), *Educational Regimes in Contemporary India*. New Delhi: Sage Publications.

———. 2007. 'Ducked or Bulldozed? Education of Deprived Urban Children in India', in W. T. Pink and G. W. Noblit (eds), *International Handbook of Urban Education*, pp. 285–304. Dordrecht: Springer.

———. (2009) 2010. 'An Indigenous Discourse to Cradle our Cognitive Heritage and Script our Aspirations: Reflections from India and South Africa', in R. Cowen and A. M. Kazamias (eds), *International Handbook of Comparative Education*. Dordrecht: Springer.

———. 2010. 'Curriculum: Economic and Cultural Development', in B. McGraw, P. Peterson and E. Baker (eds), *The International Encyclopedia of Education* (3rd edn). Oxford: Elsevier.

Unterhalter, E. 2010. 'Social Justice, Development Theory and the Question of Education', in R. Cowen and A. M. Kazamias (eds), *International Handbook of Comparative Education*, pp. 781–800. Dordrecht: Springer.

United Nations Educational, Scientific and Cultural Organization (UNESCO). 2005. *Education for All Global Monitoring Report 2005 — The Quality Imperative*. Paris

Zaslavsky, C. 1973. *Africa Counts*. Boston, Mass. Prindle and Schmidt.

14

The Place and Role of Higher Education in an Evolving South African Democracy

Derek van der Merwe

We live in unsettled times, both locally and globally. The demand for paradigm shifts in the way people and the corporations, institutions and nations within which they organise themselves, relate to one another and to the environment to ensure long-term sustainability is urgent. As the primary repositories of knowledge and skills transfer in (most) societies, institutions of higher education can and are expected to be in the vanguard to respond to the challenges of wealth creation in a world of limited resources. Institutions and systems of higher education worldwide are as much in transition as the societies they serve, as fragile as they are, resilient and sustainable only if the relationship with the society they serve is overtly symbiotic. This demands structural changes, systemic adjustments, real transformation.

South Africa has been engaged in the transformation of its system of higher education and of the institutions that comprise it since 1994. Two phases of transformation can be identified. The objective of the first phase, between 1997 and 2006, was a radical transformation of the racialised and unequal system of higher education that had existed prior to 1994. Between 2004–2006, by means of a series of mergers and incorporations, the then 21 universities and 15 technikons were reduced to 23 universities with differing mandates (11 traditional universities, six universities of technology and six so-called comprehensive institutions). It also established two National Institutes for Higher Education to coordinate the provision of higher education in those provinces where universities did not exist.

Though the restructuring of higher education undertaken in the first phase was complex, far-reaching and radically transformative it was never meant to be a one-off panacea for higher education in South Africa. Massive problems remain — problems not dissimilar from those encountered in a host of other countries. A second phase of transformation commenced in 2009, with the establishment by the Zuma administration of a Department of Higher Education and Training (DoHET). This step heralded the government's intention to create a coherent and single post-school education and training system and to systematically address the many problems, structural and substantive, that bedevil post-school education and training in South Africa. The blueprint for this second phase of transformation is provided in DoHET's 'Strategic Plan 2010/11 to 2014/15', presented to Parliament in March 2010.

A Coherent and Single Post-School Education and Training System in South Africa

DoHET is responsible for post-school education and training and a Department of Basic Education is responsible for school education. Prior to the establishment of DoHET, administrative responsibility for higher education and training was dispersed among two national departments (Education and Labour) and nine provincial departments. A single department responsible for the entire post-school system has created opportunities for improved coordination and interaction between the sub-systems within the sector, and for improved progression of learners between the sub-systems. The post-school education and training system comprises universities, further education and training colleges, skills development, adult basic education and training and the National Qualifications Framework. DoHET is also responsible for managing the Human Resource Development Council (HRD Council) for which the Deputy-President, under the leadership of the Presidency, is responsible.

DoHET's 'Strategic Plan' is embedded in a 20–30-year strategic perspective. This long-term perspective emphasises the fundamental importance of a clearly articulated human resource development strategy (for which the HRD Council is responsible) — it calls human resources development a 'central pillar' of DoHET's strategic planning ('Strategic Plan: 34') — and clearly articulates the place and role of post-school education and training in this developmental trajectory ('Strategic Plan: 17'; see too HRD Council speech 1).

In 2009 the national government adopted the Medium-term Strategic Framework (MTSF) for 2009–2010 to 2014–2015. It enumerated a number of strategic priorities for the five-year period of the MTSF, and allocated resources to these priority areas in accordance with the Medium-term Expenditure Framework (MTEF). Strategic Priority Number 4 of the MTSF is to 'strengthen the skills and resource base'. The special remit of DoHET is the two key goals for 'broadening access to post-secondary education and improving graduation rates' and 'ensuring that the country's training and skills development initiatives respond to the requirements of the economy, rural development challenges and social integration' ('Strategic Plan: 40–42', see too Budget speech: 2). For the 2010–2011 financial year a massive 19.9 per cent of the National Budget was allocated to education and training. The portion of the education and training budget allocated to higher education and training increased by almost 40 per cent over a three-year period, although in this same three-year period, higher education's share of the annual budget for education had declined by 20 per cent (Budget vote 2010: 2; NSFAS Review Report: xiii).

This, then, is the national strategic context within which the post-school education and training sector functions. It is driven by the twin imperatives of *transformation* (redressing the imbalances and inequalities of the past) and *development* (acquisition of knowledge and skills for future employment), and by integrated, coordinated and coherent sub-systems enhancing access and broadened economic activity. It is a hugely ambitious project.

The new post-school education and training dispensation has three identifiable sub-systems:

(a) *Higher education*, which comprises the following:

- 23 publicly-funded higher education institutions (11 traditional or general universities, six comprehensive universities and six universities of technology);
- two National Institutes of Higher Education (earmarked for development into fully-fledged universities);
- 78 registered and 22 provisionally registered private higher education institutions;

- nursing colleges;
- agricultural colleges.

Higher education in South Africa is governed by the Higher Education Act (No. 101 of 1997). The Council on Higher Education is the ministerial advisory body for higher education. Quality assurance for higher education is the responsibility of the Higher Education Quality Committee.

(b) *Further Education and Training*, which comprises 50 Further Education and Training Colleges (FET Colleges) with 263 campuses, as well as a large number of private FET providers. Further education and training is governed by the Further Education and Training Colleges Act (No. 16 of 2006). The National Board for Further Education and Training is the Ministerial advisory body for FET Colleges. Umalusi is the quality assurance council for further education and training (alongside basic and general education).

(c) *Skills Development and Training* which comprises the following:

- 21 Sectoral Education and Training Authorities (SETAs);
- Government Trade Test Centres;
- Skills Development Institutes.

Skills development and training in South Africa is governed by the Skills Development Act (No. 97 of 1998) and the Skills Development Levies Act (No. 9 of 1999). The National Skills Authority is the Ministerial advisory body for skills development. The Quality Council for Trades and Occupations (established in 2010) is responsible for quality assurance of workplace training, and for its accreditation and certification.

Some of the features of each of these sub-systems are discussed below.

Higher Education Sector

Both a development agenda and a transformation agenda dominate policy formulation and implementation in this sector. Both agendas seek to address the range of challenges that continue to confront higher education. The following may be said to be the most pressing:

(a) student access and success;
(b) funding, both in respect of financial aid for students and the physical infrastructure of universities;
(c) quality of higher education provision;
(d) persistent discriminatory practices in institutions; and
(e) differentiation within the university sector to meet the demands for skills, innovation and high-level knowledge.

The provision of increased access to higher education for learners has been a pivotal component of higher education policy for many years. Indeed, access to higher education institutions for African, female and poor students has grown dramatically over the last number of years (a recent study shows that there has in fact been a four-fold increase in the number of Black African graduates since 1991 — Dell 2011). Providing access to universities has become very much an art form in recent years, driven by institutional three-year Enrolment Plans approved by DoHET. A range of factors contribute to enrolment patterns and the ability of universities to set and meet enrolment targets. These include the availability of state funding to subsidise student places; (physical and human resource) capacity of the institution to accommodate an increasing number of students; financial means of students to pay for their studies and of the state to provide them with financial aid; and a schooling system that still fails to adequately provide learners from disadvantaged backgrounds with learning opportunities that will give them access to universities. The reality is that all universities are at full capacity and beyond, and are unable to absorb significantly more students.

Student success is similarly driven by a range of policy determinants. Targets for success rates, measured as graduation rates and throughput rates, are set for each university by DoHET and sanctioned by means of subsidy allocations. Universities are allocating ever more of their resources to student development and support programmes to increase their chances of success. The state is making ever more funding available to support these interventions (R451m was made available for teaching development in the 2010–2011 budget — Budget vote 5). Universities generally express concern about the quality of the students who enter the system from the schools. Minister Nzimande tellingly stated in his opening speech at the April 2010 Higher Education Transformation Summit that 'we are not likely to get a radically different type of student anytime soon' (Summit speech 2010: 3) and therefore, student development and support will continue to absorb a significant component of university resources for some time to come. In furtherance of the national transformation agenda, universities will increasingly be expected to create legitimate learning pathways for students from disadvantaged backgrounds to give them the means and the support to remain in the system beyond a first qualification.

State funding of higher education is a matter of grave concern. Funding levels are woefully inadequate to achieve the magisterial strategic objectives outlined above. A case in point, if only to illustrate how deeply dependent the achievement of transformational and developmental objectives are on adequate funding, is the bitter-sweet saga of the National Student Financial Aid Scheme (NSFAS). State-funded financial aid to students is provided by NSFAS. This scheme, implemented in 1999, has the eminently laudable objective of providing loans and bursaries to poor students who qualify for financial aid on the basis of a means test. In 2010, R2.7bn was available for disbursement to poor students, up from the mere R441m available in 1999 (NSFAS Review Report: x). Many universities also provide millions from their own funds to augment NSFAS funding. NSFAS provides financial aid to 17 per cent (or some 660,000) of higher education students (including students in FET colleges). And yet this is not enough, not nearly enough. The Ministerial Committee appointed in 2010 to review NSFAS states in its Report that '[i]t would probably need to triple its budget to meet even current demands' (ibid.: x, xiii, 106). Severe financial constraints are exacerbated by the poor results of students who benefit from the Scheme. The Ministerial Committee reports a 72 per cent drop-out rate of students supported by the Scheme since 1999, and a graduation rate of only 19 per cent. In an effort to encourage NSFAS students to complete their studies, final-year undergraduate students who qualify for NSFAS support will in 2011 receive a full-cost loan to be converted into a bursary if they graduate. This model, if successful, will be phased in over the next few years to include poor students in earlier years. Thus the ruling party's election promise, namely to provide free higher education at undergraduate level — a demand vociferously voiced by student and youth organisations — would be kept. This is also the recommendation of the Ministerial Committee, that the state should provide free higher education to poor students and students from working class backgrounds (ibid.: 105–6, 124). It must be said that the Ministerial Committee recognises the huge financial burden involved in bringing this to fruition and has suggested additional sources of income, such as a social security tax or a payroll tax on employers.

Quality is a perennial concern for higher education in South Africa, as elsewhere. South Africa has a relatively sophisticated system of quality assurance (based largely on the UK's system of higher education quality assurance). It is managed by the Higher Education Quality Committee (HEQC), a committee of the Council for Higher Education. By the end of 2011 every higher education institution would have been subjected to a quality audit managed by the HEQC. Each audited institution is obliged to present an Improvement Plan to the HEQC. Recently the HEQC indicated that, in preparation for a second round of audits, it wished to adopt a different strategy. The first round of audits had focused strongly on governance concerns and had created an atmosphere of compliance rather than engagement. In the next round, the HEQC wishes to pursue a developmental agenda, in which the focus is on interactive engagement around the core functions of teaching and learning and quality enhancement that directly benefit the student.

Higher-education institutions continue to be bedevilled by persistent discriminatory practices based on race and gender. A pervasive sense of alienation that existed in all institutions (some more so than others) was identified among staff and students by the Ministerial Committee on Transformation and Social Cohesion and the Elimination of Discrimination in Public Higher Education Institutions, which published its (not entirely uncontroversial) report in 2008. Transformation/Diversity Offices exist in all institutions and are seen as essential to the establishment of a sustainable culture of respect for diversity and difference.

Institutional *differentiation*, as a means to promote transformation and opportunities for development, has been a topic of scholarly debate for some years. The need for differentiation is universally acknowledged, the nature of the differentiation and the means to achieve it, is not. The national government created three types of universities in South Africa: traditional universities, providing professional and general formative degree programmes; universities of technology, providing vocational education; and comprehensive institutions, providing a combination of vocational and traditional degree programmes. Within this basic typology much scholarly debate (and not a little sophistry) has taken place on the identification of categories of differentiation. At the heart of the matter is the approval of — and the provision of funding for — academic programmes (and their accompanying qualifications) for each university, in order to optimise the efficient distribution of scarce resources, enhance quality, create synergies for innovation and the advancement of knowledge and increase learning opportunities for students that are readily translatable into skills transfer and employment. The question of the most appropriate allocation of resources between the ostensibly competing demands of research productivity (and accompanying postgraduate training) and (undergraduate) teaching support and development (and allied concerns such as subsistence, housing and transport), also features prominently in these debates. There is much to be said for an approach that encourages partnerships and regional collaboration between universities, without detracting from the autonomy institutions cherish (Stoop 2010).

Further Education and Training Sector (FET)

The public 50 FET colleges have performed poorly in the new democratic dispensation. There are some exceptions, but by and large the colleges have significantly underperformed and many colleges, especially those in rural areas, are dysfunctional. The FET colleges have certainly been the poor cousins of the higher education sector. In 2001, a policy document published by the then Department of Education, *A New Institutional Landscape for FET Colleges*, paved the way for the reconfiguration of some 150 technical colleges into 50 FET colleges spread over 263 sites of delivery. A National Plan for FET colleges was announced in 2007, but its implementation has been characterised largely by procrastination and an inability to fully comprehend their new training mandate. Less than half the number of students registered at the 23 public universities (some 800,000 in 2008) were registered at FET colleges. There is general consensus that this ratio should in fact be inverted. The National Plan for FET Colleges committed government to an increase in the number of FET college students to 1 million by 2014 — a pipe dream at this stage (NSFAS Review Report: x; Stumpf et al. 2009: 7; 'Strategic Plan: 25'). There are many reasons why the FET college sector is in this current moribund state. The sector has struggled with the transition from technical colleges to FET colleges and, as a result, suffers from an opaqueness of identity and a lack of purpose. Until their transfer to DoHET they were managed like schools by the nine provincial education departments, but expected to provide skills training to adults and to interact with the world of work in a manner for which they were ill-equipped. The result has been mismanagement, low morale, poor quality, poor results, institutional instability, labour instability and severe financial constraints. The governance, curriculum and funding challenges they face are severe ('Strategic Plan: 24–26'; Stumpf et al. 2009: 6–9).

The Minister of Higher Education and Training has committed to a radical strengthening and improvement of the quality and functioning of this sub-system, so vital to the achievement of the national human resource development objectives and a critical component of the post-school education and training sector. It is meant to be 'a significant locus of delivery of vocational and continuing education with strong links to industry in order to meet critical skills shortages' (SAGCCI speech 2010: 2; see too 'Strategic Plan: 24–25').

A FET Roundtable was held in April 2010 with key stakeholders in this sub-system, to debate the many challenges facing the colleges. This was followed by a FET Summit that took place in August 2010 and a programme of action for the FET colleges (FET Summit Report: 25). The most important challenges facing this sub-system are the following:

(a) Balancing the demand for rapid growth of student numbers in the system — at least doubling the student numbers in the next five years (Media statement, November) — with the massive transformation demands in a very fragile system;

(b) the introduction of a more flexible approach to the scope of learning programmes offered by FET colleges, and a more differentiated FET college sector that allows for greater variety in the level of programmes offered by the FET colleges;

(c) financial aid to students at FET colleges; and

(d) creating coherence among the three sub-systems in the post-school system by means of collaboration and the introduction of clear articulation pathways.

Rapid growth in the system is really an economic and developmental necessity, despite the fragility of the system within which it must happen. Significant progress has already been made in this regard. It was announced in January 2011 that opportunities for learners who had passed the 2010 school-leaving examinations of 2010 have grown by 56 per cent over 2010. Most of these places were in the further education and training sector. A considerable challenge facing the government is the widely held perception that the FET sector is a poor second prize for students who fail to gain entry to a university. This stigma will not disappear overnight.

Programme diversity and the creation of articulation pathways goes to the very heart of the government's ambitions to afford further education and training a place at the high table of post-school education and training and the human resource development of the country. The National Qualifications Framework Act (No. 67 of 2008) provides for a 10-level National Qualifications Framework for South Africa. Higher education provides qualifications at levels 5–10 and FET colleges at levels 2–4. As from 2007 only one qualification, the National Certificate (Vocational), can be conferred by a FET college, for learning programmes designed to cover specific career areas at NQF levels 2–4. FET colleges, therefore, do not provide education and training beyond level 4. In exceptional cases, however, on the basis of a provision in the FET College Act, a FET college may offer programmes at a NQF level higher than 4 under the authority of a higher education institution and with the permission of the Minister. The National Plan for FET Colleges allows for a maximum of 30 per cent of students to register for programmes beyond NQF level 4, which are under the authority, not of a higher-education institution, but of a Sectoral Education and Training Authority.

A clear delineation between the levels at which, and the institutions at which, trade and occupationally directed learning takes place has been established. This should allow for meaningful collaboration between FET colleges and higher education institutions (particularly between universities of technology and comprehensive institutions where vocational education and training programmes are offered) to create relatively seamless vocationally-oriented learning pathways from lower to higher NQF levels for students. The constricted and exceptional circumstances under which FET colleges may offer programmes at higher education NQF levels does, however, entrench FET colleges into a role of continued subservience to higher education, and adds to their stigmatisation. Given the scarcity of skills in the country, a more flexible and enabling regime for FET colleges, one that broadens the mandate of some FET colleges to offer post NQF level 4 trade and occupationally directed learning with differing modes of collaboration with higher education institutions, is surely appropriate (Stumpf et al. 2009: 7–9, 10, 13–26; 'Strategic Plan: 24–25').

A core component of the training that takes place in FET colleges is workplace learning. It is widely recognised that a serious bottleneck exists in the availability of structured, quality workplace experience (SEIFSA speech 2010: 5). Collaboration with Sectoral Education and Training Authorities to facilitate opportunities for workplace experience on a massive scale is essential if FET colleges are to assert themselves in the policy space created for them.

Financial aid to students is an obvious means to incentivise students to register at FET colleges. President Zuma recently announced that poor students (as defined in accordance with the NSFAS means test) would be fully exempt from paying fees and would receive a 15 per cent subsidy for transport costs — all of this to be funded from monies made available via the National Skills Levy (MacGregor 2011). It is, of course, a bold first step but it remains to be seen whether this is a sustainable strategy.

Skills Development and Training

Responsibility for skills development and training was transferred from the Department of Labour to DoHET to establish the third of the sub-systems comprising the post-school education and training sector. The purpose is to 'effectively [connect] education to technical training, to labour market entry, to the workplace and to lifelong learning', to sustain productivity ('Strategic Plan: 27').

226 *Derek van der Merwe*

Underpinning the drive for a cohesive and coherent skills development strategy, incorporating the whole of the post-school education and training sector, is the National Skills Development Strategy, the third review of which is currently under discussion. It provides the policy framework within which partnerships between the Sectoral Education and Training Authorities (SETAs), employers and education and training institutions are fostered, and the development of credible, widely-consulted sectoral skills plans. It also proposes an innovative project called PIVOT, which seeks to develop programmes that combine course work at higher education institutions and FET colleges with structured workplace learning in the form of professional placements, work-integrated learning, apprenticeships, learnerships and internships (SEIFSA speech 2010: 5; 'Strategic Plan: 21, 28–29').

It is envisaged that the SETAs, funded from skills levies paid by employers into the National Skills Fund, will facilitate education and training into and within the workplace, expand access to structured and quality-assured workplace learning and close collaboration between individual workplaces and the higher education and FET sectors. They have been referred to as a 'nerve centre' of skills development alongside artisan training (*Budget Vote* 2010: 3). Widely criticised for underperformance, they have been significantly restructured into 21 SETAs, with clear mandates and approved governance structures. The National Skills Fund, itself suffering embarrassingly from a chronic inability to disburse its funds, is subject to review and a closer alignment of its objectives with those of the human resource development strategy of the country, and of education and training capacity-building in the post-school sector (see, generally, SEIFSA speech 2010: 4–5; 'Strategic Plan: 29–31').

Concluding Remarks

Although exact figures are hard to come by, in 2007 an estimated 2.8 million South Africans between the ages of 18–24 were not in employment, education or training (NEETs). Despite a huge growth in excess of 50 per cent in post-school educational opportunities for 2010 school-leavers, some 20 per cent (or 76,000) school-leavers will still not have a place. These are truly sobering statistics and a measure of the challenges facing the government intent upon the pursuit of a development agenda in which education and training is pivotal to job creation, enhanced economic activity and reduction in poverty levels. A massive increase in opportunities for post-school education and training, particularly in the further and continuing education and training environment, is planned ('Strategic Plan: 18'). Given the virtual saturation of the existing 23 public universities it makes sense to plan for the conversion of the two national institutes for higher education into new universities (Media statement December; HE Summit speech 2010: 3).

Expanding access to higher education and training opportunities is one thing; achieving a return on such investments in the form of qualifications that translate into a skilled and knowledgeable workforce is quite another thing. The challenges are enormous. The deep social inequalities that pervade South African society (in the NSFAS Review Report: x reference is made to evidence — dubious, one surmises — that suggests that South Africa is now the most unequal society in the world) means that significant resources have to be expended on the pursuit of a transformation agenda that redresses past injustice, and depletes much needed future-oriented developmental resources. These deep inequalities are mirrored in the glaring disparities between universities in virtually every institutional activity. To illustrate, research output statistics for 2009 recently released indicate that five universities produce 60 per cent of South Africa's university sector research output, while 11 (or almost 50 per cent) produce only 8 per cent of the sectoral research output (Research Outputs 2009 Report 16 and Annexure 1).

Without doubt, severe underfunding is the biggest obstacle to the successful implementation of the strategic objectives for the post-school sector. Despite significant increases in funding for higher education in recent years, funding levels are still way below the norm for a middle-income country (NSFAS Review Report 106). Long-term underfunding has had a pernicious effect on higher education, and in particular it has entrenched the deep divide that exists between richly-resourced and poorly-resourced universities. The demand for free higher education from the populist left is insistent, and the ruling party has in fact committed itself to its progressive realisation. The cost will be astronomical and many believe it to be a bridge too far for the South African economy.

Higher-education institutions have notoriously high dropout rates (a study by the Council for Higher Education concluded that only 44 per cent of students registered for university programmes in 2000 would go on to graduate (Summit speech 2010: 3; see too HRD Council speech 2010: 2) and ever more funding is being invested both by the State and by the institutions themselves in learning development and support — necessarily at the expense of investment in research infrastructure and support. Institutions now recognise that development and support cannot be limited to teaching and learning only, but encompasses the full complement of academic, social, financial and emotional support.

The deep-seated chauvinism in favour of universities that permeates the choices learners make in respect of the post-school educational opportunities available presents a formidable challenge to policy makers in creating an enabling environment to channel literally hundreds of thousands of learners away from universities and into skills-based training. Part of this challenge is to respond effectively to the many deeply-rooted governance problems facing the sector — and the Department itself, understaffed and subject to internecine battles, is not immune. Governance concerns permeate the entire post-school education and training sector.

The litany of woes can be extended. There is no need to do so. There is a remarkable resilience to higher education in South Africa, this despite the 'change-fatigue' that is apparent everywhere. It continues to produce graduates who are globally competitive. Its research output continues to show steady annual growth — though admittedly from a low base. There is no lack of initiative and commitment from high-level decision makers. It is the sheer magnitude of the developmental challenges that confront the South African post-school education and training sector, the perennial sense of catch-up that pervades the sector and darkens the mood of even the most optimistic. It is scant solace to know that similar challenges are faced by many other societies globally. Sustained wealth creation is deeply dependent on a workforce that is skilled, knowledgeable and innovative; but wealth (resource abundance) is required to educate and train such a workforce, and that abundance of wealth is not present. It is the cruel paradox of modern societies in a developmental state. It is a challenge no one dare give up.

References

Dell, S. 2011. 'South Africa: Black Graduates Quadruple in Two Decades', *University World News Africa Edition*. Accessed 31 January 2011.

MacGregor, K. 2011. 'South Africa: Massive Growth in Post-school Places', *University World News Africa Edition*. Accessed 21 January 2011.

Stoop, L. 2010. 'Measuring and Increasing Diversity in the South African Higher Education System', *South Africa-Norway Tertiary Education Development Programme*. Close-out Conference, University of Johannesburg. November.

Stumpf, R., J. Papier, S. Needham and H. Nel. 2009. *Increasing Educational Opportunities for Post NQF Level 4 Learners in South Africa Through the Further Education and Training College Sector*. Committee for Higher Education Transformation and Further Education and Training Institute. May.

Department of Education. 2001. 'National Plan for Higher Education in South Africa'. February.

———. 2008a. 'National Plan for FET Colleges in South Africa'.

———. 2008b. 'Report of the Ministerial Committee on Transformation and Social Cohesion and the Elimination of Discrimination in Public Higher Education Institutions'. November.

Department of Higher Education and Training. 2010a. 'Report of the Further Education and Training Summit Steering Committee', FET Summit Report, September.

———. 2010b. 'Report of the Ministerial Committee on the Review of the National Student Financial Aid Scheme', *NSFAS Review Report*.

———. 2010c. 'Report on the Evaluation of the 2009 Institutional Research Publications Outputs'. (*Research Outputs 2009 Report*). November.

———. 2010c. 'Report on the Stakeholder Summit on Higher Education Transformation' (HE Summit Report). April.

———. 2010d. 'Strategic Plan 2010/11 to 2014/15' ('Strategic Plan'). 'Transformation and Restructuring: A New Institutional Landscape for Higher Education'. Government Notice No. 855 in *Government Gazette* No. 23549 of 21 June 2002.

Ministerial Media Statements and Speeches

Media statement, Department of Higher Education and Training (DoHET). 2009. 'Ministerial Statement on the Transfer of the Skills Development and Training Sector to the Department of Higher Education and Training'. November.

———. 'Ministerial Statement on Higher Education Funding 2009/10 to 2011/12'. December.

Budget Vote. 2010. Speech. March.

Inaugural Plenary Meeting of the Human Resource Development Council (HRD Council speech). 2010. March.

Keynote Address: Stakeholder Summit on Higher Education Transformation
(Summit speech). 2010. April.
Steel and Engineering Industries Federation of South Africa Annual
Conference (SEIFSA speech). 2010. May.
Southern African-German Chamber of Commerce and Industry Luncheon
(SAGCCI speech). 2010. July.
Sugar Industry Trust Fund for Education Induction Function (SITFE speech).
2010. July.

15

Urban Dreams and Realities

Kalpana Sharma

India still lives in its villages. But within the next four decades, half the country's population will be living in its megacities and towns. Indeed, the Indian city is the most appropriate symbol of a changing India and of an India where some things never change. So the picture of urban India consists of high rises, flyovers, roads jam-packed with every model of automobile and also slums and poverty, people lining up to collect water from water tankers, huge piles of garbage, potholed roads and beggars. All of it is true and all of it coexists within the same frame.

Currently, almost one-third of India's population, or 340 million people, lives in its towns and cities. By 2030, nearly 590 million people, or 40 per cent of the population will be urban. By 2050, half the population is projected to be urban.

The shape of urbanisation ranges from megacities like Mumbai and Delhi that have populations in excess of that of some smaller nations to small towns with between 5–20,000 inhabitants. The number of million-plus cities has increased from 24 in 1901 to 393 in 2001 and their share of urban population has increased from 26 per cent in 1901 to 69 per cent in 2001. The remaining 30 per cent are distributed in 3,979 towns and cities (Roychowdhury PowerPoint presentation).

The rate of urbanisation poses a major challenge for India in more ways than one even as some consider this as an opportunity for accelerated economic growth. Urbanisation is in some ways a double-edged sword. As countries grow economically, they urbanise. That has been the pattern of growth in the industrialised North. But in India's case, and also in China, the problem is not just urbanisation, but the pace at which it is accelerating (McKinsey Global Institute 2010: 13).

According to a report by the McKinsey Global Institute, 'It took nearly 40 years (between 1971 and 2008) for India's urban population to rise by nearly 230 million. It will take only half the time to add the next 250 million' (2010: 13). The urban population has increased 10 times between 1901 and 2001 while the total population has grown five times (MoEF, GoI 2009: 134). Also, for the first time in India's history, the five large states of Tamil Nadu, Gujarat, Maharashtra, Karnataka and Punjab will have more of their populations living in cities.

The increase is not principally due to migration, as was the case several decades back. Today, much of it is due to natural growth in the urban population as well as the expansion of urban areas. So while between 1961–70 expansion of urban boundaries accounted for only 3 per cent of growth of urban population, by 1991–2002 it had increased to 13 per cent while migration as a factor grew only from 19 per cent to 21 per cent over these four decades.

So why is this accelerated rate of urban growth a problem in the Indian context? There are several reasons, principally the absence of adequate foresight in urban planning. This is the underlying cause of the two issues I want to address. One, while urbanisation traditionally represents economic growth, in India it is also exacerbating inequity, both in economic terms and in access to basic urban services like water, sanitation and housing. And two, the current pattern of urban development and growth will be costly to the environment not only in the cities and towns but also in the surrounding countryside.

Inequity

An ideal that can realistically be accepted for our cities is one that has been termed 'harmonious', a term that envelops several concepts as is evident from the following quote:

> A society cannot claim to be harmonious if large sections of its population are deprived of basic needs while other sections live in opulence. A city cannot be harmonious if some groups concentrate resources and opportunities while others remain impoverished and marginalised. Harmony in cities cannot be achieved if the environment pays the price of urban living. Reconciling contradictory and complementary elements is critical to creating harmony within cities. A harmonious city promotes unity within diversity. Harmony within cities hinges not only on prosperity and its attendant benefits, but on two pillars that make harmony possible: equity and sustainability (State of the World's Cities 2008–2009).

The contrasts between the haves and have-nots are the leitmotifs that distinguish Indian cities today from many others around the world. On an average, at least a quarter of the population of any Indian city lives in slums and impermanent housing. Even if poor people living in cities manage to earn more than their counterparts in the villages, they face another type of deprivation, that of denial of basic services like water and sanitation apart from secure and affordable housing. In cities like Mumbai the problem is acute with roughly half the population, or an estimated 6.5 million people, living in slums.

Will growing cities, given the current dominant pattern of growth, be able to deal with such glaring inequities? Here is an issue that draws considerable attention of policy makers and civil society but so far little dent has been made on the problem.

The lack of affordable housing is a key feature of most Indian cities. Mumbai is a case in point where real estate prices are so high that only the rich can afford to live anywhere close to their place of work. The poor occupy only 10 per cent of the land but constitute 50 per cent of the population of the city living in informal shantytowns. This has happened not by accident. It is the consequence of an urban development policy that does not acknowledge the presence of millions of people who need affordable housing. As a result, speculation on real estate has fuelled an urban economy that has virtually made the presence of poor people untenable in megacities like Mumbai and Delhi.

In 1995, the Maharashtra government did come up with a plan that, if it had been effectively implemented, could have made a dent on the problem of slums. The scheme envisaged bringing in the private sector by giving them incentives to redevelop land occupied by slums. Those residing on the 'encumbered' plot were assured free housing of a specified size and in return the builder could use the area freed up to construct housing or commercial property for sale. Thus a system of cross-subsidy was put in place that should have been beneficial to all three parties involved — the state, the private developer and the slum resident.[1] The aim, when the scheme was launched, was to build 800,000 houses in 10 years. In 15 years, barely 200,000 houses have been built. In the meantime, more slums have emerged on vacant lands.

Without going into too many details, it will be sufficient to state that the scheme has worked patchily for a variety of reasons. One, developers were only interested in those parcels of land where they could make maximum profit, that is those located on high value land, and not all slums. Two, slum dwellers were not always united — after all, they are not a homogenous group and represent as many political, caste and religious groups as society in general. So often they could not agree and as two-thirds of them had to sign up a developer, several schemes failed to take off. Three, the state itself was inconsistent and kept changing the ground rules — for instance, redefining eligibility criteria. As a result, although a substantial number of slum families have benefited, many more are still waiting.

The main plus point of the Maharashtra Slum Redevelopment Scheme, whatever its shortcomings in implementation, is that many slum dwellers are able to continue living in the same neighbourhood where they are currently located. As a result, their livelihoods are in place, their children's schooling is not affected and, most important, they have security of tenure for the first time in their lives. The free house, given in recognition of the fact that slum dwellers have contributed to adding value to the land on which they squat and have been paying their dues to the city government in various ways, is an asset that they would never have succeeded in getting in a lifetime given real estate prices in a city like Mumbai.

By way of contrast, in New Delhi, the national capital, a different strategy has been followed, that of moving slums out of the city. In a city where public transport has been woefully inadequate — although steps have now been taken to improve it — this is an extremely thoughtless and cruel strategy. It deprives the poor of access to jobs, places an additional burden on them of time and money to commute over vast distances to the city, and places them in a virtual no-man's land without services such as schools or hospitals.

In their book *Swept off the Map, Surviving Resettlement and Relocation in Delhi*, Kalyani Menon-Sen and Gautam Bhan (2008) paint a grim picture of what happens to such people. The book is based on a study of 2,577 families who were forcibly relocated from the banks of River Yamuna, within Delhi, to Bawana on its outskirts. The alternative accommodation, consisting of plots of land of varying sizes, was not free. Everyone paid. Furthermore, no security of tenure was guaranteed, only a lease for five years.

The result of this relocation was that people moved from an area in close proximity to their place of work to another where there were no equivalent jobs available. To retain their jobs in the city they had to commute long distances, thereby eating into their already meagre earnings. There was a 40 per cent school dropout, as children could not get admission to schools close to where the families lived. The area they were forced to vacate could have been used for low-cost housing. Instead it was marked for high-end commercial use, including shopping malls. In the vision for the city, there was literally no place for the poor.[2]

Slums are the direct consequence of the absence of a policy on affordable housing. Currently, there is considerable talk in India about 'slum-free' cities without a determined push to create adequate low-cost housing at the speed at which it is needed. What I have cited are just two examples from Mumbai and Delhi that illustrate why the solutions have not worked. There are some successes but precious few. And in any case, none of them are on a scale that could make a difference. In India, although housing falls under the jurisdiction of state governments, for the first time the central government is intervening with a housing subsidy scheme for the urban poor. But even optimists will acknowledge that this is a drop in the bucket.

If future Indian cities do not accelerate plans to build affordable housing, the stark inequities visible today will continue and could even lead to violence and disruption on a scale that should make planners worry. On current trends, harmony is not something one can relate to the growth pattern of an Indian city.

Basic Services

Urbanisation is premised on the belief that greater densities and economies of scale facilitate provision of basic services such as water and sewage. Currently, even if we take much lower benchmarks than accepted worldwide, Indian cities fall far short on every parameter in the provision of these services. For instance, if the ideal for water supply at this pared-down standard is 150 lpcd,[3] in India it is 105 lpcd. Of course, this figure is an average. The reality is that there are cities that get water only on alternate days, some only twice in a week and large sections of the poor get barely 50 lpcd at the best of times.

Only 30 per cent of sewage is treated in urban India and sewage and septic coverage is only 67 per cent, leaving close to one-third of the urban population without this essential facility. In fact, one of the more shaming statistics about India, that illustrates the appalling lack of sanitation, is that virtually one out of every two Indians is forced to defecate in the open. Just over 70 per cent of solid waste is collected, the rest visible in the garbage heaps that have become the quintessential statement of a modern-day Indian city (McKinsey Global Institute 2010: 54). Can these gaps be bridged?

It is evident that there needs to be huge investment in urban infrastructure to prevent Indian cities from becoming completely unliveable. According to the McKinsey report, at the current rate of investment, in 20 years time urban infrastructure will fall very short of the need to sustain a 'prosperous city'.

India is likely to invest $300 billion in urban infrastructure in the next 20 years which is a two-fold increase in per capita spending of $17 today. But even with such large investment programme, capacity building in India will not come anywhere close to the surging demand for services (McKinsey Global Institute 2010: 19).

Apart from fresh investment in infrastructure, we also need a reality check about the availability of resources, like water. According to one study, 56 per cent of Indian cities and towns are dependent on groundwater either fully or partially. Smaller towns are almost completely dependent on groundwater, one reason being their inability to leverage the investment required to transport surface water (Krishnan and Patel 2009).

With the smaller towns growing at a faster rate than the megacities, a water crisis is already evident in many parts of urban India. This is the consequence of overdrawing of groundwater as demand grows resulting in saline ingress. Without adequate planning to ensure replenishment of underground aquifers that feed the wells and water sources in cities, such a situation is inevitable. As a result, there are hundreds of towns in different parts of the country that are entirely dependent on water transported by tankers. Once thriving small towns have been reduced to dormitory towns for bigger cities, because the lack of water discourages industry and investment.

The larger towns that get municipal water, either through groundwater sources or surface water ferried from dammed rivers outside the town limits, have to contend with water for a few hours perhaps once or twice a week. Those with the ability to arrange for private storage get by. But the poor, who cannot store more than what they use each day, are left to beg, borrow or buy water at prices they can ill afford. In the summer months, 'water riots' are a regular occurrence in many small towns across the country.

The environmental cost for the ever-growing thirst for water in cities is being paid by people living in rural areas, whose perennial sources of water, such as rivers or deep wells, are being dammed and diverted so that water can be transported over long distances to urban areas. Dammed rivers, for water or electricity, then become the reason for forced migration of displaced communities to nearby urban areas. Thus is completed the circle of deprivation where those who lived off natural and freely available resources like water are forced to live without adequate shelter or water in a city that has taken this very resource from them.

As urbanisation spreads, water shortages will grow and even the current average of 105 lpcd of water per resident is likely to come down to 65 lpcd by 2030 (McKinsey Global Institute 2010: 55). If this is the average, we can imagine how little will be available for the urban poor.

As with housing, steps to conserve water, cut leakages and theft and build in equity into distribution systems have either not been taken or pursued half-heartedly. Thus, lack of affordable housing and water are only two of several components that illustrate the unsustainable pattern of urban planning and development currently being followed in India.

Sustainability

A useful definition of sustainability in the urban context is:

> Sustainable development means attaining a balance between environmental protection and human economic development and between the present and future needs. It means equity in development and sectoral actions across space and time. It requires an integration of economic, social and environmental approaches towards development. Sustainable urban development refers to attaining social equity and environmental protection in urbanization while minimizing the costs of urbanization (Chattopadhyay 2009).

The pattern of growth that most Indian cities have adopted is quite the opposite. For instance, it has become increasingly evident that the most liveable cities across the world are those with efficient, affordable, environmentally benign public transport systems that ensure that people do not have to use privatised motor transport. This not only improves the quality of the air but also increases the efficiency of the city and creates greater equity. If we look at this requirement and at the way Indian cities are growing, then we see the complete opposite.

On the government's own admission,

'Transport ... has been a victim of ignorance, neglect, and confusion. As far as the public transport system in Indian cities is concerned, dedicated city bus services are known to operate in 17 cities only and rail transit exists only in four out of 35 cities with population in excess of one million (GoI 2009: 141).

With liberalisation in 1991 and the opening up of the economy, there has been a huge boom in the automobile industry. From a time when Indians had access to only three or four models of cars they can now buy any brand ranging from the indigenous Tata Nano and Maruti Suzuki to Mercedes, BMW, Volkswagen, etc. In Delhi, for instance, a city that has more motorised private vehicles than Mumbai, Chennai and Kolkata put together, between 2001–2002 and 2005–2006 car sales increased by 73 per cent and the sale of two-wheelers by 68 per cent. While its road network grew three times between 1971 and 2001, the number of motorised vehicles increased 16 times (Roychowdhury PowerPoint presentation). Not surprisingly, Delhi now has the distinction of being one of the most polluted cities in the world even after it took the important step of mandating that all public transport, including buses, taxis and auto-rickshaws use CNG (compressed natural gas) instead of petrol or diesel. If air quality improved initially because of this, it soon took a downward plunge as the sheer number of private motorised vehicles continued to grow at a frightening pace.

According to a report by the Ministry of Environment,

In Delhi, one out of ten school children has asthma. According to a World Bank–Asian Development Bank study, premature deaths due to air pollution in Indian cities were estimated to have increased by 30 per cent between 1992 and 1995. High levels of lead pollution in the air lead to stunted growth in children, as well as hyperactivity and brain damage (GoI: 140).

Global warming and the inevitability of climate change seem to have prompted a shift in the thinking of urban planners in India. As a result, there is fresh investment in public transport systems in many cities including metro rail and the Bus Rapid Transport System (BRTS) that has transformed cities like Curitiba in Brazil and Bogota in Colombia. Unfortunately, this is not accompanied with a proactive policy to discourage private automobiles. Instead, even as dedicated bus lanes are built, wider roads, flyovers and freeways are being constructed as well as multi-storied car parks for the private car owner. The virtual gridlock in most cities during peak hours, where the optimum speed at such times is barely 15 km/hour, illustrates the foolhardiness of following such a policy — one that builds public transport without discouraging private transport. Levels of air pollution in Delhi are an example of the direct environmental fallout of such a policy (Sharma 2010).

Conclusion

The picture painted above of urban India is rather depressing. It is like an express train hurtling in the wrong direction. The problem lies in the belief that a 'global city' is the aspirational model, that this will be delivered by building capital intensive infrastructure like modern airports, expressways, special economic zones, Shanghai-type business districts, glitzy retail outlets like shopping malls, etc. Such a model denies the realities of poverty and inequity and of the need for environmental sustainability. It overlooks the strengths of existing forms in our cities that work — such as mixed-use areas, low-rise buildings requiring less energy, spaces for people to walk and use non-motorised forms of transport. Instead of building on these strengths, our planners are destroying them and replacing them with a style and pattern that has already been rejected in the very places where it was devised — the industrialised North.

The strength of cities and their dynamism lies in a healthy mix of population, opportunities to work and prosper and densities that allow access to services to all. But the downside as we see in our cities is the price of wrong planning being paid by the poor, unsanitary living conditions in the quality of the air and water they breathe, and in their access to services.

The challenge, I believe, is pushing for an environmentally sustainable model of urban development. Ultimately only that kind of vision can benefit everyone, and not just those who can sanitise themselves against the disease and dirt in our cities by creating their private bubbles within which they live.

Notes

1. For details of the scheme check http://www.sra.gov.in/.
2. See review of this book on Infochange India: http://infochangeindia.org/200806027158/Urban-India/Analysis/Swept-off-the-map.html.
3. Litres per capita per day.

References

Chattopadhyay, Basudha. 2008. 'Sustainable Urban Development in India, Some Issues'. 1 August. http://www.indiaenvironmentportal.org.in/content/sustainable-urban-development-india-some-issues. Accessed in August 2010.

Krishnan, Sunderrajan and Ankit Patel. 2009. 'Groundwater Situation in Urban India'. http://www.carewater.org/UGW.pdf.

McKinsey Global Institute (MGI). 2010. 'India's Urban Awakening, Building Inclusive Cities, Sustaining Economic Growth', p. 13. April 2010.

Menon-Sen, Kalyani and Gautam Bhan. 2008. *Swept off the Map, Surviving Resettlement and Relocation in Delhi*. New Delhi: Yoda Press.

Government of India (GoI). 2009. 'State of Environment 2009'. Ministry of Environment and Forests (MoEF), Government of India..

Roychowdhury, Anumita. 2009. 'Challenges of Urban Growth in India', PowerPoint presentation. http://www.slideshare.net/equitywatch/4-ifej-media-workshop?src=related_normal&rel=44619.

Sharma, Kalpana. 2010. 'Motorised Mayhem'. http://infochangeindia.org/Urban-India/Cityscapes/Motorised-mayhem.html. March.

State of the World's Cities. 2008–2009. UN Habitat. Earthscan.

16

Contesting Conservation: Nature, Politics and History in Contemporary India

Mahesh Rangarajan

Making space for nature in India today is no easy task. But opportunities in a liberal democracy with nearly six decades of adult franchise open up possibilities for new kinds of engagements of citizens with issues of ecology and justice. Writing at the onset of the era of neoliberal reform, two leading scholars of ecology and equity had argued there were two kinds of development choices before the country (Gadgil and Guha, Ramachandra 2000). One was highly centralised and resource-extensive use and abuse and the other founded on devolution, intensive resource use and regeneration.

It is now possible to take a more nuanced view wherein the choices are not so stark. This is not because the deeper contradictions have become less pronounced; it is more due to the emergence, though in a very incipient form, of a middle ground. This is still an emerging and often ambiguous space, and its contours and shape differ in various regions. But it is possible to argue that many of the alternative currents that were visible two decades ago are now more mature, complex and diverse. This does not mean the challenges are any easier.

The task of reconciling regeneration of the life-cycles of rivers and forests, ponds and mountains is still not easy given the geophysical and historical constraints of the country. For a start, it has twice as many people today as it did four decades ago: population density has risen five-fold since 1881 (Guha 2001). Such a country cannot be an easy place to retain landscapes with mostly natural vegetation. It is common place to assume the landscape was like this across the centuries but the reverse is also true. It is only over the last two centuries that the cultivated arable land has grown to occupy nearly half the land mass. For centuries, it was the ebb and flow of the line of forest and arable land that was a decisive and continuing trend (Deloche 1993: 1–10). The growth of modern industry, of railway lines and mines, highways and new townships has also been a major ecological factor. Economic growth, even as it creates wealth, exacerbates conflicts between rival uses for the land and waterscapes. Since 1980, the Indian economy has been the second fastest growing in the world. The Gross Domestic Product has doubled since 1991. The expansion of industry or the conflicts within and between urban and rural society over access to and control of resources are not new, but have grown sharper in recent times.

The socio-cultural milieu and political landscape are also in a state of flux, more so due to an increasing awareness of rights among the under privileged and the complex relationship of this process to unequal access to natural resources and to economic and social opportunities. The scale and extent of controversy over forest clearances, the issue of land rights of those whose livelihoods or habitations are displaced are now issues of prime political importance. How far will the accumulation of wealth be reconciled with the clash of rights of those directly reliant on resources is a major issue of political import in forest and coast, dam site and river front? This simple question resonates in a myriad forms across the country.

Traditionally, discussions about the conservation of nature, and particularly of wildlife, have gravitated towards creating and maintaining nature reserves. Several national parks and tiger reserves, Elephant Reserves and wildlife sanctuaries have been established or expanded since the early 1970s. Many such sites had their origins in the princely or imperial past when they were hunting grounds for the landed aristocracy, princes and British imperial officials. Around four decades ago, a new 'ecological patriotism' combined with deep concern about extinction of rare fauna impelled a major emphasis on saving nature. The acreage of Protected Areas went up 10-fold from 1969 to 1989. Indian parks are still small, an average size of about 200 sq. km, and there is nothing to compare with Kruger (Rangarajan 2001; Saberwal and Rangarajan 2007). But at a larger level and anticipating developments in eastern and western Africa, the imperial state had by a century ago annexed over 600,000 sq. km of forest. Even more land, some 735, 000 sq. km, are to this day owned by state forest departments, a pattern with roots in the colonial past. It is such administrative mechanisms that India's new rulers turned to in the 1970s as they gave preservation a place in the sun (Beinart and Hughes 2007; Rangarajan 2009).[1]

The strategy of preservation was simple. Spaces on land and water of intrinsic ecological worth were delineated and protection was made the explicit management priority. Preservation was the way to safeguard ecological integrity. Competing social, economic or cultural claims were shut out by law and executive fiat. Much of conservation, then, has been about the vigorous defence of these reserves and their protection from any activity that compromised wildlife and nature. It is crucial to stress that the vast majority of the forest estate was open to economic exploitation. The forester to this day is less a planter of trees and more a complex land manager: mobilising labour, laying roads and bridges, cutting fire lines and supervising contracts, regulating the clearance of forest or its regrowth. It may escape memory but nobody should forget what the famous wolf-boy Mowgli did at the end of Rudyard Kipling's well-known *Jungle Book*: he became a forest guard!

Protecting nature has primarily meant locking human influences out in a small but significant area of land. The limitations of the preservationist approach are self evident. Vital as they are for heritage and science, such reserves cover a mere 5 per cent of the country's landscape. They do not exist in ecological or economic isolation from a wider matrix. In turn, the parks and sanctuaries are part of a larger network of government forests which are also increasingly sites of contest. Crises of survival of rare fauna such as the tiger have resurfaced, leading to debate, controversy and, to some extent, introspection among decision makers. They are increasingly embattled and under pressure, with Task Forces having been set up on key flagship species such as the tiger (2005) (MoEF 2005) and the elephant (2010) (Rangarajan et al. 2011). Significantly, both these Task Forces had two features in common: they called for more integration of science in policy making and for greater transparency, dialogue with and participation of those living in and around Protected Areas (Madhusudan and Sankaran 2010).

Critics have rightly pointed to the limitations of such piecemeal reform, even as they acknowledge it has some elements of a long overdue paradigm shift in the interrelationship of nature, knowledge and power. The conflicts such initiatives aim to defuse are acute: two of every three kills of elephants by people in India are by cultivators defending crops. In turn, 400 people a year, mostly farm labourers and farmers, are killed by elephants. But at a wider level, this will only work if protection (for both animals and people) and compensation are made accountable at the local level, preferably via the elected representatives. This will call for an overhaul not merely of the forest departmental machinery but the revenue administration in general.

Yet, this points to a larger scenario where fluidity is a fact and interventions are rigid. Lines on the land rarely mean as much as they seem. Animals and birds, water and wind do not obey the boundaries people draw. In any case only 25 of the 650 Protected Areas in India are more than 1,000 sq. km, a far cry from Selous Game Reserve in Tanzania which is over 40,000 square kilometres. Often, a park's wildlife populations can be imperilled by what happens beyond its borders. The catastrophic population crash of the three most common vulture species, first documented in Bharatpur's wetlands, had its origins in the changing practice of veterinary medicine across India. Tigers or elephants may be marooned in small reserves as mega-development projects cut off corridors that animals can now walk across. Reserves with sharp boundaries hold even less meaning in arid or montane land-scapes where species share their ranges with human communities. Wolves or snow leopards, for instance, can hardly be contained within park boundaries. Big cats, especially leopards, survive in stable populations in sugar cane fields calling for strategies that go beyond simple seclusion (Athreya et al. 2010). Even in urban spaces, remnant nature can persist both in form and substance. As for rivers and the sea, the vitality of the larger waterscape hinges on much more than policing the extraction of biomass. Large dams have often significantly altered the ecology of several rivers, while the coastline is being rapidly transformed by new ports, increased pollution and urban expansion. The earlier notion of secluded reserves has little meaning given the fluidity of natural systems. It is not without value but it does need careful rethinking especially given the ways in which the viability of reserves is under threat from actions well beyond their boundaries.

If nature's processes span borders, so too do the webs of human actions. The recent wiping out of the tiger population of a well-known Indian tiger reserve, Sariska, owed as much to pressures on the habitat from mining and commercial firewood trade from outside the tract as it had to do with the work of poachers (Shahabuddin et al. 2007). Similarly, river pollution is an ever-present threat to unique reptiles and mammals, the gharial in the Chambal river and the Gangetic dolphin in the Ganga (Kelkar et al. 2010; Lenin 2007).[2] The creation of wealth and waste, the movement of goods and people, all combine to limit if not totally undermine the value of enclave-centred conservation. This is no new phenomenon: captive elephants were a major item of trade for over two and half millennia, while horses, another vital auxiliary of war, were bred or maintained in grasslands. India, for centuries, imported ivory from Africa and shatoosh wool from the Tibetan plateau. The pace and scale of such exchange or extraction has radically changed in the recent past.

So make no mistake: reserves are not *passé*, and still need priority. Preservation remains a valid and worthwhile ideal to strive for. The larger projects of cleaner air and water, sustainable farming and eco-friendly urban spaces will gain immeasurably from safety sites where we can learn about the workings of nature. The idea of *in situ* preservation has special significance in a country with a population density of nearly 400 to a square kilometre. It is equally vital because India, with just 2 per cent of the earth's land surface has a fifth, no less, of its domestic ungulates. Unless some areas are kept free of biomass extraction, it will be difficult to get a sense of how nature's system of renewal or repair works. But the matrix requires active intervention, care and thought. The reserves and the larger landscape milieu are different parts of a spectrum that complement each other.

But there is little doubt that nature reserves are in crisis for reasons well beyond the circumstances responsible for their insular character. Often, the reserves are contested spaces and the present model that tries to render them inviolate works, but only fitfully. Powerful economic factors were checkmated a quarter century ago when a hydel power plant in Silent Valley was scrapped to save a rainforest (D'Monte 1985). More recently, a major nuclear research facility was disallowed in a critical forest adjacent to Mudumalai Tiger Reserve, and a bauxite mine disallowed in the Niyamgiri Hills, Orissa. The former were mostly about ecological integrity and the latter also about rights of the Scheduled Tribes under a key piece of recent legislation, the Forest Rights Act, 2006 (Padel and Brody 2010). The latter has been crucial in halting the grant of a bauxite mining lease in the Niyamgiri Hills of Orissa for a major international aluminium company. The ability of the Gram Sabha or the village hamlet council to draw on provisions of the Act were central to this denouement thought it is too early to see how far this will be a precedent in other, less publicised conflicts. The Niyamgiri case had important implications for nature protection, as the Hills are part of a key elephant landscape.

Tiger reserves, national parks and wildlife sanctuaries still slow down if not hamper such major changes in the land in parts of India. But the larger web of the economy cannot but intrude on the world of nature. The market economy has long done so but in recent decades such pressures have grown manifold even in frontier states, and interior hill regions (Saikia 2011). The complex of parks in the Nilgiri Biosphere Reserve is a case in point. [About] 150,000 people have relied on Bandipur Tiger Reserve alone for firewood. Over 100,000 cattle graze in it every day. For those eking out modest livelihoods, energy and cash are vital for sustenance, and the forest is a source of both. If the parks do sustain the people, the harvest of fuelwood and fodder also does undermine its fragile ecology. Conversely, animals like elephants and wild boars raid crops in the adjoining farmlands, while cattle vie with wild grazers or browsers for fodder in the reserved forests. Most conservation efforts here as elsewhere are directly in conflict with the survival needs of such farming communities. Increasingly able to assert their rights, and as active voters, they cannot be stopped from regular ingress on the park. It is a fragile balancing act. The park as an entity survives and the livelihoods do too, but the idea of a strict nature reserve is realised only in part. This remains the case even though — unusually for an Indian park — it has no residents within its perimeter. To add to pressures, large infrastructure projects in the greater Nilgiris remain a major issue that threaten to slice up this contiguous forest tract.

Conversely, the displacement of resident peoples, whether through physical relocation to create 'inviolate spaces for wildlife recovery' or in a more indirect sense via the denial of usufruct rights to access forest produce has been a major locus of tensions. The displacement on more than one occasion of fishers, cultivators and woodcutters in the Sundarbans mangroves in 1978 even entailed direct confrontations, with loss of lives in police firings. Elsewhere, as in the central Indian forest of Kuno where the

Sahariya Scheduled Tribes were relocated, their economic condition has deteriorated rather than improved. In the recent past, a far better economic package has been made available by the Union (or federal) Government to the tune of one million rupees per family. Even prior to this in Bhadra, Karnataka, independent studies indicate higher incomes for most people relocated from a Tiger Reserve. There is a caveat: unlike in the other two cases cited here, most of the displaced in Bhadra were not Scheduled Tribals or Scheduled Castes, but mainly from a dominant peasant community. Whether such a practice can be replicated elsewhere is, therefore, an open question (Jalais 2009; Kabra 2009).[3] The issue is of central importance as over 50,000 families are set to be relocated from Tiger Reserve core areas in the next few years.

There are indeed ways to intervene that alleviate distress. Efforts to facilitate alternate energy and to evolve better farmer-maintained fencing address some of the issues in an innovative way and take the sharp edge off conflict. Perhaps if extended more widely, they can do more than just buy time. They can create or secure conservation spaces via cooperation, widening the constituency for conservation beyond those who make gains (or limit losses) arising from protection. Such efforts outside the parks are as integral to making space for nature as creating parks in the first place.

Such efforts are admittedly on a small scale but they may well be harbingers of change. This will of course only be so if they are scaled up and become the nucleus of new and livelihood-friendly conservation practice. Insurance for herders to protect sheep from wolves and snow leopards have worked in the western Himalayas and are being expanded under Project Snow Leopard (Bhatnagar 2010; MoEF 2008).[4] Farmers' cooperative fences to keep out elephants have worked well near Bandipur, Karnataka and hold promise elsewhere. Cooperation to save adjacent wetlands and continuing age-old tolerance may be the key to saving the largest crane in India, the sarus. Similarly, the Bodoland Autonomous Council in Assam has enabled the recovery of a major biodiversity site, Manas, as it is seen as an integral heritage of the Bodo Scheduled Tribe which has gained autonomy over the region that contains the Reserve. These are but small initiatives, often led and worked on by exceptionally motivated individuals or groups.

Elsewhere, there has been an efflorescence of small community-run 'no-go' sites and areas where limited extraction is permissible. Can they be scaled up fast enough? This hinges on legal and administrative changes that enable these to have the stable basis they now lack. And even if they are, will it simply gain some space, win some time but not much more?

But as argued above, the larger ecological and economic fabric is under strain and can do with more than just tending fences at the forest edge. It may defy commonly held premises, but recent ecological and social research has shown that significant spaces continue to remain for nature *outside* reserve boundaries. This is true even for charismatic vertebrates such as Asian elephants, and even more so for biomes like wetlands, dry savannah and scrub jungles. An obsession with reserves alone may do these species and habitats grave injustice. For many smaller taxa, habitats outside reserves may often be far more crucial than what may be found inside them.

Policy and practice vis-à-vis the lands and waters outside reserves still has crucial implications for conservation. Yet, we cannot overlook the fact that outside reserve boundaries, economic, social and cultural demands will take priority. Thus, on the ground, it is often difficult to view the reserve boundary as a line that clearly separates conservation opportunity from conservation threat. Making space for nature seemed easier in the imperial or princely case, but then the hierarchies of men were reproduced when it came to access to nature.

Should these continue in a democratic society? That they do is undoubtedly true, but democracy is on trial here as much as on other issues of justice. A just society or a state by just means has today to grapple with how to achieve peace with nature. But the burdens of the peace cannot be uneven or the fruits unequally shared. To do so conservation has to delink itself from its more conservative roots, and perhaps the constructive efforts mentioned here or the more active, grass roots movements of protest both have critical role to play (Jacoby 2001).[5]

For these hopes to be made reality, change is a must. Just as conservation must grapple with the serious challenges within reserve boundaries, it must equally embrace the opportunities outside them. To accomplish such a metaphorical blurring of the reserve boundary, we must first transcend the more entrenched ideological boundaries as well. If nature spills beyond borders, thought, policy and action too must follow suit. This is *not* a prescription to let go of nature reserves. We would contend against a 'let's forget nature reserves' stance with all the emphasis at our command. But conservation, whether protection or ecological restoration, cannot stop at reserve boundaries. Nor can it treat the wider matrix as orphaned ecological space.

Such a wider platform for ecology is easy to speak about but harder to create or sustain. Like any other school of thought, the conservation community too is riven across many ideological lines. Biocentric ideologies of *preserving* nature are locked in contest with anthropocentric ideas of *using* nature (Gadgil 2001; Karanth 2006).[6] Landscape-level approaches conflict with those who want a hard, sharp edge for reserves to the prime field of focus (Karanth and DeFries 2010).[7] Some focus on small species or reserves as worthwhile and others remain focused on big animals and landscapes to play an umbrella or flagship role. Captive breeding and *ex situ* means of conservation vie with the needs of protecting species *in situ*. Some leverage emerging markets for conservation, others favour a systematic delinking of nature from markets. Some see inclusive, democratic processes that involve a cross-section of society as anchor; others yearn for an earlier age when power and wealth were concentrated with a few, and conservation rolled out quickly.

Conservation practitioners have defied all manner of typecasting and continue to adopt a mélange of shifting positions. They have cut the cloth to the occasion. Like any crisis-driven response, conservation has often involved on-the-spot responses with the theory later playing catch-up. Many sharp edges in conservation arise from the novelty of the conservation enterprise itself. Managing runaway growth to minimise long-term negative impacts on ecology in a disparate society is hard enough. With so many voices, many strident and each more vocal with time, the task becomes even more complex.

To rethink conservation is to reorder our ideas about nature as much as society. To use Deng Xiao Peng's phrase, it is about crossing the river while feeling the stones. The journey must not be broken but has to negotiate the hidden real-life obstacles. For conservation, the crossing has to be in the mind and heart as much as by how the feet walk the river bed. Ethics and economics, political and social concerns, all have to blend with ecology. The structures and functions of nature do matter but so too the ways in which institutions work or cultures change.

These newer engagements can complement older approaches. This may not be easy especially when the proponents of the older guns and guards approach see any change as the start of the deluge. The deep attachment to the strict enforcement model has been reinforced by recent crises, especially so with threats in the wild to the national animal, the tiger (Chundawat 2009; Thapar 2006, 2008).[8] In a routine all too familiar in South Africa, the emphasis on enforcement can all too easily become a means to simply reinvigorate bureaucratic stranglehold on rural economies and ecologies without addressing threats to ecological integrity. Further, recent campaigns to save imperilled species, ecologies and habitats have derived substantial support from the corporate sector, audio–visual media and film fraternity. What is significant is the counter-positioning of threats to nature (in the most recent case represented by a young tiger cub) with its converse, the strong enforcers, hence, the call for more contributions for purchase of equipment for enforcers.[9]

There is a significant critique of such centralisation of power and the many abuses that accompany it. But what is more crucial is that stringent anti-poaching campaigns in a country such as India hardly begin to address critical threats to the larger flora and fauna complex. Conservation is about the wider ecological integrity of the landscape and even scientists who are proponents of strict preservation do not see poaching as *the* major issue at hand (Watson et al. 2010). Proponents of hard-edged reserves are themselves divided on whether the core response is better policing versus poachers or a more integrated habitat preservation model.

But there is also a pragmatic view that is a critique of the preservation via firm borders position. As the Bandipur case shows, the best armed guards cannot keep out village cattle. As anthropologists have argued, the forest guard is not merely an agent of government: he is likely to be also a villager with deep social roots (Vasan 2008). Even were the enforcement of authoritarian agendas possible as they often are, it raises a critical question of who is to save what and from whom. The idea of nature is after all deeply contested and how one responds to the issue of where repair and renewal is to begin is a deeply, implicitly political question.

It is more difficult in forest and other such landscapes beyond the urban spaces and intensely cultivated areas. Whereas agrarian rights have been devolved downward — though in an uneven way and save for certain regions not equitably — it is true that the government as property owner and regulator looms larger in the life of basic producers who are in hill, forest and dry regions. In addition to the Forest Department there are a host of other government agencies that impinge on the lives and livelihoods of those who herd, fish, hunt, gather or cultivate a crop once a year. It is no surprise that the intensity of conflicts in forests is equalled by those on the coast or in dry rangelands and hill pastures (Centre for Science and Environment 1982; Gooch 2009).[10]

How can we advance nature-friendly agendas on a wider social and ecological canvas? This requires engagement not only with protection but production, not only 'inviolate spaces' but also with human settlements. Often, they try going beyond small nuclei of middle class, bureaucracy and science to reach out to larger political constituencies. There are intimations of change not only in citizen groups and academia, but also in government. It calls for a paradigm shift that there is a challenge for the larger political system (Shahabuddin and Rangarajan 2007).

Whether they will be a counteracting force to the more destructive trends unleashed by larger economic forces is an open question. The deepening of democracy as in the case of the Forest Rights Act is a positive trend. But it sits uneasily with the greater centralisation of power and the reinforcing of market-led growth both within and without the country. Similarly, the greater transparency and accountability due to recent changes in policies is displacement of people from parks is a vast improvement but whether it changes forester–citizen interaction on the forest floor is yet to be seen. The promise of law-governed democratic state runs counter to so much in the daily, more crude and brutal realities of grids of power (Chhatre and Saberwal 2006; Gopalakrishnan 2010).[11] Iconic animals have indeed made a transition to becoming symbols of ecological awareness, but there is a troubling past of repressive measures to protect hunting grounds that is in danger of being played out in a new setting (Gold and Gujjar 2003).

Conservation in practice has to combine ecological sanity with justice, a space for nature with one for livelihoods. There are working approaches with different and often more effective ways of drawing on knowledge and institutions, processes and practices to create more not less space for nature. Many of these initiatives lie at points in the spectrum that is neither fully statist and centralised nor completely community centred and locally rooted. There is a space that combines elements of both but mixes and matches them in new ways.

It is possible here to draw on Ajantha Subramanian's insightful work on the fishers of the Coromandel coast of Tamil Nadu where she concludes that the state system does more than merely create docile subjects or insurrectionary 'others'. In the case of the fishers, decades of political activity have opened up new spaces for a kind of collectivity that is deeply engaged within state spaces. These dynamic, contested processes which are the subject of her study are deeply relevant to the debate on the future of nature in India. In fact, the Forest Rights Act has led to consideration of a similar legislative measure providing for legal basis for fisher rights on coast and in the sea. Of course, as she observes, resource renewal will involve a different set of priorities for production (Subramanian 2009). It is also important to acknowledge that the south-west coast, with its long history of radical social reform and upheaval over the last century, may not in every way be typical of many other regions in the country. But there is reason to argue that the level and extent of attempts to redefine democracy in a way inclusive of rights to forest or coast do have the potential for new engagements with nature as much as among people.

It is important to note that such a cautiously positive view of the present scenario is not shared by many seasoned observers. The frictions around Maosim and related radical currents are often seen as fundamentally challenging the present socio-political order. Bastar, the central Indian region in Chhattisgarh, which is an epicentre of the often violent encounter between the government and armed rebels, is a well-known forest tract. It has had a long history of upheaval and a century ago witnessed a major rebellion which contested imperial control of the forest and curbs on swidden cultivation. Its major chronicler and historian is also a leading scholar of the politics of forestry. It was here and elsewhere in the central Indian forest tracts that that writers and journalists have written extensively and human rights activists raised issues of abuse of the law by police and paramilitary forces. What is crucial is that there is a sharp contest not only for the wealth of the forest but for the minerals that lie beneath the soil, bauxite, iron ore and coal. Yet, it would be misleading to ignore the struggles to protect the forest cover from encroaching mines and industry that are waged on a peaceable basis. It is such protests that played a key role in the denial of the mining lease for bauxite in the Niyamgiri Hills. To date, this point is not disputed by Maoist sympathisers not a single mine has been closed by extremist groups. In fact, peaceful but often militant movements in these very regions have borne the brunt of both government and Maoist violence. Such struggles are replete with potential for they often engage those whose work and livelihood depends centrally on the continued existence of the forest (Roma 2010).

But for that, the need to think afresh and create anew has never been more urgently felt. There is no doubt conservation or ecology, as with any social entity, is a house divided. Which current will prevail and for how long will have much to do with the new denouement. To strive for nature without borders is not just about more of the same. It is about some of the new. This is part of the larger challenge of crafting a more just society but in a manner that respects and builds on livelihoods as much as it allows nature's systems space and time for repair and renewal. Making space for the cycles of earth and water, forest and mountain hinges on how people combine peace among themselves with the search for a justice with nature.

Notes

1. The contrasts between South Asia and Southern Africa in differing imperial legacies of conservancy are explored here.
2. On the gharial see Lenin (2007); on the dolphin, see Kelkar et al. (2010).
3. On the Sundarbans, see Jalais (2009); on Kuno and Bhadra see Kabra (2009).
4. MoEF (2008); for innovative insurance schemes, see Bhatnagar (2010).
5. This term 'delinking conservation' from conservative owes much in intellectual terms to the work of Jacoby.
6. These are two different views by two leading Indian ecologists.
7. See the papers in the special section of the journal *Biological Conservation* edited by Karanth and DeFries (2010), especially their own introduction, 'Conservation in Human-dominated Landscapes in India', pp. 2865–69.
8. Valmik Thapar is an author, photographer and naturalist. For a different view that is far more critical of the breakdown of governance in a central Indian Tiger Reserve, see the work by ecologist Raghuram S. Chundawat (2009).

9. The reference here is to the Aircel 'Save our Tigers, campaign, launched March 2010 (see www.saveourtigers.com, accessed 20 September 2011) and to the recent Tigerathon with Amitabh Bachchan on NDTV.

10. The most compelling portrait emerging from studies and first rate journalism are the State of the Environment's Citizen's Reports, published since 1982. On pastoralists, see Gooch (2009).

11. Gopalakrishnan (2010); for a critique of a park, see Chhatre and Saberwal (2006).

References

Athreya, V., Morten Oden, John D. C. Linell and K. Ullas Karanth. 2010. 'Translocation as a Tool for Mitigating Conflict with Leopards in Human-Dominated Landscapes in India', *Conservation Biology*, 25: 1133–41.

Beinart, William and Lotte Hughes. 2007. *Environment and Empire*. Oxford: Oxford University Press.

Bhatnagar, Yashveer. 2010. 'Project Snow Leopard, *Seminar* (603): 44–48. September.

Centre for Science and Environment. 1982. 'State of the Environment', Citizen's Reports. Delhi.

Chhatre, Ashiwini and Vasant K. Saberwal. 2006. *Democratizing Nature*. New Delhi: Oxford University Press.

Chundawat, S. Raghuram. 2009. *Panna's Last Tiger: How the Management Fails to Protect Our Wildlife*. Delhi: Baavan.

Deloche, Jean. 1993. *Trade and Transport Routes in India Before Steam Locomotion: Volume I, the Land Routes*. New Delhi. Oxford University Press.

D'Monte, Darryl. 1985. *Temples or Tombs? Industry or Environment, Three Case Studies*, Delhi: Centre for Science and Environment.

Gadgil, Madhav. 2001. *Ecological Journeys, Science and the Politics of Conservation*. Ranikhet: Permanent Black.

Gadgil, Madhav and Ramachandra Guha. 2000. *The Use and Abuse of Nature*. Incorporating *This Fissured Land* (1992) and *Ecology and Equity* (1995). New Delhi. Oxford University Press.

Gold, Ann Grondzins and Bhoju Ram Gujjar. 2003. *In the Time of Trees and Sorrows*. New Delhi: Oxford University Press.

Gooch, Pernille. 2009. 'Victims of Conservation or Rights as Forest Dwellers: Van Gujjar Pastoralists between Contesting Codes of Law', *Conservation and Society*, 7 (4): 239–48.

Gopalakrishnan, Shankar. 2010. 'Blame the Forest Management System', *Economic and Political Weekly*, 46. December.

Guha, Sumit. 2001. *Health and Population in South Asia from Earliest Times to the Present*. New Delhi: Permanent Black.

Jacoby, Karl. 2001. *Crimes Against Nature, Poachers, Squatters, Thieves and the Hidden History of American Conservation*. Berkeley: University of California Press.

Jalais, Annu. 2009. *Forest of Tigers: People, Politics and Environment in the Sundarbans*. New Delhi: Routledge.

Kabra, Asmita. 2009. 'Conservation Induced Displacement: A Comparative Study of Two Indian Protected Areas', *Conservation and Society*, 7 (4): 249–67.

Kelkar, N., J. Krishnaswamy, S. Choudhury and D. Sutaria. 2010. 'Coexistence of Fisheries', *Conservation Biology*, (24): 1130–40.

Karanth, K. Ullas. 2006. *A View from the Machan: How Science can Save the Fragile Predator*. New Delhi: Permanent Black.

Karanth, Krithi and Ruth DeFries (eds). 2010. 'Conservation and Management in Human-dominated Landscapes: Case Studies from India', *Biological Conservation*, 143: 2865–69.

Lenin, Janaki. 2007. 'Song of the Ganges Gharial', *Seminar* 577: 34–38.

Madhusudan, M. D. and Pavithra Sankaran. 2010. 'Seeing the Elephant in the Room: Human–Elephant Conflict and the ETF Report', *Economic and Political Weekly*, 47.

Ministry of Environment and Forests (MoEF). 2005. *Joining the Dots: Report of the Tiger Task Force*. New Delhi: Government of India.

———. 2008. *Project Snow Leopard*. New Delhi: Government of India.

Padel, Felix and Hugh Brody. 2010. *Sacrificing People: Invasions of a Tribal Landscape*. Delhi: Orient Black Swan.

Rangarajan, Mahesh. 2001. *India's Wildlife History: An Introduction*. New Delhi: Permanent Black.

———. 2009. 'Striving for a Balance: Nature, Science, Power and India's Indira Gandhi, 1917–84', *Conservation and Society*, 7 (3).

Rangarajan, M. et al. (MoEF). 2011. *Gajah: Securing the Future for Elephants in India: The Report of the Elephant Task Force*. New Delhi: Government of India. September.

Roma. 2010. 'Forest Justice Movements', *Seminar*, 613: 75–77. September.

Saberwal, Vasant K. and Mahesh Rangarajan (eds). 2007. *Battles over Nature*. New Delhi: Permanent Black.

Saikia, Arupjyoti. 2011. *Forests and the Ecological History of Assam*. New Delhi: Oxford University Press.

Shahabuddin, Ghazala. 2010. *Conservation at the Cross Roads: Science, Society and the Future of India's Wildlife*. New Delhi: Permanent Black.

Shahabuddin G., R. Kumar and M. Shrivastava. 2007. 'Creation of Inviolate Space': Lives, Livelihoods and Conflcit in the Sariska Tiger Reserve', *Economic and Political Weekly*, 42 (2), 1855–62.

Shahabuddin, G. and Mahesh Rangarajan (eds). 2007. *Making Conservation Work: Securing Conservation in this Our New Century*. New Delhi: Permanent Black.

Subramanian, Ajantha. 2009. *Shore Lines: Space and Rights in South India*, pp. 253–54. Stanford: Stanford University Press.

Thapar, Valmik. 2006. *The Last Tiger*. New Delhi: Oxford University Press.

———. 2008. *Ranthambhore: Ten Days in the Tiger Fortress*. New Delhi: Oxford University Press.

Vasan, Sudha. 2008. *Living with Diversity*. Shimla: Indian Institute of Advanced Studies.

Watson, Joe, John G. Robinson, Elizabeth L. Benneth, Urs Breitenmoser, Gustavo A. B. da Fouseca, John Goodrich, Melvin Gumal, Luke Hunter, Arlyne Johnson, K. Ullas Karanth, Nigel Leader-Williams, Kathy MacKinnon, Dule Miquelle, Anak Pattanavibool, Colin Poole, Alan Rabinowitz, James L. D. Smith, Emma J. Stokes, Simon N. Stuart, Chanthavy Vongkhanheng and Hariyo Wibisono. 2010. 'Bringing the Tiger Back from the Brink — The Six Percent Solution', *PBLOS Biology*, 8–9. http://www.plosbiology.org/article/info%3Adoi%2F10.1371%2Fjo urnal.pbio.1000485. Accessed 20 September 2011.

Part III

Relating to Each Other as Regional Nation-States

17

Globalising World and the Changing Dimensions of Indo–South African Ties

Rajen Harshe

This article captures diverse dimensions of Indo–South African ties in the context of globalisation. It initially reflects on the essence of globalisation and proceeds to analyse a few basic similarities as well as differences between India and South Africa that could form a viable basis to build their mutually beneficial ties. Subsequently, it underscores a number of concrete areas where the two countries have and could cooperate in the globalising world.

Globalisation and its Essence

The term 'globalisation' signifies multilayered processes that are shrinking distances, especially after the disintegration of the Soviet Union in 1991, to an extent where the world is being gradually conceived as a single unit. Consequently, capitalism, for the want of formidable developmental alternative, has emerged stronger as a mode of development and a world system. Although globalisation need not be reduced to capitalism, an intertwined association between the two is undeniable. In the twilight of such association, several issues of global concern such as nuclear proliferation, global environmental and climatic conditions, international trading arrangements and human rights are being collectively deliberated and resolved by emerging configurations of powers. Such configurations, apart from the USA, its western allies and Japan include China, and the middle-ranging rising powers such as India, South Africa and Brazil. The latter three powers, which appear developed among developing countries and developing among developed countries, have become significant in major international forums like the World Trade Organisation (WTO) or the

G20. Furthermore, globalisation has facilitated asymmetric forms of interdependence between developed and developing countries through free flow of trade, finance, technology, knowledge, ideas, information, arms, drugs, diseases and people across the world.

With the unfolding of the processes under globalisation they have had their critics like J. Stiglitz and as also sympathisers like J. N. Bhagwati (Bhagwati 2004; Stiglitz 2002). Stiglitz, after his initial criticism of globalisation that subjected developing countries to severe financial hardships, eventually began to construe ways of making globalisation work (Stiglitz 2006). In contrast, Bhagwati, by and large, celebrated the notion of free flow of trade and resources to uplift the plight of even developing countries. In substance, globalisation has not only unleashed the path of integration but has strengthened international regimes such as the WTO, the World Bank (WB) and the International Monetary Fund (IMF). In addition, it has facilitated the growth of transnationally mobile capital with the rise of multinational banks and firms (MNCs) through well-spread-out global networks and transformed the character of the world political economy. By now, apart from the developed industrialised countries, countries such as China, India, South Africa and Brazil also have their share of MNCs. Consequently, intra-industry trade plausibly is becoming as important as the international trade. Moreover, multiple ways of promoting networks of cooperation in areas such as trade, banks, insurance, business commerce and information have become possible owing to Information Communication Technologies (ICT). Further, cross-border movement of capital has been much speedier than any cross-border movement of labour. In fact, the unprecedented flow of finances during the last two decades coupled with the lack of sound regulatory mechanisms over finances can potentially accentuate financial crises. Even the ardent defenders of capitalism like Soros are critical of the manner in which the unregulated form of capitalism has been causing unbridled exploitation of the poor in the post Cold-War years (Soros 1997). Evidently, this phase has witnessed the burgeoning of a wide variety of international non-governmental organisations (NGOs) that are fighting for environmental and human rights of individuals and communities across the world. They have also fought for the right to be decision makers in the WTO summit at Seattle in 1999 (Kaldor 2000). What is more, globalisation has also magnified the radius of interstate and inter-societal terrorist outfits including a major multinational terrorist organisation such as the Al-Qaeda. The Al-Qaeda sprang up with the advent of the USA-backed mujahedeen groupings in Afghanistan and by now it has built a worldwide network of activities (Cooley 2000; Gunaratna 2002; Harshe 2008). The process of building transnational coalitions to fight terrorism is integral to globalisation.

In addition to these developments, the resurgence of regions and constitution, and reconstitution of regional organisations could as well be construed to a response to globalisation. In the process, powerful capitalist countries such as the USA, Germany and Japan have emerged as leading giants of major world trading blocs such as North American Free Trade Agreement (NAFTA), European Union (EU) and Asia-Pacific Economic Cooperation (APEC). Moreover, there are several other organisations such as Association of South East Asian Nations (ASEAN), South Asian Association of Regional Cooperation (SAARC) and Southern African Development Community (SADC) that are contributing to the rise of the making of the 'regions'. If we extend the notion of regions to religious and cultural identities, institutions such as Organisation of Islamic Countries (OIC) could also be conceived as a region.

Obviously, the nation-state is witnessing existential strains under globalisation due to pressure from the international and regional organisations from above and challenges posed by the separatist ethno-nationalist movements from below. For instance, states in western and central parts of Europe have achieved transnational integration in key economic and commercial areas while with the disintegration of the former Soviet Union and Yugoslavia in the 1990s there is resurgence of ethnic nationalism in Eastern Europe and Central Asia. Actually, states in both developed as well as developing countries including Canada, Spain, the UK, India, Sri Lanka, Iraq, Turkey and several African countries have been handling secessionist movements. Since transnational, subnational and non-state actors, in their own ways, have come into the foreground, nation-states will continue to struggle to reinvent themselves. Irrespective of such existential challenges, the sovereign territorial state continues to be the primary and indispensible de jure unit to negotiate with the phase of globalisation. In view of this, some light needs to be shed on commonalities as well as differences in the evolution of India and South Africa.

India and South Africa: Areas of Convergence and Divergence

To begin with, independence in India and post-apartheid South Africa was preceded by protracted struggles launched by major mass movements cum parties such as the Indian National Congress (INC) and the African National Congress (ANC). Both the INC and the ANC also combined complex and diverse ideological strands within their fold and the ANC functioned almost like a 'state in exile' (Lodge 1988). While democracy in independent India witnessed one-party dominant rule for the initial two decades, post-apartheid South Africa continues to be led by the ANC with its repeated victories in the general elections. Both the countries are relatively stable representative democracies.

The central features of India's development model were protection of infant industry from outside competition, public sector with commanding heights of the economy leading towards the state as a major source of employment, growth of private sector under the shadow of public sector, a parliamentary democracy, a partially planned economy and policy of non-alignment in external affairs. Although this model was designed to bring about a socialist pattern of the society owing to an unprecedented economic and financial crisis triggered by the paucity of foreign exchange reserves during 1991, India had to embrace economic reforms to bring about macroeconomic stability in its malfunctioning economy. Reforms subsumed rolling back of the state sector, cutting expenditures on salaries and subsidies and even closure of the sick public sector units, promotion of private initiatives and liberalisation of trade. Thus, India systematically began to work towards integration of its economy within the world economy (Harshe 2000). Even if reforms have led to sustained economic growth at an annual average between 6–8 per cent, for more than 15 years, they have stimulated glaring social and economic inequalities and uneven developments of the sectors and regions.

Unlike in India, in South Africa under successive apartheid regimes there was an inextricable link between race and the development of capitalism. A few conglomerates such as SANLAM, Rembrant and Volkaskas witnessed spectacular growth due to official policy of promoting Afrikaner capital. The capitalism in South Africa, in turn, was integral to world capitalism as multinationals and banks from major industrial economies were operating in South Africa on a massive scale. The Anglo-American corporation of South Africa offered an example of symbiotic association between the state and private capital in South Africa and transnational firms and banks. Besides, South Africa also was the beneficiary of nuclear cooperation and sophisticated weapons from France. The military–industrial complex in South Africa had made the apparatus of apartheid formidable. It was against this formidable strength of the apartheid regimes that the ANC and other parties were fighting to establish a non-racial society as also a socialist order. Paradoxically, post-apartheid South Africa under the ANC regimes also diluted its socialist moorings and chose to opt for reforms. While going through reforms, post-apartheid South Africa has been undergoing several developmental problems such as extreme forms of inequalities, poverty, racial tensions, bad governance and corruption (*The Economist* 2010).

Both India and South Africa are engaged in working out innovative federal arrangements. There is uneven development within and among states in India, especially the northern states comprising Hindi-speaking states, on the one hand, and those from the south and south-west, on the other (Ahluwalia 2000). Besides, the rising demands for formation of the new states as well as secessionist movements like those in Kashmir or north-eastern states have been rocking the quasi-federal structure of India. Despite the overall control of the centre over economic, financial, commercial and foreign affairs, the states are independently vying for foreign investments and loans from donor agencies like the World Bank. In contrast, in South Africa, after the abolition of homelands and formation of nine provincial units, the new Constitution has given space to the units to pursue independent foreign economic policy (Harshe 2001). Even if there are no overt secessionist movements in South Africa, the Inkatha Freedom Party (IFP) and the ethno-nationalism of the Zulus do pose occasional irritants to the overwhelmingly dominant position of the ANC-led regimes.

Owing to their plural social settings, India and South Africa have been grappling to come to terms with the politics of identity (Harshe 1999). Identities, more often than not, are socially constructed around continuities in similarities within the social groups. They tend to aggravate the distinction between the 'self' and the 'other'. The social processes in India have been witnessing an anarchy of identities constructed around birth, blood, territory, ethnicity, religions and languages. Indeed, the hierarchical and unequal social structure of Hindu society rampant with caste discriminations has virtually fuelled a revolt among downtrodden castes in India. Their urge to find a just social order has led to social tensions and disharmony. Unlike in India, the dimensions of racial identity in South Africa have had international ramifications. In fact, the racial identities such as the white and the blacks along with their vices or virtues were socially, culturally and intellectually constructed over long span of history (Manzo 1992). These identities were not merely internalised but they signified power relations in very crude forms. Moreover, legally supported institutionalised inequality under apartheid regimes did leave its indelible impact on the post-apartheid state in South Africa. To overcome the bitter memories of the past the Republic of South Africa launched a commendable experiment in the history of mankind through the formation of the Truth and Reconciliation Commission where the perpetrators of injustice apologise to the victims of unjust system. In a word, in the light of their democratic and socially plural settings both India and South Africa can draw from each other's experiences in democratising their democracies by promoting human rights and innovative federal arrangements by reorienting their developmental agendas. In the globalising world such agendas could be translated into action with the help of suitable foreign policies built around serving mutual national interests.

Revisiting Indo–South African Ties

Indo–South African ties took off on a sound footing as India was among the first countries that opposed racism at international forums such as the United Nations (UN) immediately after its independence. Further, India raised a flag of revolt against racism and apartheid at the Afro–Asian conference at Bandung in 1955 and played an important role in ousting the apartheid South Africa from the Commonwealth of Nations in 1961. Along with other non-aligned countries India condemned and urged to boycott apartheid South Africa in the successive summits of the Non-Aligned Movement (NAM). What is more, India became chairman of the NAM-sponsored Action for Resisting Invasion, Colonialism and Apartheid Fund (AFRICA Fund) in 1986 and advanced $50 million to southern African countries to reduce their dependence on South Africa for trade and infrastructure. India's continued moral and material support to the ANC as well as for the release of Nelson Mandela had already built a bond of cordiality between the two countries.

Moreover, in the phase of reforms India began to recast its Africa policy. To make its high growth rates sustainable India is looking for new sources of energy. Evidently, countries with rich mineral resources including Nigeria, Angola, Sudan and the entire range of countries from the gulf of Guinea have acquired added importance in India's foreign policy. Apart from gaining oil supplies from West Asian countries, India has chosen to diversify its sources of obtaining oil. It has been importing oil from Nigeria and the Oil and Natural Gas Corporation — ONGC Videsh has invested $1 billion dollars in Sudan and is working in partnership with Sudanese, Malaysian and the Chinese oil companies. Even though South Africa has deployed Sasol Company to produce petrol and diesel it does not have adequate energy security. However, South Africa is enormously rich in mineral resources such as platinum, gold, diamond, chrome, manganese, uranium, etc. India needs platinum, uranium and thorium to develop its own nuclear energies. In their gradually consolidating trade ties gold bullion constitutes more than one-third of India's imports from South Africa. India also polishes diamonds from South African mines. In its turn, India has been exporting 26 diverse products including vehicles, petroleum products, textiles, iron and steel, cereals (rice) and pharmaceuticals to South Africa.

India's recorded trading import from South Africa was worth $2.5 billion in 2006 while South Africa's recorded import during the same year was $1.6 billion. This meant that South Africa enjoyed comfortable surplus in its trade of $900 million. On the whole, India is South Africa's 13th largest trading partner (Alves 2007). The volume of such trade has grown phenomenally over the years. For instance, in 1993, it was US$13 million; in 2008–2009 it was $.7.6 billion and by 2012 it is likely to be $10 billion. The growth of trade between the two countries is hindered by India's relatively high tariff barriers. What is more, there were at least four Indian business exhibitions in South Africa in 2007 and under INDE-2007 a large number of Indian engineering firms came to South Africa.

Likewise, roughly 40 South African business firms have investments in India. South Africa construes India as a potential investment space in wide-ranging sectors such as infrastructure, financial services, retail, tourism, automotives and mining. The company with the largest potential investment in infrastructure is Sasol with around $6–8 billion. Apart from being a large market, India has a large population that speaks in English to facilitate the Indo–South African business deals. In fact, after President Zacob Zuma's visit to India in May 2009 the trade between the two countries has gained further impetus. Subsequently, in June 2010, Rob Davies, Minister of trade in South Africa, held talks with the representatives of Confederation of Indian Industries and the Federation of Indian Chambers of Commerce. Both the countries have been actively working towards bilateral investment promotion and protection agreement.

Indeed, the entire range of trade ties between India and South Africa has to be viewed in the context of Focus Africa programme — successfully launched after 2002 — and India's overall policy to expand its ties with African countries. The programme was initially launched with seven African countries including Nigeria, South Africa, Mauritius, Tanzania, Kenya, Ghana and Ethiopia but as its scope widened, more than 20 African countries from different regions of Africa became a part of it. Through this programme the government began to assist exporters and Export Promotion Councils. India's move to sign preferential trade agreement with Southern African Customs Union (SACU) comprising Botswana, Lesotho, Namibia and Swaziland will settle tariff and regulatory issues and further firm up its trade ties with the region. In fact, South Africa is a bridge that can link India with the entire southern African region.

South Africa has been among the most powerful states within the African Union (AU). South Africa's penchant for African renaissance has invariably prompted it to play a pre-eminent role in organisations like the AU through projects like the New African Partnership for Development (NEPAD). Like South Africa, India has also supported the NEPAD and invested over $200 million in the NEPAD infrastructure and helped in launching Pan African Parliament (PAP) (Alves 2007). It is this association with South Africa that would give India an opportunity to play an enhanced role in the AU countries as well. The PAP is a major AU project signifying inter-governmental ICT network. India's strength in ITC can hardly be underestimated.

Strategic Partnership

India's strategic relationship with South Africa is integral to its overall Africa policy. India has trained defence forces in several African countries, participated in UN peacekeeping operations in Congo, Namibia, Mozambique, Somalia, Rwanda, Liberia, Angola and Sierra Leone. Likewise, the Indo–South African defence pact of 2000 has facilitated their cooperation in peace building; weapons procurement and combating terrorism (Harshe 2005: 455). There have been moments when the defence cooperation was damaged between the two countries. For instance, the South African state-owned arms company, Denel, was implicated in corruption by the India's Central Bureau of Investigation and ever since this has been a sensitive issue in the electoral politics in India. As far as nuclear weapons are concerned, South Africa has voluntarily signed the Nuclear Non-Proliferation Treaty (NPT) while India has stubbornly resisted signing discriminating treaties like the Comprehensive Test Ban Treaty (CTBT).

In addition, areas such as terrorism, narcotics and allied issues related to small arms proliferation, human trafficking and border control are also being explored for Indo–South African cooperation. In fact, India has had to face terrorism during the past three decades from diverse dissident groups such as the Maoists, and from separatist groups in Punjab, Kashmir and the north-eastern states. By now, subversive activities of the radical Islamic groupings including Lashkar-e-Taiba (LET) and Jaish-e-Mohammad (JEM), that have been connected to terrorist outfits such as the Al-Qaeda, have become frequent in India. Pakistan-sponsored terrorist attacks exposed India's vulnerability on 26/11 when people in major hotels like the Taj in Mumbai were fatally assaulted. Currently, if South Africa is free of problems related to terrorism, it has legal expertise in handling terrorism which could be useful in dealing with the terrorist outfits and their activities legally in the context of India.

As India's economy integrates with the world economy, its trade via the sea routes is growing. Being the major Indian Ocean Rim states, both India and South Africa have a stake in fighting the menace of pirates. Also in the Indian Ocean Region (IOR) they both have to work with other countries to maintain the IOR as a zone of peace. Apart from ensuring peace on the seas the issues related to non-traditional security involving Narcotics Trafficking (NT) and Organised Transnational Crime (OTC) warrant consideration. In fact, after the arms sale the NT and the OTC are the second-largest industry in the world. More often the production, refinement and the consumption of drugs happen in two different areas. There have been instances where narco-trafficking harms a state because money laundered, directly or indirectly are used to fuelling separatist groups, insurgents and terrorists. Sandwiched between the 'Golden Triangle' in the north-east and 'Golden Crescent' in the north-west' India has become a hub of the drug trade-India is not only exporting locally-grown and/manufactured drugs but it is also at the receiving end of the trade and serves as a major transit hub in the global narcotics trade network (Babuna 2010). Actually pockets of African communities in Goa, Rajasthan and the South are linked with drug trade. While handling the aberrations of terrorist activities the role of India and South Africa as regional powers also merits consideration.

Regional Powers Pause

It needs to be underscored that India and South Africa are dominant powers in their respective regions: South Asia and Southern Africa. Any form of regional cooperation in these respective regions is inconceivable without active cooperation or participation of these two powerful states. India plays a pre-eminent role in organisations like the SAARC. India has religious, linguistic and cultural commonalities with all the surroundings countries of South Asia. India's geographical size, location, resources, the size of its market, number of trained manpower and nuclear arsenal constitute the core of South Asia. South Asia has been an Indo-centric region and owing to India's military intervention in SAARC states such as Maldives (1988) and Sri Lanka (1987–90); the neighbouring states have often been apprehensive of India's hegemonic designs. What is more, due to differences over Nepalese foreign policy, India had abrogated its trade and transit treaty with Nepal, a landlocked state, and virtually strangulated its economy in 1989. Despite these differences, India has been able to win over most of the neighbouring countries, except Pakistan, while building trade and economic ties through the Gujral doctrine of 1996.

The doctrine stands for non-reciprocity of ties between India and its neighbours and India chose to open up its market for the neighbouring countries by offering tariff concessions. India also shares water with Bangladesh after the Ganga Water Treaty became operative in 1997. Moreover, irrespective of the protracted differences between India and Pakistan over the status of Kashmir, the SAARC has been gradually moving towards the establishment of the free trade area. It is also expanding with new members like Afghanistan and observers including Iran, China, USA, Japan and South Korea (Rao 2008). Thus, trends in Asian politics could be reflected in the functioning of the SAARC.

Like India, within the 15 members the SADC, South Africa is the most dominant player. South Africa has the region's most developed economy. Its Gross Domestic Product is roughly $213.1 billion, which is almost double of the rest of the economies of Southern Africa put together. The relationship between practically all the neighbouring countries and South Africa has been asymmetrical. In fact, resource-rich Namibia functioned as the fifth province of South Africa till it achieved independence in 1990. Southern African countries depend on South Africa for infrastructure, trade routes, market and a substantial number of migrants from neighbouring countries including Mozambique, Lesotho Malawi, etc. depend on South African mines for employment. Under apartheid South Africa the migrants were inhumanly exploited. Post-apartheid South Africa has been trying to bring about harmony between its declared policy to promote and protect human rights while handling migrants. And yet in 2006, over 260,000 migrants working without documentation were deported from South Africa. In addition, the countries of the region also aim at collaborating in the area by sharing resources like water, power, energy, goods and services.

Being regionally-dominant powers with growing economies, India and South Africa have certainly asserted their presence in the power configurations of the world. Under the NAM or any other forum from the South they both have to be reckoned with as the dominant middle-ranging powers with ever-spreading influence. Moreover, among the dominant Latin American countries, Brazil too has joined them to make the presence of this trio obvious in international forums.

The Rise of Middle-ranging Powers

The rise of China, India, Brazil and South Africa has prompted scholars to examine whether these powers are likely to be potential engines of growth and their likely impact on the world political economy (Nayyar 2008). In fact, middle-ranging powers such as India, South Africa and Brazil and their evolving ties in trade, investment, trilateral exchange of information and best practices and cooperation in broad areas for mutual benefit has the potential to change the complexion of world politics. Out of these, India is the largest democracy; South Africa stands for promoting racial equality and human rights and Brazil has been sustaining its development model. Such tri-continental cooperation between the three major regional powers, however, can develop only gradually. After the Brasilia Declaration between the three countries of 2003 they are focusing on issues of common concern, including the reform of the UN, threats to security including those emanating from terrorism, agriculture, climate, social equity and inclusion, racial discrimination, trade, science and technology and gender equality. Their trilateral alliance will matter in forums like the WTO because these states have opposed heavy subsidy given to agrarian products in developed countries to protect the interests of farmers in developing countries. Although such cooperative endeavours are at the incipient stages, the middle-ranging powers could reform organisations such as the NAM and the UN.

International Forums: The NAM and the UN

As an international forum, the NAM has been working towards reducing the structural imbalances within the world economy between the developed and developing countries since the Lusaka summit of the NAM in 1970. It has addressed this issue by supporting the mechanisms to transfer technology, credit and by supporting the demand of the developing countries to obtain better prices for their products, agrarian or mineral. As significant members of the NAM, India and South Africa have been working together through the NAM to redress economic imbalances in the world economy even if it is not easy to subvert the structures of dominance established by advanced capitalist countries.

In contrast to the NAM, the UN is a universal international organisation. This is evident from the fact that the number of sovereign member states in the UN have consistently increased after every wave of decolonisation in the post-war period. Apart from Palestine, there are no residual political problems of the Cold-War phase that preoccupy the UN seriously. With their overwhelming majority in the UN General Assembly, multitudes of developing countries continue to oppose the dominance of the developed world in practically all the domains and demand for their representation in the powerful organs such as the Security Council (UNSC). Both India and South Africa have been working to be included into the UNSC. Actually, more than South Africa, India has been clamouring to enter the portals of the UNSC initially as a non-permanent member and subsequently as one of its permanent members. In the pursuit of this objective it has been seeking support from countries such as the USA, Russia and France and several other developing countries. Since the so-called international liberal order with its rules, procedures and notions of international law has gradually acquired shape during the past six decades, India's legitimate aspiration, as one of the rising powers, ought to find an appropriate expression at the UN. However, a pyramid-like power structure of world politics has not made India's entry easy. In fact, to attain nuclear status India has had to consistently fight against the discriminatory use of the CTBT. With the signing of the Indo–US nuclear deal in 2008, the major world powers have by now reconciled to India's nuclear status. Once India captures privileged space among the dominant powers in the UNSC it can become a major player in shaping world policy.

Further, the scope of UN activities has widened and deepened from managing interstate disputes, ensuring decolonisation to managing intra state political processes. For instance, referendums were held in Namibia (1990) and Eritrea (1993) under the auspices of the UN, and the UN also intervened in civil wars in countries including Angola, Mozambique and Somalia. Actually, by using the UN as its instrument the USA under Clinton administration (1992–2000) intervened in Somalia to bring about peace among warring factions. By defying the UN, the USA went as far as to intervene in Iraq militarily in 2003. In view of such brazen policies the entry of countries like India and even South Africa in UNSC is essential because both these countries through their strategic partnership can shape the outcome of several major decisions that have wide-ranging repercussions, on the domestic and foreign policy of the UN member states.

Concluding Remarks

Briefly, globalisation and its intertwined association with capitalism do represent a complex set of processes that are shrinking distances and making new forms of cooperation and conflicts possible. India and South Africa have had a lot of similarities as also differences in the manner in which they have been handling their domestic and foreign policies. They could draw from each other's good practices and eventually forge closer strategic partnership to promote political, economic and military cooperation in different spheres of bilateral and multilateral activities.

References

Alves, P. 2007. 'India and South Africa Shifting Priorities', *South African Journal of International Affairs*, 14 (2): 87–109.

Ahluwalia, M. S. 2000. 'Economic Performance of States in Post Reforms Period', *Economic and Political Weekly*, XXXIV (19): 1637–48.

Babuna, M. 2010. 'Indo–African Narcotics Ties', Indian Institute of Defence Studies and Analysis, Event. www.idsa.in. Accessed 29 January.

Bhagwati, J. N. 2004. *In Defense of Globalization*. New York: Oxford.

Cooley, J. 2000. *Unholy Wars: Afghanistan, America and International Terror*. New Delhi: Penguin Books India.

Devji, F. 2008. *The Terrorist in Search of Humanity Militant Islam and Global Politics*. New Delhi: Foundation Books.

Economist, The. 2010. Special report on South Africa, pp. 1–14. 5–11 June.

Gunaratna R. 2002. *Inside Al Qaeda Global Network of Terror*. New Delhi: Roli Books.

Harshe, R. 1999. 'State Structures and Identities in India and South Africa', *Indian Social Science Review*, 1 (1): 67–85.

———. 2000. 'Reconstructing the Links between Domestic and Foreign Policy of India under Liberalisation', *Indian Social Science Review*, 2 (1): 147–64.

———. 2001. 'The South African Experiment in Coalition Building', *Seton Hall Journal of Diplomacy and International Relations*, 2 (2): 87–96.

———. 2005. 'Recasting Indo–African Development Cooperation', in R. Harshe and K. M: Seethi (eds), *Engaging With the World: Critical Essays on India's Foreign Policy*, pp. 442–48. New Delhi: Orient Longman.

———. 2000. 'Unveiling the Ties between US Imperialism and Al Qaeda', *Economic and political Weekly*, 43 (51): 67–72.

Kaldor, M. 2000. 'Civilising' Globalisation? The Implications of the Battle in Seattle', *Millennium*, 29 (1): 105–14.

Lodge, T. 1988. 'State of Exile: The African National Congress in South Africa 1976–86', in P. Frankel, N. Pines and M. Swilling (eds), *State, Resistance and Change in South Africa*, pp. 229–48. New York: Crom Helm.

Manzo, Kate. 1992. 'Global Power and South African Politics: A Foulcaultian Analysis', *Alternatives*, 17 (1): 23–66.

Nayyar, D. 2008. 'China, India, Brazil and South Africa in World Economy Engines of Growth?' Discussion Paper No. 2008/05. U.N. University UNU-WIDER. www.wider.unu.edu. Accessed February 2009.

Rao, P. V. 2008. 'Expansion of SAARC: Political and Economic Implications', *South Asian Affairs*, 1 (1): 17–34.

Soros, G. 1997. 'The Capitalist Threat', *Atlantic Monthly*, 297 (2): 45–58.

Stiglitz, J. 2002. *Globalization and Its Discontents*. New Delhi: Penguin Books India.

———. 2006. *Making Globalisation Work*. New York: Allen Lane.

Walters, D. 2010. 'Indo–African Relations: Is Elephant Playing Catch Up with the Dragon?'. www.consultancyafrica.com. Accessed 30 January 2011.

18

IBSA in the Foreign Policy of a Rising India

Priya Chacko

India's rise as a major economic and political power is said to be leading to dramatic transformations in its foreign policy (Kahn 2009). Such an interpretation, however, is misleading and partial. While it may be true that India has signed strategic partnerships with the United States (US) and the European Union (EU), that it has joined the group of 20 major economies and has a higher profile in multilateral forums such as the World Trade Organisation (WTO), it is also the case that India remains committed to Southern multilateralism.[1] It continues as a leader in the Non-Aligned Movement (NAM) and the Group of 77 (G77) and has participated in the creation of new Southern multilateral groupings such as the IBSA (India, Brazil, South Africa) forum. This article seeks to examine why India has continued to prioritise and, indeed, reinvigorate Southern multilateralism despite being a rising state with growing international economic and political power.

The Emergence of IBSA

IBSA was established at the instigation of today's leading Southern actors with the exception of China in 2003. The exclusion of the non-democratic China from IBSA immediately gave it a normative gloss that is apparent in the Brasilia Declaration which established the forum in 2003: '[t]his was a pioneer meeting of the three countries with vibrant democracies, from three regions of the developing world, active on a global scale, with the aim of examining themes on the international agenda and those of mutual interest'. Nonetheless, discussions of IBSA have tended to emphasise its economic implications rather than its normative or identity drivers and have focused on a highly general level of analysis instead of a specific examination of its place in the foreign policies of the individual countries involved (Cornelissen 2009: 12; Shrivastava 2008: 136, 2009: 127; Taylor 2009: 47, 45). Those scholars who have focused on the states' motivations for establishing IBSA argue that India, South Africa and Brazil 'see in the application of regional representivity' a way of relegitimising the institutions of global governance while, 'positioning themselves therein in a leadership role' (Alden and Vieira 2005: 1090–92). There is little evidence provided, however, that IBSA is tied to India's claim to regional leadership or that the latter is the basis of India's claim to representation in institutions of global governance. In fact, while India supports the principle of regional representation from Africa and Latin America on the Security Council, for instance, it justifies its claim to a permanent seat on the basis of its status as 'the largest democracy on the planet' and the strength of its economy, which together with China's, 'constitutes an international public good' (Sharma 2008; Singh 2008).

India's involvement in IBSA has also been explained as a part of a balancing strategy that involves deepening its relationship with the US and at the same time forging coalitions with other states in favour of a multipolar world order (Beri 2008: 811). Yet, this explanation also raises questions. Given that the US has repeatedly committed to helping India become a global power, India could arguably achieve its goal of being one of the major poles in the emerging world order without pursuing a counter-balancing strategy (Obama 2010). Moreover, why does India persist in pursuing Southern coalitions when seeking a closer relationship with, for instance, the EU would also serve the purpose of counter-balancing? Given that trade between India, Brazil and South Africa remains small compared with India's trade with the US, China and Europe, would not a rising India be better served in its economic interests by focusing its diplomatic efforts on these countries and regions?[2] As Amrita Narlikar argues,

> It would be reasonable to expect this new, rising India to have devised new foreign policies, and new negotiating strategies to implement them. It might also seem likely that these policies would incline towards greater engagement with the country's economic partners, less emphasis on Third World rhetoric ... (2006: 59).

Narlikar notes that, despite launching a programme of economic liberalisation, India continues to pursue high-risk, defensive negotiating strategies in multilateral trade negotiations and, despite embarking on new relationships, such as its strategic partnership with the US, it has further institutionalised its relationships with countries of the South. She argues that neither an explanation centred on domestic political imperatives nor the entrenched culture of bureaucratic politics can fully account for this behaviour. There is little evidence that domestic interest groups exercise much influence on foreign policy and while India's bureaucratic institutions are famed for their predilection for 'getting to no', this characteristic requires explanation. Both Narlikar and Stephen Cohen argue that the main sources of India's negotiating behaviour are a political culture which includes a mindset that valourises self-sufficiency and anti-imperialism and a perception among state officials that they represent a civilisation which deserves respect and deference (Cohen 2001: 84–87; Narlikar 2006: 72). What requires further explanation, however, is precisely why this political culture persists in a rising India whose economic and political power is now acknowledged, and how this mindset influences India's choices in Southern coalition-building. India has not simply chosen 'the Non-Aligned Movement and Third World collectivism as its pathway to power' as Narlikar suggests; it is increasingly prioritising the selective Southern multilateralism of coalitions like IBSA, which implies an important shift in its normative priorities (Narlikar 2006: 75).

Identity and Foreign Policy in Postcolonial India

Understanding the way in which Indian nationalist leaders negotiated the colonial encounter is central to understanding the nature of postcolonial identity and its relationship with foreign policy in contemporary India. In particular, the views and beliefs of India's first Prime Minister and Foreign Minister, Jawaharlal Nehru, are significant. In the strand of nationalism epitomised by Nehru, the colonial encounter gave rise to a perception of backwardness as well as a sense of what might be called India's 'civilisational exceptionalism' and these perceptions produced specific understandings of how postcolonial India should engage with the world. For Nehru, the history of Indian civilisation was a source of internal critique as well as a source of possibility for the future. To him, India was a great civilisation that went into decline. He wrote, for instance, that India's 'progressive deterioration during the centuries' could be seen in the loss of a 'rational spirit of inquiry' that was 'so evident in earlier times' and 'which might well have led to the further growth of science' but was 'replaced by irrationalism and a blind idolatry of the past'. Those factors that contributed to its decline could be overcome through a selective appropriation of 'western' modernity while those that made it great, its 'civilisational exceptionalism', which Nehru described as a 'certain idealist and ethical background to the whole culture', could be used to construct an ethical modernity as opposed to a modernity fashioned only along western lines (Nehru (1946) 1982: 54, 95).

While Nehru is often presented as a straightforward modernist nationalist (Chatterjee 1993), he was, in fact, a critic of western industrialism and western modernity and nowhere is this clearer than in Nehru's writings on foreign policy, which became a key site of Nehru's critique of Western modernity and his assertion of India's civilisational exceptionalism (Prakash 1999: 109, 202). '[T]here can be no real cultural or spiritual growth based on imitation', he argued, but in addition to this, he regarded western modernity as being deeply flawed — it had given rise to a rapacious imperialism and it had a self-destructive quality because of the rise of virulent nationalisms combined with an exploitative capitalism (Nehru (1946) 1982: 546). The combination of these factors, according to Nehru, had resulted in the world wars, imperialism and colonialism and the development of the atom bomb (Nehru 1934–35 1996: 399, 402, Nehru (1946) 1982: 33, 506–7). Thus, rather than accepting the universal nature of the European experience, Nehru sought to ground India's postcolonial identity in a better, more ethical modernity and international relations was central to this project. Fortunately, this could be facilitated by 'the essential basis of Indian thought for ages past, though not its later manifestations' which 'is based on a fearless search for truth, on the solidarity of man, even on the divinity of everything living, and on the free and co-operative development of the individual and the species, ever to greater freedom and higher stages of human growth' (Nehru (1946) 1982: 514–15).

In the post-independence period, Nehru's normative commitments helped to shape foreign policies such as non-alignment,

'*Panchsheel*' or peaceful coexistence, the rejection of collective defence pacts, active involvement in the United Nations (UN) and economic policies aimed at self-reliance — most of these policies entailed close collaboration with other newly independent states.

India and Southern Multilateralism

The countries of the global South, especially those in Asia and Africa, played two key roles in fashioning India's postcolonial foreign policy/identity — they were partners in the efforts for global reform and arenas for India's foreign policy activism. Nehru sought to repudiate colonial geopolitics and what he viewed as the dominance of the 'fear complex' in world politics while strengthening the UN and establishing norms of human rights. India played an active role in opposing the emerging apartheid regime in South Africa from 1946 to 1948, supporting anti-colonial movements in Asia and Africa and providing leadership at the Geneva Conference in 1954 that was convened to find a resolution to the first Indo–China War. It also played a pivotal role in the UN peacekeeping operation in the Congo from 1960 to 1964 and helped organise the Asian Relations Conference in 1947 and the Bandung Conference in 1955. These activities were guided by a foreign policy framework underpinned by the ideas of non-alignment and *Panchsheel* which, I would suggest, should be seen as policies that were originally intended to further a radical internationalist vision through a conception of security that did not depend on generating insecurity in others and, at the same time, promoted an understanding of national autonomy that re-sisted interactions with individual countries and groups that were inherently unequal. Non-alignment and *Panchsheel* were built on a social ontology drawn from Buddhist and Gandhian thought which emphasised the interdependent, impermanent nature of the Self and the multi-dimensional and plural nature of truth (Chacko 2011). Specifically, non-alignment was a means of creating an environment in which dialogue and equality with all parties was possible and *Panchsheel* was aimed at fostering interdependence between states (Nehru 1961: 78–79). Both were a part of a 'deliberate policy of friendship' that challenged the assumption of fear, enemies and 'threatening Others' are the most important factors governing relations between states. For Nehru, the modern nation-state was prone to cultivating a 'narrow nationalism' and an exploitative industrial capitalism. His alternative was a nation-state underpinned by an internationalist outlook that would strengthen international institutions and, more radically, work toward the establishment of a world federation (Bhagavan 2008).

Nehru viewed the countries of Asia and Africa as vital to achieving the broader goal of constructing an identity for India that was rooted in an 'ethical modernity' because they shared a common experience of having been subjected to colonial rule and had drawn 'mentally ... psychologically and morally, nearer to one another' (Nehru 1999: 559). This was buttressed by ancient historical and cultural ties which had been broken in the past — by choice, because Indian civilisation had withdrawn 'into her shell, intent on preserving herself', but also by compulsion because the British had 'barred all the doors and stopped all the routes that connected us with our neighbours ...' — and contributed to India's decline and stagnancy (Nehru (1946) 1982: 54, 149).

Nehru's knowledge of Africa's history, by his own admission, was more limited although he assumed the existence of close historical ties, for 'Africa, though separated by the Indian Ocean from us, is in a sense our next door neighbour' (Nehru 2000: 627). He was also convinced that together with Asia, Africa would 'play an increasing role in the conduct and destiny of the world organization' and that India and Africa would 'inevitably be thrown more together' (Nehru 1964: 74). For Nehru, Asia had 'special responsibility to the people of Africa' which had suffered 'infinite tragedy', because 'we are sister continents' (ibid.: 14, 19). Such statements have been treated as evidence of paternalistic attitudes toward Africa and it has been suggested that 'ideas of "Afro-Asian" solidarity largely focussed on the symbolic politics of public friendship' and were 'form with little content' (Hoymeyr 2007: 80). However, even if they can be deemed paternalistic, Nehru's attitudes toward Africa were not premised on a belief in Africa's cultural inferiority, and India's leading role in the UN peacekeeping mission in the Congo from 1960–64 and its activism against the apartheid regime in South Africa shows that Afro–Asian solidarity did, in fact, have tangible consequences (Nehru 1964: 74). India's involvement in the Congo was a key moment in the fashioning its postcolonial identity as one grounded in an ethical modernity for it provided it with an opportunity to showcase an

'Afro–Asian approach' to conflict resolution and to exercise the 'responsibility' that Nehru argued had been cast on India, given its commitments to the UN, non-alignment and anti-colonialism (ibid.: 65, 70). The issue of apartheid, on the other hand, gave Nehru the opportunity to give substance to his philosophical commitments to interdependence and universal human rights and saw it as a test case for advancing the idea of the UN as a 'world republic in which all States, independent States are represented and to which they may be answerable on occasions' (Nehru 1984: 216–17).

While some economic cooperation with other states, and especially the Southern states, was encouraged during the Nehru era, this dimension was secondary to encouraging economic self-reliance and preventing conflict. From the mid-1960s, however, international activism on economic issues began to figure prominently in India's foreign policy. During this period, India moved from economic self-reliance and global political universalism to a form of 'collective self-reliance' at both the global political and economic levels in which the South played a central role (Kothari 1988: 2223).

The shift away from the universalism of the Nehru era can partly be attributed to the détente between the USSR and the US, which rendered Nehru's concerns about nuclear war less urgent, and to India's disillusionment with the UN, which began building in 1948 as the perception grew of the Security Council's bias toward Pakistan on the issue of Kashmir (Behera 2006: 35; Kochnek 1980: 53; quoted in Rana 1970: 71–72). Moreover, while concerns about the injustice of lingering international political and economic hierarchy was present during the Nehru era, they only came to the fore in the 1960s and 1970s when it became clear that there was little impetus in the North to address the procedural and substantive justice claims of the South. Thus, India shifted from embedding Southern multilateralism in a broader universalism to promoting Southern multilateralism in its own right by helping to establish the United Nations Conference on Trade and Development (UNCTAD) and the G77 at UNCTAD's first session in 1964. It also took a greater leadership in committees and study groups at the UN from the mid-1970s, and joined in the Declaration calling for a New International Economic Order (NIEO) in 1974. The NIEO placed issues of economic sovereignty at the forefront, tying it closely to political sovereignty, human rights and the introduction of a principle of solidarity (Nations 1974). Moreover, it mounted a challenge to the legal positivism which underpins international law on economic matters and ignores the global power imbalances that entrench Northern control (Otto 1999: 156).

Indian diplomats were active in the drafting of NIEO documents and often provided technical and secretarial assistance to the NAM and the G77 at the UN and the newly established Conference on International Economic Cooperation, which aimed to give the South a greater voice on trade issues (Mansingh 1984: 368). To label this period as one in which there was 'a drift toward third world radicalism' is misleading, for India pursued an active but restrained style of multilateral diplomacy with a 'preference for exacting but inconspicuous committee work' and tended to occupy the middle ground between North and South and East and West, refraining from supporting resolutions explicitly designed simply to censure the Western powers or the Socialist Bloc (ibid.). As in the past, India presented itself as a mediator and facilitator of dialogue and cooperation on North–South issues, such as UN financing and the desire by African states, in the face of resistance from the western bloc, for an arms embargo against apartheid South Africa (Kochnek 1980: 59–62; Rana 1970: 72–73; Mansingh 1984: 368).

Ultimately, however, India's desire for an ethical modernity as a marker of its postcolonial difference was the product of a double bind in which it remains a mimetic subject split between the 'western' subject of 'western modernity' and a figure of backwardness (Chakrabarty 2000: 40). As an ethico-political project and an act of agency, therefore, India's postcolonial identity remained circumscribed by the anti-colonial politics of negotiating the colonial encounter and the conceptual vocabulary of 'western modernity' itself. Hence, while Nehru was cautious about western science and industrialism, he was also committed to the idea that India should pursue nuclear technology, large-scale industrial projects and a strongly centralised state structure which resulted in outcomes far removed from the vision of a tolerant and democratic ethical modernity that would mitigate the potential for violence and oppression.[3] Likewise, despite its opposition to western domination, the G77's reliance on liberal legal concepts such as development and state sovereignty meant that its call for an NIEO 'remained uncritical of modernity itself' and failed to reveal the 'mechanisms of hierarchy and exclusion that made third world identification possible' (Otto 1999: 159, 166).

IBSA and a Rising India

The 1990s and 2000s raised a new set of domestic and international challenges for India. The end of the Cold War, the decline of the Congress Party's dominance on Indian politics and economic liberalisation changed India's foreign policy. Despite these structural changes, the normative project established in the immediate post-independence period continues to play a defining role in the construction of India's postcolonial identity. Indian leaders still express doubts about dominant conceptions of power, assert India's 'civilisational exceptionalism', discuss the merits of the concept of non-alignment, are resistant to the idea of alliances and, as noted above, India continues to participate in anti-hegemonic coalitions in international organisations at considerable cost (Gandhi 2006; Nath 2008). Similarly, an examination of India's representations of IBSA shows that the South continues to be a marker of India's postcolonial difference as a state pursuing an ethical modernity.

Indian officials explain IBSA's character as a 'dialogue forum' rather than a coalition and they are careful to highlight the fact that its inception in June 2003 was not reactively driven by the collapse of the WTO Cancun talks in September 2003, but by a broader positive desire for an 'effective forum for South–South cooperation' (Shashank 2004). As detailed in the 2006 IBSA Joint Declaration, 'South–South cooperation' is seen to encompass 'strengthening the multilateral trading system', the reform of the IMF, the UN and the Security Council to include greater Southern representation, the expansion of South–South trade and the establishment of a development aid facility for funding projects related to the alleviation of hunger and poverty. In addition, the Declaration highlights universal human rights, including the right to development, sustainable development, nuclear disarmament, the 'inalienable right of all States to the peaceful application of nuclear energy' and the need to resolve the Israeli–Palestinian conflict (2006). While an IBSA Dialogue Forum on Defence Cooperation has also been established, an analysis of speeches and statements reveals that this aspect receives much less attention than the role of IBSA in fostering civil society interaction. According to Manmohan Singh: 'IBSA is largely a peoples [sic] project' (Singh 2010a, 2010b). Speeches and statements also portray the forum as an 'interactive element' that has been added to the 'more declaratory' G77 and they place IBSA within a UN framework (Shashank 2004).

Representations of IBSA thus remain partly within older foreign policy discourses. However, the selective Southern multilateralism of IBSA and its promotion of a South–South development aid facility with the potential challenge this presents to Northern dominance of debates on development and governance, suggests a reversion to a more vocal style of engagement and the positioning of India together with Brazil and South Africa, in an explicit leadership position within the global South. India's leadership in Southern multilateralism during the Nehru era was encompassed within its commitment to the transformation of the UN into a world federation and its moral responsibility to those who had, like India, suffered colonial oppression and with whom it shared long historical ties. India's contemporary claims to leadership are still based on the need for UN reform and moral responsibility toward other Southern countries — albeit in the areas of democratising its power structures and increasing the effectiveness of its development agenda, and in the context of the negative effects of globalisation rather than colonialism (Shashank 2004).

India's IBSA discourse often highlights the democratic character of the three members. Democracy promotion has long had an ambiguous place in Indian foreign policy discourse (Mohan 2007: 99). For Nehru, democracy was central to the creation of an ethical modernity and he made a strong link, in particular, between social democracy and internationalism on the one hand, and capitalism, imperialism and a narrow nationalism on the other (Nehru (1936) 1942: 166). His foreign policy discourse prioritised the promotion of the values associated with democracy, such as tolerance, restraint, dialogue and equality, rather than the institution itself. During the 1970s and 1980s, democracy became a key distinguishing feature between India and its neighbours and India's interventions in Pakistan's civil war in 1971 and Sri Lanka's civil war in the 1980s were partially justified by the failure of democracy in these countries. Nonetheless, democracy was not a core part of India's foreign policy discourse during this period.

It has only been in the past decade that India has explicitly and consistently raised its democratic character and promoted democracy as a political virtue. C. R. Mohan attributes this shift to 'intensive engagement with the United States', which took to highlighting the common bond of democracy it shared with India in the 2000s (2007: 99). This was not, however, the first time the US has attempted to construct a shared democratic identity with India. In the 1950s the US tried, and failed, to fashion a common identity based on a shared multicultural democratic ethos because it also sought to link this shared democratic identity to the broader US Cold War project in which the Soviet Union was rendered into the Other and the US was the main defender of democratic principles and political freedom (Muppidi 1999). For Nehru, the logic of the Cold War generated an 'us and them' mentality that thrived on fear and hostility and his foreign policy was aimed at undermining this (Nehru 1961: 68). There was, moreover, an inherent resistance to the idea that postcolonial India should subordinate its identity to a shared identity defined predominantly by the US (Muppidi 1999: 136). The end of the Cold War and the US's heightened willingness to endorse India's self-image of civilisational exceptionalism, in particular, by signing an agreement on civil nuclear cooperation and deeming it 'a responsible state with advanced nuclear technology', has, however, led to a significant improvement in relations and has made it more legitimate to highlight a shared democratic identity with the US (United States and India 2005).

Yet, what Mohan's US-centric analysis ignores is that democracy has not just appeared in India's foreign-policy discourse on the US–India relationship, but rather, as shown above, has simultaneously arisen in India's discourse on IBSA. Indeed, whereas India's involvement in democracy promotion with the US has been limited to the membership of both countries in the UN Democracy Fund, Manmohan Singh has proclaimed that 'IBSA is a strong moral force in today's unsettled world' (Singh 2010a). India has thus gone much further in adding a normative element to its relationships with South Africa and Brazil than it has with the US and what this indicates is that rather than 'shedding some of its past burdens of Third World ideology'; as Mohan claims, India continues to value Southern solidarity and multilateralism as central components of its postcolonial identity and continues to view the North, as a normative partner, with some ambivalence (2007: 114).

While ensuring that India does not over-identify with Northern liberal democracies, IBSA also allows it to distinguish itself from that other rising power, China. Indian leaders are well aware of the role of perception in how rising powers are treated. According to Singh, '[u]nlike China's rise, the rise of India does not cause any apprehensions' for, '[t]he world takes a benign view of India. They want us to succeed' and 'we should take advantage of it. This benign mood cannot last' (2010). Hence, when recently asked about the possibility of a merger between IBSA and BRIC, the grouping of Brazil, Russia, India and China, during the 2010 IBSA Summit, Singh replied in the negative, and in a way that emphasised the democratic collective identity of IBSA: 'IBSA has a personality of its own. It is three separate continents, three democracies. BRIC is a conception devised by Goldman Sachs' (quoted in Bagchi 2010).

Yet, while democracy has been a consistent theme in India's discourse on IBSA, it continues to appear as a depoliticised ethics. IBSA may well bring 'together three dynamic democracies from three continents bound together by shared values and a common commitment to democracy, pluralism, human rights and the rule of law' (Krishna 2010), but just how this will shape 'debate on global issues' remains unclear. India's invocations of democracy in its IBSA discourse also efface the complexity of the concept of democracy itself. For instance, all three members of IBSA face challenges, exemplified by the rise of Naxalism (Maoism) in India and xenophobic violence in South Africa, that have been portrayed as a threat to democracy or a failure of democracy or development but might more compellingly be theorised as generated by and constitutive of democracy itself. As Wendy Brown reminds us, 'democracy as a concept and practice has always been limned by a non-democratic periphery and unincorporated substrate that at once materially sustain democracy and against which democracy defines itself' and far from eliminating violence, democratic politics has been shown to facilitate and provide the resources for violence (Brown 2010). IBSA's triumphalist discourse, however, reiterates a substantively empty Euro-American narrative on the superiority of liberal democracy and thus, as with prior forms of Southern multilateralism, tends to perpetuate the conceptual hegemony of 'western modernity'.

Conclusion

The purpose of this article has been to understand India's continuing commitment to Southern multilateralism and, in particular, its new focus on the IBSA forum. Since 1947 India's Southern multilateralism has served to reiterate a postcolonial identity grounded in a desire not just to become modern, but in concert with others, to fashion a better modernity based on alternative ways of regulating relations between countries. During the formative period of Indian foreign policy between the 1940s to the mid-1960s, its promotion of Southern multilateralism was embedded in a broader commitment to a universalist project of strengthening the UN and promoting human rights and was driven by the idea that given the common experiences of colonial subjugation shared by Asia and Africa, and their long-standing cultural ties, the two continents were ideal partners in global reform. From the mid-1960s to the 1980s, India shifted from promoting universal human rights and the UN toward a focus on the procedural and substantive justice claims of the South. Nonetheless, it generally retained a commitment to dialogue and mediation during this period, even while it adopted a more restrained style. In the new era of Southern multilateralism, which has seen the emergence of IBSA, India has reverted to a more vocal leadership style and taken up the promotion of normative concepts like democracy. In this way, the South and Southern multilateralism have played important parts in India's attempt to fashion a postcolonial identity grounded in an 'ethical modernity' and IBSA is viewed by India as a key normative tool in the negotiation of its rise as a major power which allows it to maintain its autonomy from the US and distinguishes it from China. It remains to be seen, however, whether IBSA will do anymore to contest the aspects of liberal modernity that have entrenched the conceptual and practical elements of Northern hegemony than older forms of Southern multilateralism. Future research will have to focus on India and IBSA's deployment of concepts such as democracy, development and security and the way in which the three individual members negotiate the tensions inherent in conceiving IBSA as an ethico-political project.

Notes

1. The 'South' is often seen as a successor to the term 'Third World' as, but like its predecessor, it is neither descriptively or analytically unproblematic. I use the term here to refer to countries of Africa, Asia and Latin America, which are all roughly located in three southern continents (India of course being a notable exception). These countries share a history of colonialism and imperialism, and a present marked by a general sense of common global problems and aims such as poverty alleviation and the democratisation of international politics. I use the term 'Southern multilateralism' to mean the coordination of relations by three or more Southern states in accordance with certain principles.
2. See the trade statistics at the Indian government's Department of Commerce website: http://commerce.nic.in/eidb/iecntq.asp, accessed 12 September 2010.
3. For instance, see the many works by Ashis Nandy, Shiv Viswanathan and Arundhati Roy.

References

Alden, C. and M. A. Vieira. 2005. 'The New Diplomacy of the South: South Africa, Brazil, India and Trilateralism', *Third World Quarterly*, 26: 1077–95.

Bagchi, I. 2010. 'PM against Merger of IBSA, BRIC Blocs' *The Times of India*. http://timesofindia.indiatimes.com/india/PM-against-merger-of-IBSA-BRIC-blocs/articleshow/5823437.cms. Accessed 16 September 2010.

Behera, N. C. 2006. *Demystifying Kashmir*. Washington, DC: Brookings Institution Press.

Beri, R. 2008. 'IBSA Dialogue Forum: An Assessment', *Strategic Analysis*, 32: 809–31.

Bhagavan, M. 2008. 'A New Hope: India, the United Nations and the Making of the Universal Declaration of Human Rights', *Modern Asian Studies*, 44: 311–47.

Brown, W. 2010. 'We Are All Democrats Now ...', *Theory & Event*, 13.

Chacko, P. 2011. 'The Search for a Scientific Temper: Nuclear Technology and the Ambivalence of India's Postcolonial Modernity', *Review of International Studies*, 37: 185–208.

Chakrabarty, D. 2000. *Provincializing Europe: Postcolonial Thought and Historical Difference*. Princeton and Oxford: Princeton University Press.

Chatterjee, P. 1993. *The Nation and its Fragments: Colonial and Postcolonial Histories*. Princeton, NJ: Princeton University Press.

Cohen, S. P. 2001. *India: Emerging Power*. Washington, DC: Brookings Institution Press.

Cornelissen, S. 2009. 'Awkward Embraces: Emerging and Established Powers and the Shifting Fortunes of Africa's International Relations in the Twenty-First Century', *Politikon*, 36: 5–26.

Gandhi, S. 2006. 'Text of Inaugral Address by Sonia Gandhi', *Hindustan Times*. http://www.hindustantimes.com/news/specials/leadership2006/coverage_17110603.shtml. Accessed 17 November 2006.

Hoymeyr, I. 2007. 'The Idea of "Africa" in Indian Nationalism: Reporting the Diaspora in The Modern Review 1907–1929', *South African Historical Journal*, 57: 60–81.

IBSA. 2003. *'Brasilia Declaration'*. Department of International Relations and Cooperation, South Africa. http://www.dfa.gov.za/docs/2005/ibsa_brasilia.htm. Accessed 26 August 2010.

———. 2006. Joint Declaration of first IBSA Summit Meeting, 13 September. http://pmindia.nic.in/visits/content.asp?id=113. Accessed 30 September 2010.

Kahn, J. 2009. 'India Cleans Up Its Act', Newsweek. http://www.newsweek.com/id/221588. Accessed 13 March 2010.

Kochnek, S. A. 1980. 'India's Changing Role in the United Nations', *Pacific Affairs*, 53: 48–68.

Kothari, R. 1988. 'Integration and Exclusion in Indian Politics', *Economic and Political Weekly*, 23: 2223–27.

Krishna, S. M. 2010. 'Remarks by EAM at IBSA Ministerial Meeting'. Ministry of External Affairs. http://www.mea.gov.in/mystart.php?id=530116524. Accessed 30 September 2010.

Mansingh, S. 1984. *India's Search for Power: Indira Gandhi's Foreign Policy 1966–1982*, New Delhi: Sage Publications.

Mohan, C. R. 2007. 'Balancing Interests and Values: India's Struggle with Democracy Promotion', *Washington Quarterly*, 30: 99–115.

Muppidi, H. 1999. 'Postcoloniality and the Production of International Insecurity: The Persistent Puzzle of U.S.–Indian Relations', in J. Weldes, M. Laffey, M. Gusterson and R. Duvall (eds), *Cultures of Insecurity: States, Communities and the Production of Danger*. Minneapolis: University of Minnesota Press.

Narlikar, A. 2006. 'Peculiar Chauvanism or Strategic Calculation? Explaining the Negotiating Strategy of a Rising India', *International Affairs*, 82: 59–76.

Nath, K. 2008. *Dinner Address — Kamal Nath*: The International Institute for Strategic Studies. http://www.iiss.org/conferences/iiss-citi-india-global-forum/igf-plenary-sessions-2008/opening-remarks-and-dinner-address/dinner-address-kamal-nath/?locale=en. Accessed 24 December 2010.

Nehru, J. (1936) 1942. *Jawaharlal Nehru: An Autobiography (With Musings on Recent Events in India)*. London: John Lane The Bodley Head.

———. 1961. *India's Foreign Policy: Selected Speeches, September 1946–April 1961*. New Delhi: The Publications Division, Ministry of Information and Broadcasting, Government of India.

———. 1964. *Nehru and Africa*. New Delhi: Indian Council for Africa.

———. (1946) 1982. *The Discovery of India*. Calcutta: The Signet Press.

———. 1984. *Selected Works of Jawaharlal Nehru*, vol. 2, Series Two. New Delhi: Jawaharlal Nehru Memorial Fund.

Nehru, J. (1934–35) 1996. *Glimpses of World History: Being Further Letters to His Daughter Written in Prison, and Containing a Rambling Account of History for Young People*. New York: Jawaharlal Nehru Memorial Fund.

———. 1999. *Selected Works of Jawaharlal Nehru*, vol. 24, Series Two. New Delhi: Jawaharlal Nehru Memorial Fund.

———. 2000. *Selected Works of Jawaharlal Nehru*, vol. 24, Series Two. New Delhi: Jawaharlal Nehru Memorial Fund.

Obama, B. 2010. 'One of the Defining Partnerships of the 21st Century': President Obama's Address to Joint Session of Parliament'. *Outlook*. http://www.outlookindia.com/article.aspx?267820. Accessed 8 November 2010.

Otto, D. 1999. 'Subalternity and International Law: The Problems of Global Community and the Incommensurability of Difference', in E. Darian-Smith and P. Fitzpatrick (eds), *Laws of the Postcolonial*. Ann Arbor: The University of Michigan Press.

Prakash, G. 1999. *Another Reason: Science and the Imagination of Modern India*. Princeton, NJ: Princeton University Press.

Rana, S. 1970. 'The Changing Indian Diplomacy at the United Nations', *International Organization*, 24: 48–73.

Sharma, A. 2008. 'Interview of Minister of State, Shri Anand Sharma on the Africa Summit — 18 February 2008'. Ministry of External Affairs. http://meaindia.nic.in/indafrica2008/18ia01.htm. Accessed 29 August 2010.

Shashank. 2004. 'On the Meeting of IBSA Dialogue Forum by Foreign Secretary Shri Shashank': Ministry of External Affairs. http://www.mea.gov.in/mystart.php?id=53037624. Accessed 29 September 2010.

Shrivastava, M. 2008. 'South Africa in the Contemporary International Economy: India's Competitor or Ally?', *South Asian Survey*, 15: 121–42.

———. 2009. 'India and Africa: From Political Alliance to Economic Partnership', *Politikon*, 36: 117–43.

Singh, M. 2008. 'Joint Press Interaction by Prime Minister Dr. Manmohan Singh and British Prime Minister Dr. Gordon Brown — 21 January 2008'. Ministry of External Affairs. http://meaindia.nic.in/pressbriefing/2008/01/21mi01.htm. Accessed 29 August 2010.

———. 2010a. 'PM's Address at the Plenary Session of the IBSA Summit, 15 April'. http://pmindia.nic.in/visits/content.asp?id=329. Accessed 30 September 2010.

———. 2010b. 'Prime Minister's Opening Remarks at the Press Conference after the IBSA Summit, 15 April'. http://www.mea.gov.in/mystart.php?id=530115728. Accessed 30 September 2010.

Taylor, I. 2009. 'The South Will Rise Again? New Alliances and Global Governance: The India–Brazil–South Africa Dialogue Forum', *Politikon*, 36: 45–58.

United Nations 1974. '3201 (S-VI). Declaration on the Establishment of a New International Economic Order'. United Nations. http://www.un-documents.net/s6r3201.htm. Accessed 23 September 2010.

Times of India, The. 2010. *'World has Benign View of India's Rise: PM Manmohan Singh'*. http://timesofindia.indiatimes.com/india/World-has-benign-view-of-Indias-rise-PM-Manmohan-Singh/articleshow/5825572.cms. Accessed 17 April 2010.

United States and India. 2005. 'Joint Statement Between President George W. Bush and Prime Minister Manmohan Singh'. The White House. http://www.whitehouse.gov/news/releases/2005/07/print/20050718-6.html. Accessed 24 April 2007.

19

Scientific, Environmental and Agricultural Collaboration within the IBSA Dialogue Forum, 2003–2010

David Fig

Has the IBSA Dialogue Forum served the peoples of its constituent countries, especially in the areas of science, technology, environment and agriculture? To answer this question requires an examination of the purpose, workings and stated aspirations of IBSA and an examination of the challenges of forming a trilateral partnership embracing key countries in three regions of the world. In this article, particular attention will be placed on understanding the workings of IBSA in relation to some of the controversial technologies that impact on the environment, such as agrofuels and genetically modified (GM) seed and crops.

The Emergence of IBSA

The IBSA Dialogue Forum was created in June 2003, by the Declaration of Brasília signed by the foreign ministers of India, Brazil and South Africa (Brazil, Ministry of External Relations 2003). The Declaration went much further than the purpose of IBSA as a trilateral cooperation within global trade talks. It was a forum for stimulating greater South–South collaboration in the spheres of defence, trade, transport, social development, science and technology, agriculture and environment. IBSA emphasised multilateral diplomacy to change the structure of the UN and other institutions like the NAM, UNCTAD and G77 to reflect the emergence of the global South.

IBSA emerged at a time when both Brazil and South Africa had 'normalised' their political situations after years of military dictatorship and apartheid racial oligarchy. Both countries were now constitutional democracies, eager to join forces with India, the world's largest democracy, with commitment to strengthen the democratic vision. There are similarities among the three countries: immense problems of poverty and inequality, and a sizeable middle class. India's middle class is as large as the combined populations of Brazil and South Africa, despite its low GDP per capita (see Table 19.1). The three countries are home to large corporations, relatively diversified industries and sophisticated capital markets. Their bureaucracies are elaborate, and they possess sufficient technical policy expertise to engage strongly at international level. Both countries have moved away from patterns of import-substitution industrialisation and strong state enterprises embracing neoliberalism, privatisation and more open markets (Alden and Vieira 2005).

IBSA countries being the most significant players in their respective regions as in economic spheres also carry with them some caveats in that the other countries in the respective regions may resent the hegemonic role of the larger players. This is certainly true in the case of Brazil–Argentina and India–Pakistan, where rivalries have at times ruined the possibilities of intra-regional unity. However, with the emergence of closer regional cooperation in the southern cone of Latin America, historical rivalries have given way to closer relations.

In Southern Africa, the existence of the century-old Southern African Customs Union (linking South Africa with Botswana, Namibia, Lesotho and Swaziland) means that South Africa cannot make trade agreements unilaterally but must involve other SACU nations. Similarly, Brazil has to work through the Mercosur structures. SACU has already concluded a trade agreement with Mercosur, and a further agreement between India and Mercosur is in the pipeline. The result is that further formalisation of trade arrangements between IBSA partners requires them to ensure that their regional partners are also included. Trilateralism can therefore only work through mutual respect for the partners' existing regional commitments, adding a certain complexity to further steps towards trade liberalisation and harmonisation of standards.

The economies of Brazil and India are around three times the size of South Africa's, and their populations are far greater. This begs the question of whether South Africa is a significant partner

Table 19.1: Values and Global Rankings of IBSA Members with Respect to Physical Area, Current and Projected Populations, and Various Economic Indicators

	India		*Brazil*		*South Africa*	
Area 000km^2	3287.0	7th	8512.0	5th	1226.0	25th
Population 2004	1081.2	2nd	180.8	5th	45.2	25th
Population 2050	1592.7	1st	244.2	7th	52.5	n/a
GDP US$ billion (2007)	691.2	10th	604.0	14th	212.8	28th
GDP per person (US$)	1031	139th	8 220	60th	5 824	73rd
HDI (2009)	0.612	134th	0.813	75th	0.683	129th
Gini Coefficient (2007)	0.368		0.57		0.578	

Sources: The Economist Pocket World in Figures, 2007 edition; UN Development Programme, *Human Development Reports 2007/8*, 2009; IMF; UN Population Division, *World Population Prospects*, 2008.

Table 19.2: Trilateral Meetings of IBSA

Year	*Location*	*Nature of Meeting*	*Business*
2003	Brasília	Foreign ministers	Founding declaration
	New York	Heads of Gov't	Presentation to UN General Assembly
2004	New Delhi	Commission 1	Agreement to double trade by 2007
2005	Cape Town	Commission 2	Framework for continuing co-operation Agreement to extend co-operation to agriculture
2006	Brasília	1st Summit	Support for conclusion of Doha round and Global System of Trade Preferences
	Rio de Janeiro	Commission 3	
2007	Pretoria	2nd Summit	
	New Delhi	Commission 4	Extend work to climate and environment
2008	New Delhi	3rd Summit	
	Somerset West	Commission 5	
2009	Brasília	Commission 6	Coordinate positions for Copenhagen climate talks
2010	Rio de Janeiro	4th Summit	IBSA–BRIC joint Business Council

Sources: Various IBSA communiqués, 2003–2010.

for the other IBSA members, and what it brings to the party. The initial argument was that each of the partners carries great weight in their respective regions and continents. Therefore, South Africa was regarded as a useful 'stepping stone' for the other partners into Southern Africa as well as Africa as a whole. While there is some logic to this, both Brazil and India have managed their own foreign relations with Africa, including trade, investment and resource extraction, without having to rely on South Africa's support (Gelb 2004). President Lula, during his two terms of office (2003–2010), made four official visits to over 17 African countries, and opened 13 new embassies in Africa.

Another factor is the Gini co-efficient, an index of economic inequality within a country. The higher the co-efficient, the more unequal is the income distribution. Not only has South Africa surpassed Brazil in terms of inequality in recent years, but these two societies remain ranked amongst the most unequal in the world.

IBSA in Action

It was important that the structures of IBSA facilitate the Plan of Action, rather than being another talkshop. Hence apart from regular summits of heads of government, there is an annual Trilateral Commission, led by foreign ministers and joint working groups coordinated within the relevant line ministries. Particular countries champion particular sub-themes in the case of agriculture. Instead of an independent secretariat, the foreign ministries take care of logistics. This meant that the work of the organisation became part of the normal functioning of government, rather than channelled through separate agencies. Cooperation became programmatic, and therefore continuous, independent of the political shelf life of specific politicians (White 2009).

One of IBSA's original thrusts was to press for the redesign of global institutions to further the interests of the South. Given that one indication of global status is permanent membership of the UN Security Council (UNSC), the three IBSA countries have been staunch advocates of changing the rules to permit them to assume this function. However, instead of pressing trilaterally for permanent membership of the UNSC, both Brazil and India have formed alliances not with South Africa but with Germany and Japan for this purpose. This side-stepping of IBSA weakens the voice of the South on this question.

Has IBSA helped to improve trade relations between the partners? Lyal White claims that between 2003 and 2008 trade within the IBSA partners increased impressively from US$3.9 billion to over US$10 billion. While this is a low base, there is much room for improvement as against Brazil–China trade of US$43 billion in 2008.

IBSA also initially sought changes to the Bretton Woods institutions and the World Trade Organisation (WTO). However, in 2009, Brazil lent US$10 billion to the International Monetary Fund (IMF) which reinforced the institution's ability to lend to developing countries. This loan symbolised Brazil's preference for working with the unreconstructed Bretton Woods institutions, rather than attempting to boost the Bank of the South, a new institution aimed at freeing the global South from its dependency on the IMF and World Bank.

IBSA versus BRICS

The lure for India, Brazil and, most recently, South Africa of Brazil–Russia–India–China–South Africa collaboration (BRICS) connection may, in the long term, outweigh the importance of IBSA to them. South Africa joined the organisation in 2010. The original BRIC countries were identified as most likely to be the four most important economies of the world in the year 2050 by Jim O'Neal of Goldman Sachs in 2001, and could supplant the G7. South Africa's economy, population and other criteria compared to other countries is small. Its admission to the BRICS surprised some observers since the two next likely candidates whose economic importance by the mid-century was projected as significant were Mexico and South Korea.

BRICS organised three summits in Ekaterinberg in Russia in 2009, in Brasília in 2010 (back-to-back with the IBSA summit and sharing a common meeting of the two business forums), and in Sanya, Heinan province, China in April 2011. For some time, South Africa was interested in joining the group. President Zuma raised the matter during state visits to each of the BRIC countries during 2010. However, it was only after his visit to China that he received a letter of invitation to join the group from President Hu Jintao in late December.[1]

The response in Pretoria was official delight: International Relations Minister Maite Nkoana-Mashabane greeted the invitation as 'the best Christmas present ever. We will be a good gateway for the BRIC countries. While we may have a small population, we don't just speak for South Africa, we speak for Africa as a whole' (Seria 2010). A number of analysts have been less upbeat about the move.[2]

Jim O'Neal, who had put forward the concept of BRIC, fulminated because 'South Africa's economy is very small. For South Africa to be treated as part of BRIC doesn't make any sense to me. But South Africa as a representative of the African continent is a different story' (Seria 2010). Since the other members do not need South Africa as an intermediary for their economic penetration of the African continent, South Africa's membership should be seen more as a symbolic gesture of including an African representative amongst the more important emerging economies.

Will BRICS eclipse IBSA? This depends on the way in which BRICS evolves as an entity. While BRICS can encompass broad positions, it is IBSA which is set to do detailed trilateral projects on the ground. IBSA has form and function, largely through inter-ministerial cooperation, whilst BRICS is still fairly amorphous. The political tensions, say, between India and China, do not inhibit the work of IBSA. Nevertheless the BRICS may, through inclusion of South Africa, help to consolidate existing hegemonies, such as China's trade and investment strengths in Africa. China is likely to tender for the construction of large infrastructural projects in South Africa, for example, new nuclear reactors, and inclusion in BRICS may have helped provide some leverage in the bidding process.

What is the glue that holds IBSA together? For the present, the IBSA project seems more systematic and focused on results, while BRICS is still a very loose arrangement rather than a formal alliance. IBSA has a strong programme of action and a plan of action to realise its agenda. Its joint working groups have met regularly to accomplish some strategic goals.

IBSA has been reinforcing bilateral and triangular relations and common actions in a number of arenas. This has increased interaction among member countries. This was first noticed at the 2003 WTO ministerial at Cancún, where the three countries formed part of the leadership of the G20 and later G20+. Although condemned by significant sections of civil society, the IBSA countries acted together at Copenhagen to deliver a loose and essentially minimalist agreement.

While the culture of trilateral collaboration, still only eight years in the making, is maturing and is especially notable within some government departments and in the business community, the challenge will be how to use the synergies of IBSA to create more equitable societies.

Technological Collaboration in IBSA Countries

Agroenergy

The global move towards conversion of agricultural crops and biomass to energy has resulted largely from attempts by countries to become less dependent upon fossil fuels. Their motivation may be to address climate change, to become less economically dependent on petroleum imports or to cut the costs of such imports. Agrofuels[3] such as ethanol and biodiesel are mostly drawn from crops such as sugar cane, maize, soya, sweet sorghum, jatropha (an oily nut), coconut, palm oil, sugar beet, sunflower and canola. Energy can also be extracted from different forms of biomass, such as bagasse, other crop residues and even genetically modified trees. New global demand has led to great competition between production of food crops and agrofuels, leading to higher food prices, greater hunger and insecurity, land grabs and weakening of food sovereignty across the global South.

Most critics point to the food/fuel conflict involving key staple crops such as maize, sugar, soya and palm oil, but they also note the expansion of the agrofuels frontier into crucial carbon dioxide sinks such as rainforests and wetlands. The expansion of sugar plantations, for example, compromises water-scarce areas, because each kilogram of sugar requires seven litres of water for its cultivation. Often, the planting of monocultures to meet these needs has a negative environmental impact, due to the required massive use of organophosphates and other lethal herbicides and pesticides. Most crop energy is exported, and is seldom a part of the strategy to reduce energy poverty locally. In terms of poverty alleviation, it is also well known that labour conditions on sugar plantations are dire, and wages low, leading to sugar being deemed a 'hunger crop' (Moreira 2010).

Brazil has by far the longest record of producing ethanol as a motor fuel. Initial motivation derived from the oil shocks of 1973 when world petroleum prices quadrupled overnight. Originally subsidised through the Proálcool programme, the ethanol price was capped at 59 per cent of the petrol price. From 1980 all-ethanol vehicles were produced, and by 1985 they had taken over 75 per cent of the market for new cars. However, petroleum prices dropped significantly and the government ran out of funds to provide ethanol subsidies. Ethanol production stagnated, and many cars were stranded without fuel until imports made up for the shortfall. Price controls were removed and the market for all-ethanol cars dried up, with people switching to cars that mixed petrol and ethanol in flexible ratios. From 2001, sugar harvests again increased, and ethanol demand was met from domestic production by 2009 (Suárez 2008).

The expansion of soya production led to the adoption by the Brazilian government of an agrodiesel programme from 2005, with soya as the main feedstock. From January 2010, it has become mandatory in Brazil to blend 5 per cent of agrodiesel. This is of immense benefit to the large-scale agribusiness corporations, as is the rise in soya oil prices from US$306 per ton in 2001 to US$1 343 per ton in 2008 (RSJDH and CPT 2000; see also Suárez 2008).

The Brazilian government strongly backs agrofuels, asserting them to be an answer to the energy crisis, and to problems of climate and hunger. It rejects the notion that agrofuel crops compete with food crops and place them at risk (Gonsalves 2006).[4] Brazil exports agrofuel technology and know-how, and has developing finance packages and programmes to certify the ecological sustainability of agrofuels. Much of Lula's international diplomatic thrusts in Africa have stressed the importance of agrofuels and the need for African countries to accept Brazilian expertise and investment in this area.

Table 19.3: **Ethanol Production by IBSA Country, 2004–2009**

Million US Gallons	*2004*	*2007*	*2009*
Brazil	3989	5019,2	6577,89
India	n/a	52,8	91,67
South Africa	n/a	n/a	n/a

Sources: *US Department of Energy. 2007.* Biomass Energy Data Book, World Fuel Ethanol Production by Country or Region, *Table 2.3; Earth Policy Institute. 2005.* Ethanol production examples worldwide. www.earth-policy.org/Updates/2005/Update49_data.htm. Accessed 25 August 2007.

Although very small in comparison to Brazil's agrodiesel programme, India's production of ethanol is the fourth largest in the world, and India is set on a path to produce agrodiesel from jatropha in the near future (Government of India 2003). India's diesel consumption is four times that of petrol, and government is implementing an ambitious National Biodiesel Mission which will have a 20 per cent agrodiesel blend by 2011–2012 (Gonsalves 2006).[5] India produces enough ethanol for domestic requirements, and also imports ethanol from Brazil when required (Esterhuysen 2009).

In the case of South Africa, although its sugar industry is significant and grows other suitable feedstocks, large-scale production of agrofuels has not yet occurred. By 2010 there was still no workable project from virgin feedstock, despite lobby groups, plans, policy papers and public workshops. According to Dirk Esterhuysen, '[agro]fuels continue to flounder in a morass of government inaction, lack of policy determination, and the threat to food security' (Department of Minerals, South Africa 2007).

In 2007, the government produced the first policy document on agrofuels.[6] Despite elaborate plans in the private sector for the production of ethanol from maize, the policy took into account public concerns over fuel/food competition, and rejected the use of maize, a staple food across Southern Africa, as a feedstock for agrofuels. Similarly, the policy document rejected the use of jatropha for agrodiesel, accepting the argument put forward by conservationists that the plant would be an invasive alien species and rebound negatively upon South Africa's vulnerable biodiversity. However, during 2010, a new Minister of Agriculture, Tina Joemat-Pettersson, argued that the maize surplus could reopen the question of using maize for ethanol (Black 2008).

Various plans are going ahead for agrofuel production in six of South Africa's nine provinces, including biodiesel from canola, soya and sunflower, and ethanol from sugar cane, sugar beet, cassava (manioc) and sweet sorghum (White and Costa 2009). Most projects, including the building refineries, will only come on stream from 2011, and thus far, production figures are still in the realm of planning and speculation.

In IBSA, agrofuels were clearly identified as an issue for collaboration in a number of working groups, including those for energy and climate change. This led to the formulation of a

Memorandum of Understanding on Biofuels in September 2006 (Chandrasekar and Gupta 2006), that aimed to create a trilateral task force to promote the use of ethanol and biodiesel as vehicular fuel to promote energy security (Seelke and Yacobucci 2007).[7]

Given these opportunities for collaboration, it is very hard to understand that Brazil seeks to propel its ethanol diplomacy by ignoring the IBSA structures:

(a) On 9 March 2007, President Lula signed a Memorandum of Understanding with US President George W. Bush on promoting greater cooperation on ethanol and other agrofuels in the Western Hemisphere (Westhuizen 2010).

(b) On 14 July 2010, Brazil formed a coalition with the European Union with the aim of providing development assistance on agrofuels to Mozambique (Reuters 2008).

(c) Brazil has promoted ethanol production in Africa directly during Lula's visits to African countries.

IBSA has failed to feature in all these moves. Brazil clearly needs no intermediary to broker relationships with other countries on the African continent. Alliances on agrofuels with the US and the EU mean that Brazil favours South–North networking over a strictly South–South strategy. Thus in the field of agroenergy it is difficult to see any decisive impact of the IBSA so far. The three national departments of energy have committed to drafting an action plan which might galvanise the trilateral task force on agrofuels in future.

Biotechnology and Genetically Modified Crops

Within a few years, there has been an extensive uptake of transgenic crops by the IBSA countries (see Table 19.4).

However, the Brazilian and South African governments, in succumbing to policies supporting the growing and distribution of genetically modified crops, have, in general, privileged the interests of large-scale agribusiness despite public outcries. They have allowed in their countries the rapid monopolisation of ownership of seed companies in the hands of foreign transnational corporations such as Monsanto, Syngenta, Pannar and Bayer.

In Brazil, President Lula went back on pre-election commitments to Brazil being free of genetically modified organisms (GMOs).

Table 19.4: GMO Planting by Country, Area and Crops, 2009

Country	Area in Million Hectares	GM Crops Legally Cultivated
1. USA	64	Soya, maize, cotton, canola, sugar beet, squash, papaya
2. **Brazil**	**21.4**	**Soya, maize, cotton**
3. Argentina	21.3	Soya, maize, cotton
4. **India**	**8.4**	**Cotton**
5. Canada	8.2	Canola, maize, soya, sugar beet
6. China	3.7	Cotton, poplar, papaya, tomato, sweet pepper, petunia
7. Paraguay	2.2	Soya
8. **South Africa**	**2.1**	**Maize, soya, cotton**

Source: GMO Compass. http://www.gmo-compass.org/eng/agri_biotechnology/ gmo_planting/257.global_gm_planting_2009.html. Accessed 25 August 2010.

Note: All other countries plant less than 1 million hectares.

States such as Rio Grande do Sul and Paraná tried to keep GMOs out, but with smuggling of transgenic soya from across the border with Argentina and with changes in government policy favouring the use of GMOs, their efforts to implement a moratorium failed. Brazil legalised the use of GM soya in 2005, and is now one of the world's largest producer of soya, two-thirds of which is transgenic.

Bt cotton is the only other GM crop approved for commercial cultivation. Despite this approval, the Ministry of the Environment, as well as NGOs, continue to oppose the planting due to the possibility of crossing with indigenous cotton species.

In February 2007, the São Paulo-based Cane Technology Centre (CTC) obtained approval for field trials of three varieties of GM sugar cane, modified to exhibit sucrose levels 15 per cent higher than normal. It was expected that these could be commercialised within three years (GMO Compass, 8 March 2007). In 2008, Brazil's National Council for Biosafety gave permission for the planting of two varieties of GM maize (Burke 2010).

India is the world's largest cotton producer. By 2006, 39 per cent of the Indian cotton crop was made up of GMOs. GM cotton was not cultivated in northern India, but even in southern India the state of Kerala prohibited its cultivation because it was seen as a threat to biodiversity. Kerala's Chief Minister V. S. Achuthanandan stated that GM foods would lead to the 'colonisation of the food sector. We should not be part of a system that will destroy traditional seeds and allow [transnational corporations] to infringe on the agriculture sector.' This was said in the context of the application for approval of the commercial release of Bt brinjal (aubergine/ eggplant) (Shiva and Jafri 2004). Brinjal is widely used in Indian cooking. In February 2010, the government rejected Monsanto's application.

Vandana Shiva and other critics have pointed to the failure of Bt cotton in India, in terms of yield, impact on pests and the social impact of foisting debt onto many small farmers whose crops failed and they commited suicide (African Centre for Biosafety 2010).

South Africa's regulators have allowed the commercial release of GM white maize, yellow maize, soya and cotton since 1996. In addition, field trials for potatoes, tomatoes, canola, apples, honey and 'super' sorghum have also been sanctioned. By 2010, 62 per cent of all maize, 80 per cent of all soya and 90 per cent of all cotton crops were transgenic (Food First 2009). Maize is a staple food for most of South Africa's 50 million people. In 2009, it was reported that three varieties of Monsanto GM maize failed to seed properly over 82,000 hectares. A minimum of 280 farmers (out of 1,000 who cultivated the varieties) had to be compensated (Mittal and Moore 2008). Monsanto also attempted in 1999 to provide small farmers with Bt cotton, the first such small growers' scheme in Africa, in the Makathini flats area. At first the yields were greater and there was lower use of pesticides; however, over a number of growing seasons, the farmers found that pest resistance increased, they fell into greater debt and the scheme had to be abandoned (Witt et al. 2006).

Monsanto has also provided the Eastern Cape, South Africa's poorest province, with free seed for what was called a Massive Food Production Programme. This also failed because of weak extension and other services. It had been implemented as part of developing a new 'green revolution' among Africa's small farmers. All over the continent the Bill and Melinda Gates Foundation is supporting Monsanto and the Alliance for a Green Revolution in Africa, ostensibly to bring about higher yields and to commercialise small farming. However, the scheme ties farmers into debt, dependency on GM seed and unaffordable inputs from large corporations (Genetic Resources Action International 2008).

Can it be said that there has been collaboration on GMOs within IBSA? The documentary record looks is dismal. The IBSA

Memorandum of Understanding on agriculture is somewhat hollow on the question of content, and does not refer directly to GMOs. In Article 3 ('Areas of Cooperation') it lists as its four common areas of interest:

(a) research and technical capacitation;
(b) trade in agricultural products, including sanitary and phyto-sanitary issues;
(c) rural development and poverty alleviation; and
(d) any other issues agreed to by the parties (IBSA Dialogue Forum 2006: 3).

The New Delhi ministerial communiqué in 2007 expanded to the following agricultural issues, with subgroups formed to realise projects within each of them:

(a) animal health and animal production;
(b) biofuels in the context of agriculture;
(c) sanitary and phyto-sanitary issues;
(d) agro-processing and agro-business;
(e) research and capacity building; and
(f) policy identification of joint projects (IBSA Dialogue Forum 2007: 7).

With regard to the latter issues, cooperation is referred to largely in the future tense. For example, there is reference to 'potential areas for future agriculture' co-operation in IBSA (IBSA Dialogue Forum 2010: 2–3).

Under the question of joint Research and Development (R&D), the following is stated:

New issues are emerging (for instance climate change, emergence of GMO crops, increasing role of biotechnology and nanotechnology), which may have far-reaching implications in the agricultural sector. A common strategy for tackling such issues may be developed. An IBSA fund for promoting joint R&D could be set up to initiate such activities (IBSA Dialogue Forum 2010: 3).

From this statement it can be concluded that IBSA has not yet been utilised as a vehicle for joint collaboration on GM crops, which are only being flagged for vague future trilateral cooperation.

In referring to GMOs as a 'new issue', the statement seems a little naïve (Campbell 2010).

Science and Technology

Perhaps it is in the sphere of science and technology that IBSA's working groups have made the most progress.

Science and technology cooperation was stressed in IBSA's Brasília Declaration of 2003 (IBSA Dialogue Forum 2003).[8] The establishment of a joint working group on science and technology led to a division of labour in subgroups, with each country leading two of the subgroups. Three were linked to the combatting of major diseases through medical research. The sub-topic of Antarctica has also been added to the list and linked to the theme of oceanography.[9]

Table 19.5: Lead Countries in IBSA's Science and
Technology Sub-areas of Research

Area of Research	Lead Country
HIV/AIDS	India
Tuberculosis	South Africa
Malaria	Brazil
Nanotechnology	India
Biotechnology	South Africa
Oceanography	Brazil

Source: Chevalier, Romy, Christian von Drachenfels and Andreas Stamm. 2008. 'India-Brazil-South Africa (IBSA): a new geography of trade and technology cooperation?' *Zeitschrift für Wirtschaftsgeographie* 52 (1): 46.

Thomas Auf der Heyde, deputy director-general in the South African Department of Science and Technology (DST), in an extensive interview in March 2010, felt that there had been renewed vigour and a reassessment of strategic science and technology links within IBSA over the previous 2–3 years. Both Brazil and India want the space for collaboration with South Africa on science and technology to grow, both bilaterally and within IBSA. At first, claimed Auf der Heyde, science diplomacy was made subservient to economic diplomacy, but a new kind of momentum has emerged, recognising a broader strategic engagement. Trilateral priorities include nanotechnology, biotechnology (including agrofuels) and a joint conceptual framework on innovation. A raft of practical modalities to implement these have included joint research programmes, scientific exchanges, conferences, summer schools, setting up calls for research and policy dialogues. Obstacles included limitations on funding (each country has put forward US$1 million for trilateral S&T research), identifying mutual priorities and creating a practical framework for collaboration, which could take another 5–8 years. South Africa sees its role in IBSA as providing some of the conceptual leadership, especially on areas such as innovation. Its science system is small enough to understand at an intimate level, yet large and productive enough to be able to measure benefits.[10]

DST staffers responsible for relations with IBSA reported that although no concrete projects had yet been completed, there had been engagement in the form of various workshops. For example, the first nanotechnology 'schools' had taken place in Brazil and India, grooming postgraduate students to link with scientists from the three countries. South Africa had also allocated US$475,000 to host IBSA calls for research over the next three years. All this indicates that IBSA is growing and dynamic within the sphere of science and technology.[11]

Assessment

Functional collaboration on specific themes, such as those raised above, is in its infancy within IBSA, despite the Dialogue Forum having completed seven years of its existence. Some small steps have been taken, but within a highly bureaucratised framework, and without setting up common and realisable policy goals. While intentions may be there, these have seldom been matched by significant action.

On agroenergy, local initiatives are on different scales utilising different feedstocks. There is no privileging of IBSA partners, no serious technological exchanges or transfers, no common plans on how to relate to the questions of regulation, exports or sustainability. Instead of working through IBSA or South Africa, Brazil has, for example, preferred to partner with the EU in its efforts to work with Mozambique on agroenergy.

Similarly, on GMOs, there is yet to be any policy harmonisation or common stances. India seems to have a much more precautionary approach to the uptake of GMOs, while South Africa and Brazil have been extremely liberal in meeting the needs of the transnational GM corporations, despite the potential negative impact on their mega- and agro-biodiversity. Thus a common trilateral posture may be difficult to forge.

Finally, on broad approaches to science and technology, there has been some initial movement, but once again, there is more potential than results. India and Brazil have very large science establishments, and South Africa would need to punch above its weight in order to add value to what can be achieved trilaterally.

Can IBSA achieve more than the sum of healthy bilateral relations between the three countries? The following section raises the issue of whether inclusion of a broader civil society component could improve IBSA's potentialities.

With the end of Lula's presidency in January 2011, the last of the original champions of the IBSA Dialogue Forum has left the political stage. It will be interesting to see whether IBSA's political momentum is maintained, or whether most of the efforts of India, Brazil and South Africa are incorporated into BRICS, a looser, less bureaucratic structure than IBSA, which may mean it can more readily represent its members.

IBSA has, since the Cancún ministerial meeting of the WTO, not been a strong vehicle for organising the interests of the South in the Doha round of negotiations. This round has lost much of its impetus, and proposals to go forward are not being produced by IBSA countries acting in tandem in a leadership role.

IBSA no longer represents the radical rise of the South in global politics. This mantle of the Nkrumahs, Sukarnos and Nassers has perhaps been snatched up by the new coalition of Latin American nations including Venezuela, Bolivia and Ecuador. For example, with the failure of the 16th Conference of the Parties to the UN Framework Convention on Climate Change at Copenhagen in December 2009, a counter-conference was organised in Cochabamba by the Bolivian government (Pressend 2010). IBSA governments had supported the weak unofficial accord coming out of the Copenhagen meeting.

At the same time, IBSA is not the vehicle being used by its members to support reform of the United Nations Security Council. Brazil and India are, instead, working with Germany and Japan, while South Africa is reluctant to be seen to be lobbying outside the framework of the Africa group in the UN.

Trilateral trade has increased significantly during the short life of IBSA, but pales when compared with bilateral trade between individual members and China. To date, the legacy of joint projects is weak. One of the projects involves providing development aid to fourth countries in the South, such as Guinea-Bissau, the Palestinian authority, Haiti and Timor Leste. IBSA member countries are each said to be putting up US$1 million a year to fund this programme. However, they rely on the United Nations Development Programme to be the implementing agency, so it is not clear whether the aid is being acknowledged as coming from IBSA countries.[12]

While some dividend may result from exchanges, joint research and joint projects, no attempt is being made at trilateral policy integration. Individual countries — especially Brazil and South Africa — have greater commitments to policy integration within their respective regions. Trade agreements have, to date, been organised bilaterally and on an inter-regional basis, rather than utilising the IBSA framework.

The IBSA Dialogue Forum is likely, therefore, to remain in essence a consultative body, which, to extend its coherence, has established some collaborative programmes. It does not really play a role as spokesperson for the global South, nor is it essentially involved in producing a coherent South position on key global issues such as UN reform, to fulfil Millennium Development Goals, or combatting global poverty, inequality and injustice.

Since it is does not promote the values of its national civil society organisations in key spheres like energy, climate, environment and agriculture, the IBSA Dialogue Forum is unlikely to put forward a new global vision for sustainability and planetary justice. Its summits and ministerial consultations may increasingly provide, however, a focal point for civil society from the three nations to put forward their shared alternative vision through coordinated actions and interventions.

Notes

1. Chinese Foreign Minister Yang Jiechi in a statement made on his ministry's website, reported in Seria (2010).
2. South Africa, Government Communication and Information System, 'South Africa must Proceed Cautiously with BRIC Countries, Say Analysts', 25 January 2011. http://7thspace.com/headlines/370691/south-africa-

sa-must-proceed-cautiously-with-BRIC-countries-say-analysts. Accessed 1 February 2011.

3. The terminology used here prefers the prefix 'agro-' to denote that these fuels are provided by agricultural activities. It is preferred to the prefix 'bio-' (Greek for 'life') which may be misinterpreted by some into thinking that the fuels have some kind of biological mandate, i.e., are life-affirming or ecologically sound. This distinction has been proposed by La Via Campesina and some of its constituent social movements in Latin America, such as the Brazilian Movement of Landless Rural Workers (MST).

4. Speaking at an FAO conference in Brasilia in April 2008, Brazilian President Lula claimed that allegations that global food prices were rising because of biofuels were baseless. 'Biofuels aren't the villain that threatens food security. On the contrary ... they can pull countries out of energy dependency without affecting foods. Food prices were going up,' he said, 'because people in developing countries like China, India and Brazil itself were simply eating more as their economic conditions improved' (Emilio San Pedro, *BBC News*, 18 April 2008, http://news.bbc.co.uk/2/hi/science/nature/7351766.stm, accessed 20 August 2010).

5. For example, in 2004, it imported 447 million litres from Brazil. See Gonsalves (2006: 38).

6. Hopewell Radebe, 'Rethink Likely on Ban on Biofuel Maize', *Business Day*, 11 October 2010. The minister was quoted as saying: '...with the excessive maize surplus, we as a government need to look again at our biofuels policy.'

7. The countries agreed to advance (a) research and development bilaterally; (b) help to build domestic biofuels industries in third countries; and (c) work multilaterally to advance the global development of agrofuels. See US State Department, Office of the Spokesman, *Memorandum of Understanding between the United States and Brazil to Advance Co-operation on Biofuels*, 2007 http://www.state.gov/r/pa/prs/ps/2007/mar/81607.htm, accessed 23 August 2010. Also see Seelke and Yacobucci (2007).

8. IBSA Dialogue Forum (2003). Clause 9 of the Declaration states that 'Amongst the scientific and technological areas in which co-operation can be developed are biotechnology, alternative energy sources, outer space, aeronautics, information technology and agriculture. What can be reported to date is a seminar on biosafety held under the auspices of the Science and Technology Working Group.'

9. In 2009, further research sub-areas were added after the IBSA Summit, namely: information and communications technology, food security, astronomy/astrophysics and renewable energy.

10. Interview, Thomas Auf der Heyde, Deputy Director-General, International Affairs, Department of Science and Technology, South Africa, Johannesburg, 6 March 2010.

11. Interview, Punkah Mdaka, Director for the Americas and Asia, and Portia Raphasha, IBSA Nodal Representative, both in the Department of Science and Technology, South Africa, Pretoria, 16 March 2010.
12. 'The IBSA Fund', 13 January 2010, www.ibsa-trilateral.org/index. php?option=com_content&view=article&id=29&itemid=79, accessed 29 April 2011.

References

African Centre for Biosafety (ACB). 2010. 'The Monitoring of Environmental Impacts of GMOs in South Africa: A Status Quo Report', ACB Briefing 13. Johannesburg: ACB.

Alden, Chris and Marco Antonio Vieira. 2005. 'The New Diplomacy of the South: South Africa, Brazil, India and Trilateralism', *Third World Quarterly*, 26 (7): 1089.

Black, Vanessa. 2008. *Agrofuels in South Africa: Projects, Players and Poverty*. Johannesburg: African Centre for Biosafety, 24–35.

Brazil, Ministry of External Relations. 2003. 'The Declaration of Brasília: Trilateral Meeting of the Foreign Ministers of Brazil, South Africa and India', Note 214. 6 June.

Burke, Jason. 2010. 'India to Rule on Future of Aubergine as Country's First Genetically Modified Food', *The Guardian*. 8 February.

Campbell, Keith. 2010. 'IBSA R&D Progressing but Unevenly', *Engineering News*. 15 August.

Chandrasekar, V. S. and Devidas Gupta. 2006. 'Bring Perpetrators of Mumbai Blast to Justice: IBSA', *Outlook India*. 14 September. http://news. outlookindia.com/item.aspx?415495. Accessed 23 August 2010.

Department of Minerals and Energy (DME), South Africa. 2007. *Biofuels Industrial Strategy for the Republic of South Africa*. Pretoria: DME.

Esterhuysen, Dirk. 2009. 'South Africa Biofuels Annual Report', *GAIN Report*, US Department of Agriculture. 28 May: 2. For the lobby's website see South African Bioenergy Association at www.saba.za.org.

Food First. 2009. 'Monsanto Genetically Modified Corn Harvest Fails Massively in South Africa'. 22 July. http://www.foodfirst.org/en/node/2504. Accessed 27 August 2010.

Gelb, Stephen. 2004. 'The IBSA Dialogue: A South African Perspective', paper presented to a workshop on 'The IBSA Dialogue, Global Governance and Development'. Johannesburg. 5–8 July, 13.

Genetic Resources Action International (GRAIN). 2008. 'Lessons from a "Green Revolution"', *Seedling*, pp. 22–29. October.

GMO Compass. 2007. 'Are GMOs Fuelling the Brazilian Future?' 8 March. http://www.gmocompass.org/eng/news/stories/273.gmos_fuelling_ brazilian_future.html. Accessed 26 August 2010.

Gonsalves, Joseph C. 2006. *An Assessment of the Biofuels Industry in India* (UNCTAD/DITC/TED/2006/6). Geneva: UN Conference on Trade and Development.

Government of India. 2003. 'Report of the Committee on Development of Biofuel'. New Delhi: Planning Commission.

IBSA Dialogue Forum. 2003. *Brasília Declaration*. Brasília: Ministry of External Relations.

———. 2006. *Memorandum of Understanding on Agriculture and Related Issues.* Brasilia: Itamaraty, 13 September, 3.

———. 2007. *New Delhi Ministerial Communiqué.* New Delhi: Indian Ministry of External Affairs, 7.

———. 2010. *Future of Agricultural co-operation in India, Brazil and South Africa (IBSA)*, 15 April, 2–3.

Mittal, Anurhada and Moore, Melissa (eds). 2008. *Voices from Africa: African Farmers and Environmentalists Speak Out against a New Green Revolution in Africa.* Oakland: Oakland Institute.

Moreira, José Roberto. 2010. 'Brazilian Perspectives on the development of Clean Energy', Paper presented to a multi-country research dialogue on 'Emerging Economies in the New World Order: Promises, Pitfalls and Priorities'. New Delhi. 12–13 April, pp. 10–14.

Network for Social Justice and Human Rights (RSJDH) and Pastoral Land Commission (CPT). 2007. *Agroenergy: Myths and Impacts in Latin America.* São Paulo and Recife: RSJDH/CPT.

Newell, Peter. 2003. 'Biotech firms, biotech politics: negotiating GMOs in India' IDS Working Paper 201. Brighton: Institute for Development Studies.

Pressend, Michelle. 2010. 'Charting a New Climate Change Discourse: The People's World Congress on Climate Change and Protecting Mother Earth in Bolivia', paper presented at a conference on the 'Global Economic Crisis: Challenges and Possibilities for Trade Unions and Social Movements'. 10 April.

Pschorn-Strauss, Elfrieda. 2005. 'Bt Cotton: The Case of the Makhatini Farmers', *Seedling*, pp. 12–25. April.

Reuters. 2008. 'Brazil gives Final Permit for GMO Corn Varieties'. 13 February. http://greenbio.checkbiotech.org/news/brazil_gives_final_permit_gmo_corn_varieties. Accessed 24 August 2010.

Seelke, Clare Ribando and Brent D. Yacobucci. 2007. *Ethanol and other Biofuels: Potential for US and Brazil Energy Co-operation.* Washington: US, Congressional Research Service.

Seria, Nasreen. 2010. 'South Africa Is Asked to Join as a BRIC Member to Boost Emerging Markets', *Bloomberg*, 24 December. www.bloomberg.com/news. Accessed 1 February 2011.

Shiva, Vandana and Afsar H. Jafri. 2004. 'Failure of GMOs in India', *Synthesis/Regeneration* 33 (Winter). http://www.greens.org/s-r/33/33-04.html. Accessed 27 August 2010.

Suárez, Sofia Monsalve (ed.). 2008. *Agrofuels in Brazil.* Heidelberg: FIAN International.

White, Lyal. 2009. *IBSA Six Years On.* Johannesburg: South African Institute of International Affairs, p. 2.

White, Lyal and Tatania Cyro Costa. 2009. *Biofuel Technology Transfer in IBSA: Lessons for South Africa and Brazil.* Johannesburg: South African Institute of International Affairs, p. 1.

Westhuizen, Lauren van der. 2010. 'Brazil, EU Hook Up in Mozambique', *Business Day*. 3 August. http://www.businessday.co.za/articles/Content.aspx?id=116858. Accessed 24 August 2010.

Witt, Harald, Rajeev Patel and Matthew Schnurr. 2006. 'Can the Poor Help GM Crops?: Technology, Representation and Cotton in the Makhatini Flats, South Africa,' *Review of African Political Economy*, 109: 497–513.

About the Editors

Sujata Patel is Professor of Sociology, University of Hyderabad, Andhra Pradesh and Visiting Professor, University of Johannesburg, South Africa (2010–2012). She is Editor of the series 'Cities and the Urban Imperative' (Routledge), as also 'Sage Studies in International Sociology' and 'Studies in Contemporary Society'. Her edited books include *Exclusion, Social Capital and Citizenship: Contested Transitions in South Africa and India* (2012), *Doing Sociology in India: Genealogies, Locations and Practices* (2011) and *The ISA Handbook of Diverse Sociological Traditions* (2010).

Tina Uys is Professor and Head, Department of Sociology, and Director of the Centre for Sociological Research, University of Johannesburg, South Africa. She is Vice-President (National Associations), International Sociological Association (ISA) for the term 2010–2014. She is former President, South African Sociological Association (SASA) and Research Committee on Social Psychology (RC42) as well as a member of the Executive Committee of the ISA (2006–2010). Her most recent book is an edited volume, *Exclusion, Social Capital and Citizenship: Contested Transitions in South Africa and India* (co-edited, 2012).

Notes on Contributors

Priya Chacko is Lecturer in International Politics at the School of History and Politics, University of Adelaide, Australia. She is author of *Identity and Foreign Policy in Postcolonial India* (Routledge, 2011).

Ashwin Desai is Professor of Sociology, University of Johannesburg, South Africa. His latest publications include an edited collection, *The Race to Transform: Sport in Post-apartheid South Africa* (2010) and *Many Lives: 150 Years of being Indian in South Africa* (co-authored, 2010).

David Fig is Honorary Research Associate, Environmental Evaluation Unit, University of Cape Town, South Africa. He chairs the Biowatch Trust, which defends small farmers' rights, and recently won a victory against the Monsanto Corporation in the Constitutional Court of South Africa. His research encompasses the socio-political aspects of the Southern African environment, including questions of energy, agriculture, technology, the extractive industries and corporate environmental behaviour. His most recent book is *Staking their Claims: Corporate Social and Environmental Responsibility in South Africa* (edited, 2007).

V. Geetha is a writer and translator. She writes in English and Tamil on modern Tamil society and history, gender, caste and education. She has co-authored several books on the Tamil anti-caste movement, and has written on gender and patriarchy as they have emerged in the Indian context. Her most recent publication is *Religious Faith, Ideology, Citizenship: the View from Below* (co-authored, Routledge, 2011). Active in feminist circles in India for over two decades, she is currently an editor with Tara Books, Chennai.

Janis Grobbelaar is Professor and Head, Department of Sociology, University of Pretoria, South Africa. She holds degrees from the universities of Cape Town, Stellenbosch and South Africa. In 1994 she was seconded to the then first Independent Electoral

Commission (IEC) as Deputy Provincial Electoral Officer of the Pretoria sub-province in the first ever SA democratic election. From 1996–98 she worked for the South African Truth and Reconciliation Commission (SATRC) as Information Manager in the Johannesburg office of the commission. She has taught and published within the field of the sociology of South Africa.

Adam Habib is Deputy Vice-Chancellor, Research, Innovation and Advancement, University of Johannesburg, South Africa. In the past he has held academic appointments at the universities of Durban-Westville and KwaZulu-Natal and the Human Science Research Council. He is on the editorial boards of *Voluntas, South African Labour Bulletin* and UNESCO's 2009 *World Social Science Report*. His research interests include democratisation and development, contemporary social movements, giving and solidarity, institutional reform, race, redress and citizenship, and South Africa's role in Africa and beyond. He has recently concluded a study on the state of academic freedom in South Africa.

Rajen Harshe is Professor, Department of Political Science, University of Hyderabad. He was the first Vice-Chancellor of the University of Allahabad after it became a central university (2005–2010). He is a leading scholar of International Relations Studies in India. He has an impressive and diverse range of publications covering development-related issues in areas such as South Asia, Sub-Saharan Africa, Western Europe and theories of international relations, especially those related to imperialism and globalisation. His latest book is *Reflections on Nation Building: A Gypsy in the World of Ideas* (2011).

Ravindra K. Jain is Chairman, Indian National Confederation and Academy of Anthropologists (2008–2011). He taught social anthropology and sociology at University of Oxford, United Kingdom (1966–74) and Jawaharlal Nehru University, New Delhi (1975–2002). He is on the editorial board of *Global Networks* and *South Asian Diaspora*. His recent publications include *Nation, Diaspora, Trans-Nation: Reflections from India* (Routledge, 2010), *Indian Transmigrants: Malaysian and Comparative Essays* (2009, winner of the G. S. Ghurye Award) and *Between History and Legend: Status and Power in Bundelkhand* (2002).

Brij Maharaj is a geographer at the University of KwaZulu-Natal, South Africa. He has received widespread recognition for his research on urban politics, segregation, local economic development, migration and diasporas, and has published over 120 scholarly papers in renowned journals such as *Urban Studies, International Journal of Urban and Regional Studies, Political Geography, Urban Geography, Antipode, Polity and Space, Geoforum* and *GeoJournal,* as well as five co-edited book collections. His last book, *Zuma's Own Goal — Losing South Africa's 'War on Poverty'* (co-edited), was published in 2010.

Derek van der Merwe holds the position of Deputy Vice-Chancellor (Human Resources and Institutional Planning) at the University of Johannesburg, South Africa. Prior to this he was the Pro Vice-Chancellor of UJ. He holds the degrees BA (Law), LLB and LLD, all from the University of Pretoria. Before taking up various senior management roles at the University since 2001, he was Professor, Private Law and also Dean, Faculty of Law. As a law academic, he has published in the fields of legal theory, legal history, property law, social assistance law and intellectual property law.

Lubna Nadvi teaches Political Science and International Relations at the School of Politics, University of KwaZulu-Natal, South Africa. She has served as National Secretary-General, South African Association of Political Studies (SAAPS) from 2001–2004, and was a member of the SAAPS Executive Committee and Council until 2010. As an academic, she researches and publishes in the area of Middle East and African politics, political Islam, HIV Aids, gender/feminist studies, social movements and civil society. She completed her doctorate in the field of political Islam in 2008. She is the author of an anthology of English poetry, titled *Reflections upon Water.* She has recently been a recipient of a Human Rights Award from Amnesty International.

Anita Rampal is Head and Dean, Faculty of Education, University of Delhi. She has been a Nehru Fellow, UGC Research Scientist, Chairperson of the NCERT textbook teams at the primary stage, and is a member of national task forces and the Steering Committee of the Planning Commission for Elementary Education and

316 *Contemporary India and South Africa*

Literacy. Her special interests include participatory curriculum development, cognition and communication of science and mathematics with a focus on indigenous knowledge, and policy analysis for equity in education. She has published papers, monographs and books in English and Hindi, and has produced films on women's education and political participation.

Mahesh Rangarajan is Professor, Modern Indian History. He is presently on deputation as Director, Nehru Memorial Museum and Library, New Delhi. Educated at the universities of Delhi and Oxford, he also chaired the Elephant Task Force of the Government of India in 2010. He has been a political commentator in print media and on television. His most recent work is a co-edited two-volume book, *India's Environmental History* (2012).

Mariam Seedat-Khan is a South African academic and author who obtained her undergraduate degree from York University in Toronto. In 2006 she was awarded her D.Phil. in Sociology from the University of KwaZulu-Natal, South Africa. She is currently Lecturer in Sociology, University of Johannesburg, South Africa. She is also Secretary, South African Sociological Association. Her areas of research and teaching include gender, identity and socialisation. Her book, *The Socialization Process of the Female African Domestic Worker*, was published in 2009.

Kalpana Sharma is an independent journalist and columnist based in Mumbai. She writes on environmental, developmental and urban issues as well as gender and media. She has held senior editorial positions in leading Indian newspapers including *Indian Express*, *The Times of India* and *The Hindu*. She is author of *Rediscovering Dharavi: Stories from Asia's Largest Slum* (2000) and co-editor of *Whose News? The Media and Women's Issues* (1994, 2006) and *Terror Counter Terror: Women Speak Out* (2003). In 2010, she edited *Missing: Half the Story. Journalism as if Gender Matters*.

Ujjwal Kumar Singh is Professor, Department of Political Science, University of Delhi. He is author of *Political Prisoners in India* (1998) and *The State, Democracy and Anti-Terror Laws in India* (2007).

Goolam Vahed is Associate Professor, Department of Historical Studies, University of KwaZulu-Natal, South Africa. His recent publications include *Gender, Modernity, and Indian Delights: The Women's Cultural Group of Durban, 1954–2010* (2011), and *Many Lives: 150 Years of Being Indian in South Africa* (2010).

Rehana Vally, an anthropologist at the University of Pretoria, South Africa is seconded to the Council on Higher Education as Director, National Reviews. She co-edited a volume, *Muslim Cultures* and co-authored *Viewing the New South Africa: Representations of South Africa in Television Commercials* (2006).

Padma Velaskar is Professor, Centre for Studies in Sociology of Education, Tata Institute of Social Sciences, Mumbai where she teaches courses in sociology, women's studies and sociology of education. Her research interests include the sociology of caste, class and gender, inequalities in education, education of Dalits and women's issues. She has written and published widely on these themes. Exploring the intersection between caste, class and patriarchy, she is currently working on a book based on research on Dalit women in Maharashtra.

Index